Parents, Gender and Education Reform

C RPYK

Family Life Series

Edited by Martin Richards, Ann Oakley, Christina Hardyment
and the late Jacqueline Burgoyne.

Published

David Clark and Douglas Haldane, *Wedlocked?*
Miriam David, *Parents, Gender and Education Reform*
Janet Finch, *Family Obligations and Social Change*
Lydia Morris, *The Workings of the Household*
Philip Pacey, *Family Art*
Jean La Fontaine, *Child Sexual Abuse*
Ann Phoenix, *Young Mothers?*

Parents, Gender
and
Education Reform

Miriam E. David

Polity Press

First published in 1993 by Polity Press in association with Blackwell Publishers

Editorial office:
Polity Press
65 Bridge Street
Cambridge CB2 1UR, UK

Marketing and production:
Blackwell Publishers
108 Cowley Road
Oxford OX4 1JF, UK

238 Main Street
Suite 501
Cambridge, MA 02142, USA

ISBN 0 7456 0636-9
ISBN 0 7456 0637-7 (pbk)

British Library Cataloguing-in-Publication Data
A CIP catalogue record for this book is available from the British Library.

Library of Congress Cataloging-in-Publication Data
David, Miriam E.
    Parents, gender, and education reform / by Miriam E. David.
        p.   cm. — (Family life series)
    Includes bibliographical references and index.
    ISBN 0-7456-0636-9 (alk. paper). — ISBN 0-7456-0637-7 (pbk. : alk. paper)
    1. Home and school—Great Britain.   2. Education—Great Britain—Parent participation.   3. Education—Social aspects—Great Britain.
    4. Sex differences in education—Great Britain.   5. Educational change—Great Britain.   I. Title.   II. Series.   III. Series: Family life series (Cambridge, England)
    LC225.33.G7D37   1993   92–31272
    370.19′34′0941—dc20   CIP

Typeset in 10 on 12 pt Garamond
by Graphicraft Typesetters Ltd, Hong Kong
Printed in Great Britain by T.J. Press (Padstow) Ltd, Cornwall

This book is printed on acid-free paper.

Contents

Acknowledgements

This book has been a long time in the making. Martin Richards approached me about contributing to the Family Life Series about a year after my book, with Caroline New, on childcare had been published. I was quite eager but rather felt that I had left educational issues behind and was then more interested in family policy and questions of gender. It took about two years for me to realise the extent to which these two issues were intertwined. I am most grateful to Martin Richards for his patience, forbearance and editorial support in the final stages of the preparation of the manuscript. I am also grateful to Michele Stanworth for her early very constructive challenges to my ideas and to David Held for his confidence in my project.

I am also enormously fortunate in the continuous support that I have received from a number of colleagues, students and friends. At South Bank, three of my successful Ph.D. research students – Drs Rosalind Edwards, Mary Hughes and Jane Ribbens – have been a constant source of constructive criticism and help in questioning my ideas. Working with them both individually and on our joint venture, *Mothers and Education*, has forced me to clarify my perspectives. Jane's comments and editorial advice on the manuscript were particularly useful. She, and Anne West of the Centre for Educational Research at the London School of Economics, have pressed me to continue when my spirits were flagging. The prospects of writing up our joint research report, *Parental Choice of Secondary School*, finally pressed me into action. My postgraduate students on the M.Sc. in Sociology, both the Social Policy and Sociology of Education branches, have endured my draft chapters as the basis of lectures and seminars and helped to firm up my initially hazy ideas! I am most grateful to them, especially those who graduated in the autumn of 1992.

Colleagues have also been most generous with their comments on parts or all of the manuscript. I should particularly like to thank Nick Andrew, Rosy Fitzgerald, Norman Ginsburg, Mike Hickox and Gaby Weiner who generously and unstintingly read and criticised the draft manuscript for me. Judy Allsop and Pat Ladly kindly criticised the lecture versions of draft chapters.

Sandra Acker, Madeleine Arnot, Stephen Ball, Len Barton, David Bull and the late Gail Kelly (of the State University of New York at Buffalo), Howard Glennerster, Jane Lewis, Geoff Whitty and Gail Wilson also criticised drafts of chapters that have appeared in different versions as chapters of books, journal articles or seminar papers. I have benefited from their advice and criticism. I have received help with research evidence from Michael Adler, John Bastiani, Kevin Brehony, Andrew Brown, Rosemary Deem, John Fitz, Sandra Jowett, Mavis Maclean, Ruth Merttens, Peter Moss, Geoffrey Walford and Philip Woods. Liz Bird, Naomi Fulop, Hilary Land, Ruth Levitas, Ellen Malos, Marilyn Porter, Helen Taylor, Linda Ward, Jackie West, and especially Fiona Williams and Caroline New, former colleagues and/or friends from Bristol University days, remain a constant reminder of the importance of caring and careful scholarship, which has as its aim a female-friendly future.

I should also like to thank Professors Ray Page and Jenny Levin for giving me a timely sabbatical in the autumn of 1990 to get started on thinking about and preparing the manuscript; and Judy Allsop for taking over the reins of running the Department of Social Sciences to free me to write. Sir Peter Newsam, Professors Peter Mortimore and Gareth Williams were particularly generous in facilitating my sabbatical by giving me a base in the Department of Policy Studies at the University of London Institute of Education. There I benefited from the support and advice of Julia Brannen, Lynne Chisholm, Diana Leonard, Berry Mayall, Ann Phoenix, Rene Saran, Ann Sassoon and Sylvia Walby.

Visits to the United States and Canada and to European conferences, especially in Aalborg, Denmark, in the summer of 1991, have kept me alive to the comparative dimensions of family and education. Jane Gaskell's conference on *Women and Education* in Vancouver in the summer of 1986 alerted me to some key researchers in the field, especially Kathy Rockhill and Dorothy Smith. So, too, have trips to the Ontario Institute for Studies in Education in Toronto.

It remains for me to thank Joyce Allen for her tremendous skills and word-processing expertise in preparing the manuscript for publication. Anita Bryan, Annette Lewis and Oye Odinawodu also contributed generously in typing draft chapters.

Finally, I should like to thank my family – Robert, Toby and Charlotte Reiner – for bearing with me throughout. I hope that they remain as convinced as I do of the importance of making sure that the family's relations to education are in the best interests not just of children but of us all. From a concerned and committed mother, this book is dedicated to Toby and Charlotte.

I should like to acknowledge, with thanks, the following authors and publishers for permission to reprint short extracts.

Every effort has been made to trace all copyright holders, but if any has been inadvertently overlooked, the publishers will be pleased to make the necessary arrangement at the first opportunity.

1   The Falmer Press, for permission to reprint extracts from Nicholas Beattie's (1985) *Professional Parents* (from pp. 2, 179–81, 233 and 239); Annette Lareau's (1989) *Home Advantage* (from p. 145); Harold Silver's *Education, Change and the Policy Process* (from pp. 67–9, 184–5, 194–5 and 198–200).

2   Peter Moss and the European Commission's Network on Childcare and other measures to reconcile working and family life, which is supported by the Equal Opportunities Unit of the Directorate – General V, Employment, Industrial Relations and Social Affairs, under the Third medium-term Action Programme on Equal Opportunities for Women and Men (1991–1995), for permission to reproduce Table 2.2 on *Parental Employment*.

3   Malcolm Wicks, MP, former Director of the Family Policy Studies Centre, for permission to use a modified version of his table *Key Family Indicators*, as Table 2.1, from his paper *Social Politics 1979–1992: Families, Work and Welfare*, given to the annual conference of the Social Policy Association at the University of Nottingham on 7 July 1991.

4   The Brookings Institution for permission to publish extracts from J. Chubb and T. Moe (1990) *Politics, Markets and America's Schools* from pp. 107 and 217–18.

5   Northeastern University Press, Boston for permission to use an extract from *The Everyday World as Problematic: A Feminist Sociology* by Dorothy E. Smith.

6   Oxford University Press for permission to use extracts from pp. 198–9 and 216–19 of *Origins and Destinations* by A. H. Halsey, A. F. Heath and J. M. Ridge. Copyright 1980 by A. H. Halsey, A. F. Heath and J. M. Ridge.

7   Open University Press for permission to quote from 'Parental choice and voice under the 1988 Education Reform Act' by Adam Westoby in *Educational Institutions and their Environments: Managing the Boundaries* edited by Ron Glatter, Open University Press 1989.

8   Joyce Epstein, Co-Director/Principal Research Scientist, Centre on Familes, Communities, Schools and Children's Learning, The Johns Hopkins University, Baltimore, MD 21218 for permission to use extracts from pp. 99, 108–9, 111–13, 116–17 from 'School and Family Connections: Theory, Research and Implications for Integrating Sociologies of Education and Family' published in *Marriage and Family Review*, 1990,

15, (1/2), 99–126 and in *Families in Community Settings: Interdisciplinary Perspectives*, edited by D. Unger and M. Sussman and published the Haworth Press of New York in 1990.

9   Michael Golby and Fair Way Publications for permission to use extracts from The Exeter papers in School Governorship, and specifically from pp. 1–6 of 'The New Governors Speak' and 'Parents as School Governors' pp. 140–2.

10 Rosemary Deem and the editors of *Gender and Education* for permission to publish extracts from Rosemary Deem's (1989) 'The New School Governing Bodies' (from pp. 252 and 255) and Gillian Sperling's (1991) 'Can The Barriers be Breached?' (from pp. 204 and 202).

11 The editors of *Educational Policy* at the State of University of New York at Buffalo, Graduate School of Education for permission to use extracts from Annette Lareau's article published in 1989 'Family–School Relationships: A View from the Classroom', from pp. 251–4.

12 The editors of the *British Journal of the Sociology of Education* for permission to use extracts from Kathleen Rockhill's article, published in 1987, 'Gender, language and the Politics of Literacy'.

13 Philip Woods and the editors of the *Journal of Education Policy* for permission to use short extracts from pp. 325–6 of Philip Woods' article 'A Strategic View of Parent Participation' published in 1988, 3/4.

14 Mavis Maclean for permission to publish short extracts from her articles, one with Michael Wadsworth (1986) in *Children and Youth Service Review 8* 'Parental Divorce and Children's Life Chances' and one with Diane Kuh (1991) 'The long-term effects for girls of parental divorce', in *Women's Issues in Social Policy* edited by M. Maclean and D. Groves and published by Routledge and Kegan Paul.

15 Sally Tomlinson for permission to publish short extracts from pages 5 & 6 of 'Home-School Partnerships' in *Teachers and Parents*, Education and Training paper no 7, published in 1991 by the Institute for Public Policy Research, London,

16 Valerie Walkerdine, Helen Lucey and Virago Press for short extracts from pp. 181–8 and 15–16, 82–3, of *Democracy in the Kitchen: Regulating Mothers and Socialising Daughters*, published in 1989 by Virage.

1

Introduction: Parents, Education Reforms and Social Research

Parents and education

This book is about the relations between parents and education. It explores these relations in the context of education reforms on the one hand and social changes in family life, on the other. Changes in family life, particularly those which affect women's lives as mothers, have typically been ignored as have those which affect certain ethnic minorities. My general argument is that the debates about education reforms and the part that parents should play in partnership with schools have taken place without any consideration for the various social changes that have been going on in family life. This means that the nature of education reforms, and their impact, especially on families, cannot fully be understood or appreciated. The corollary, the impact of family changes on education, also cannot fully be understood without due consideration of the interplay between the two.

I will explore the education policy debates, and review the social scientific evidence on which they have been based, over the last 50 years or so. I aim to show how the various educational and social reforms have been developed in particular political and social contexts. In particular I will review the contribution that social scientists have made to those policy formulations and evaluations. My aim is to evaluate both the policy strategies that have been developed by the right and the left and the evidence that has been produced by social and educational researchers to aid the process of social and educational reform.

The focus is on the relation between parents and education. These relations have been involved throughout the period under review, although they have often not been considered explicitly. They have often been seen as more traditional policy questions, such as about the concern to provide equal educational opportunities and to reduce disparities between families on the basis of social class, defined in terms of socio-economic circumstances, in educational opportunities. They may also have been used implicitly rather than explicitly as the basis for educational strategies, such as for socially disadvantaged children.

An interesting parallel has been the development of a partnership between educational and social reformers on the one hand and social and educational researchers on the other. This partnership mirrors that of parents and education in that their perspectives tend also to ignore questions of gender and race. Typically the dominant concern has been about how to address public policy issues, especially about education reforms.

These debates about educational policy and the role of parents will be discussed against the backdrop of changing family life – the increase in lone motherhood, the rise in maternal employment and the particular needs of some of the minority communities – and I will explore the ways in which education reforms affect parents, especially mothers, as well as their children. However, these social changes have rarely affected the public policy debates; nor have they been central to the social and educational research that has accompanied these debates and strategies.

The public agenda and political debates

In Britain, as in most other countries of the industrialised world, both education and family matters are high on the agenda for public concern and political debate at the moment. First, there is an enormous amount of public concern about how to improve educational provision and raise educational standards, in an increasingly competitive and global economy. Politicians and their advisers of right or left political persuasion tend to disagree about how this may be done. Both, however, agree on a central role for parents in the process.

The right argues that parents should be afforded the freedom to choose schools in an educational marketplace. Their demands will then improve educational standards. Schools which are not chosen by a group of parents will go out of business. This, for example, is part of the thinking behind the Parent's Charter for Education which the British Conservative government introduced in 1991. Similarly, in the United States there are a number of debates about how to make family choices more effective, especially in the central metropolitan areas. For example, Chubb and Moe (1990) have presented a most challenging polemic about how to improve America's schools by abolishing school bureaucracy and creating an educational market in its place. They have also applied their arguments, but not their very sophisticated statistical analysis of educational achievements, to the British context. They have argued that the

British Conservative government has gone much further than either the US federal or state administrations in creating a non-bureaucratic, effective system of education through the grant-maintained schools (*Sunday Times*, 9 February 1992).

The left, on the other hand, argues that parents should be given a greater role in education to ensure that schools are more effective. They too believe that parents will push for better standards for their children if they are more formally involved. The Labour party in Britain has given thought to more clearly specified contracts between 'home and school' to ensure a more equal and reciprocal relationship. These ideas are drawn from those of left political parties in other countries of Europe.

Second, much public concern focuses on changes in family structure, especially the growing rates of divorce and the increasing numbers of lone-mother families, and their likely effects on children's general and educational development. The political debates emphasise the general and ungendered role of parents. This point is well illustrated by the 1989 Children Act which has parental responsibility as its central theme and was passed by Parliament in Britain with support from all political parties.

However, wider public and political concern stresses the fact that social changes in family life have been so dramatic that they lead to the prediction that by the year 2,000 a large number of children will not grow up or spend most of their childhood in traditional family households, such as those comprising the two 'natural' parents. This excites varied political reactions, from the right's notions that children will inevitably suffer, to more measured evaluation of both the statistical predictions and their potential effects on children's lives.

Commentators on the right tend to bemoan the demise of the traditional family and argue that changes in family structure will necessarily have deleterious consequences for children, particularly in terms of their educational development. For instance, Peter Dawson, the General Secretary of the Professional Association of Teachers in Britain, raised the issue of the relationship between changes in family life and children's educational performance in his valedictory speech. He claimed that:

'By the end of this decade, most children will be brought up in one parent families . . . What are likely to be the consequences of a new social structure, with the young being raised by just one parent rather than two? . . . Professor Albert (sic) Halsey the Oxford Sociologist recently said that he shuddered for the next generation of children brought up in one parent families. They would do less well at school, be more likely to end up unemployed, be more inclined to get into trouble with the law.

Teachers are well placed to add to the list of deprivations. Children with only one parent often play truant, show signs of insecurity in their relationships with others, need more care and attention from their teachers . . . Children need two parents to grow and flourish as best they may . . .' (quoted in the *Daily Telegraph*, 8 August 1991: 12)

However, Dawson cited the figures on changes in family life and their impacts on children's educational performance as if they were unequivocally correct. As we shall see, the evidence about changes in family life is far more complex than he suggests. Moreover, the impact of such changes on children's educational performance, achievements or success in adult life has not been carefully analysed and is much more sketchy than his assertions would have us believe.

In fact, Dawson was mounting more of a moral argument than a careful appraisal of the facts. This is indicated by his prefacing comments. He noted that:

> 'The connection between children's family circumstances and their performance in school is an emotional minefield. It passes judgment on every living adult who has attempted to raise children ... Almost everything a child achieves, or fails to achieve, in school may be traced back to what happens at home.' (p. 12)

And he went on to chastise those who criticised his raising the topic publicly. He felt there had been an attempt by the 'one-parent industry' to 'justify the new social structure, and thereby a basis for insisting that the state fund it' (p. 12).

His arguments resonate with those of other writers usually seen as members of the New Right, who have mounted a defence of the traditional family. Such defences have occurred in both Britain and the US (Gilder 1981, 1982; Mount 1983; Anderson and Dawson, 1986; Scruton et al. 1987; Murray 1989, 1990). However, until now they have not usually been so clearly directed at the relationship between family changes and educational processes. In fact, Dawson's critique does not bear on recent educational reforms but continues in the traditional vein of considering only the potentially disastrous social and educational consequences of changing family structures. He does not address the implications of 'education reforms' in the context of these changing family structures.

In any event, social changes in family life may not be nearly as serious or as dramatic as these right-wing pundits would have us believe. The evidence seems to suggest that children's family experiences are rather complex. For example, in Britain in 1990, one in four children experienced parental divorce by the age of 16, but may not have spent much of childhood in a lone-parent family. They may have spent time in a step-family or with parents who cohabited rather than married. Similarly, in 1990, almost a third of all children were born into lone-mother families, although the births in some cases have been registered with both parents' names, indicating possible cohabitation instead of marriage of the parents. On the other hand, there is more evidence of child abuse or violence in families, usually two-parent households, than was the case in the past. Most importantly, there is substantial evidence of mothers' changed patterns of work and employment, whatever the type of family structure. All of these changes in family life may have impacts upon children's social and educational developments. These will be one of the subjects of this review.

Why this book?

Many of the issues about parents and education have been explored in a myriad of ways before, and the reader is therefore entitled to ask why there is a need for yet another book on this topic. There are three reasons.

First, none of the previous books has explored the relations between education reform on the one hand and changes in family life on the other hand. They have focused on one or other of these topics. The reason for this book is to bring together these debates.

Second, all the studies of education reform or the development of educational policy and strategies have tended to concentrate on specific issues within the general area. They have either focused on an issue such as parental involvement in pre-school, early childhood or primary education, or parental choice of either state or private secondary schools. They have also tended to be based on one particular geographical area or region, with the exception of official reports, mainly carried out over a decade or two ago. In Britain, the official report that launched the spate of social, sociological, psychological and educational in-quiries into parental involvement in schools and home–school relations was the Plowden report, published almost 25 years ago. It was in fact the last of the official inquiries of the Central Advisory Council for Education. And it was the last, despite its massive impact on action-research, policy developments in home–school relations for socially and educationally disadvantaged children, and fundamental as well as policy-oriented social research (Halsey 1987).

More recent official inquiries in Britain have tended to focus on specific issues, such as the Rampton report (1981) into the education of West Indian children. Its successor, the Swann report (1985), despite its all-embracing title *Education for All*, dealt mainly with the education of minority ethnic children and not with multicultural or multiracial education for all (Tomlinson 1990). None of the studies has attempted to review the available literature across the range of these issues, looking at the relevance of the various studies within the context of the contemporary policy debates. This is one of the aims of this current text.

I myself have already contributed to this literature by looking at the ways in which state policies defined and developed relationships between the family and education in historical and contemporary contexts. However, *The State, the Family and Education* was published over ten years ago and focused particularly on the evidence about the role that the state played in mediating and defining relationships between families and schools, particularly in terms of gender. It did not review the wealth of research and scholarship from within the tradition of the sociology of education, albeit that that literature has been framed within a social-democratic, policy-oriented research tradition. It also did not look at the changing debates from the New Right about giving parents a different role in their children's education. In fact, it took a longer historical time-span, looking at the origins of the British educational system. The second reason for this present book is to bring up to date the impact of a changing policy context on the range and wealth of scholarship in this area.

The third reason is to review the policy-related research and scholarship in a comparative framework, and, where possible, to draw conclusions about the current state of our knowledge about the complex relationships between parents and education highlighting the range and diversity, given current reforms. Two key research themes in this current climate are parental choice and 'school effectiveness'. There is not much consideration of what kinds of families are to be included or of the effects being sought.

Somewhat curiously, given the fact that much of the work on parental involvement has been about strategies to improve equality of educational opportunities, there have been few attempts to look at the relationships between parents and education within the context of major changes in family-life circumstances or, given those changes, to look at them from either a gender or race perspective. The intention here is to review the available evidence with these perspectives paramount in order to question the impact of such changes on the range of educational opportunities.

In most of the literature on the relations between families and education, little consideration is given to the gendered notions of parents or children in a family context. The notions of 'parent' and 'child' are seen as relatively unproblematic. It is assumed that all parents are the same social category or group, regardless of their gender and/or their legal or marital status, and that they all have the same relationship to education and formal schools for their children. Indeed, the term 'parent' has become something of a political slogan. It is used by all shades of the political spectrum as if it were unproblematic: terms such as parental choice, parental involvement, parental participation, power and control abound in the political arena. Yet there are clear differences in social and legal expectations about mothers and fathers. The aim here is to explore the varied relationships of gendered parents to education, especially to schools.

Moreover, the social, economic and racial or ethnic position of gendered parents may critically affect how they can and do relate to schools and education. This will also be explored. Similarly, children are also gendered, and there are different social and legal expectations about their education and adult roles. Where possible, the complex relations between gendered parents and gendered children over the range of issues will also be the subject of consideration. However, it must be noted at this juncture that there is a dearth of evidence about these issues.

Structure of the book

Given that the book is about the relations between parents and education, it will start by looking at the various contexts in which these relations developed. The argument is that a partnership developed between policy-makers or education reformers on the one hand and social or educational researchers on the other, in which they developed the idea of a partnership between parents and education. In other words, a clear relationship grew up between policy and research, which influenced strategic developments in education and limited the perspectives that were deployed about parents. It also influenced the form of the study of policy and its allied research.

This book will review the available evidence about the relationships between parents and education both to situate the contemporary political debates and to provide a critical perspective on those debates from the point of view of the social scientific research and evidence. It will first of all review the ways in which the policy debates have focused upon the relationships between parents and education, from pre-school to primary to secondary to higher and adult education. In this review, the critical role that social scientists have played in both forming and developing the parameters of the policy debates will be considered.

Secondly, the review will investigate the kinds of research and social scientific evidence that have been collected around key questions about the relationship between parents and education, again covering the various levels of education and education reform and looking in particular at changes in family and socioeconomic circumstances and their bearing upon a range of educational and social outcomes.

The book will conclude with a review of the contemporary public policy debates about family changes and education reforms, and the implications for the future, given those debates and the available research evidence. In particular, it will consider the broad issue of what the Americans originally termed the 'demographic time bomb' and its implications for women's educational and family lives.

The structure of the book is as follows. In chapter 2, I consider the ways in which the policy context for educational changes has been framed by debates about the nature of social welfare and education's relationships to families. I also look at the changing nature of family life in this context. I situate the evidence in terms of the ways in which social scientists have become involved in developing the policy context, providing critical evaluations of it and, more recently, developing feminist and other critiques of the relations between private families and public policies. I also briefly address the more recent critical debates about the import of changing family structures for public policies. However, the aim of this chapter is to locate the educational policy debates in a broader public and social policy context – and also to illustrate the extent to which these debates have, in fact, been pursued in parallel rather than in tandem.

In chapters 3 and 4, I consider in more detail the context and the ways in which the educational policy debates have been framed in both Britain and the US, and what their relationships are to concerns about families and parents' roles. I raise the issues of the ways in which social scientists have been involved in these processes at all levels: those of policy formulation, implementation, review and evaluation as well as critical appraisal. I borrow Brown's very useful distinction between the developments of two 'waves' of ideology in this sphere: the wave of the 'ideology of meritocracy' followed by the wave of the 'ideology of parentocracy' (Brown 1990).

In chapter 3, I look at the developments in a 'social-democratic' approach to social and educational policy, around the pursuit of the goal of equality of educational opportunity. The implementation of that goal centred on how to deal with socio-economic differences in family life, from reducing parental privilege on the basis of wealth in access to elite education to reducing parental disadvantages on the basis of poverty. The latter strategy entailed the development of notions of parental involvement through both parental participation in children's education and parent education. These ideas, as elaborated, had differential social implications for mothers and fathers. They also had effects on the development of other strategies, including ideas about political participation.

In chapter 4, I consider how these ideas were transformed from ones affecting all children into notions of parental power and control in the educational marketplace. I consider the ways in which a shift occurred from social-democratic ideologies to right-wing ideologies concerning parents' roles, rights and responsibilities in education and the ensuing 'education reforms' by which these ideologies were to be implemented. I also look at the processes in the US by way of contrast and comparison with Britain.

In chapters 5–8, I consider the ways in which the social scientific research evidence has been accumulated and collected within the context of these changing policy proposals and ideas: in other words, at the limited framing of the policy evaluation and research agendas which tend to contribute to strategic developments and debate. In chapter 5, I look at the origins of the developments in the ideas of parental involvement and participation. I focus on the ways in which they were addressed initially in the context of social-democratic policies by a concern for implementing the strategy of equality of educational opportunity. Social and educational researchers first began to aid the process of policy formulation and implementation by evaluating previous policy measures. They also proposed ways to reduce both parental privilege in access to educational opportunities and parental poverty in relation to educational and social disadvantages. At the same time a more distant and critical perspective on policy appraisal began to develop.

In chapter 6, I cover issues about developing a new form of parental participation as a 'say'. The idea of a parental 'voice' rather than a parental 'role' was developed in Britain, the US and Europe. It was about citizen or political participation and can be seen by looking at parental participation in school decision-making. I explore particularly the notions of 'parent governors' in Britain and broad 'democratic' or 'community control' issues in the US, and rely on Beattie's analysis of professional parents in Europe. I also consider the way a subtle shift to the right occurred. In chapter 7, I cover the massive research evidence collected around the idea of parental choice in Britain and family choice in the US. I explore the ways in which parental choice of school and/or education has been converted into the dominant theme of right-wing educational policy debates in the 1980s and early 1990s. I look at the narrow focus of the debates about an educational market, developed in a range of studies from the sophisticated statistical analysis of Chubb and Moe (1990) to case studies in Britain and a six-nation study conducted for the US government by Glenn. In chapter 8, I consider the question of the further and more recent elaboration of parental involvement into a variety of aspects of curricular and political issues both at school and at home. A focus on parent–school partnerships, through more legally prescribed compacts, is discussed, and typologies of different types of parental involvement and/or participation are also reviewed.

In chapters 9 and 10, I review the evidence about the implications of educational changes and reforms for mothers' involvement in their own and their children's education, and of family-life changes, especially those affecting mothers' roles, for children's educational performance and success. In these two chapters I try to highlight the accumulated evidence around questions of gendered and racialised parenthood and their future, especially given notions of the 'demographic time bomb'. In chapter 9, I am particularly interested in the ways in which women as mothers have been involved in various aspects of the educational system, both for themselves and for their children. In chapter 10, I look at the implications of changes in family life such as lone motherhood and maternal employment for children's educational success, either generally or as gendered individuals. I also review the ways in which these debates have traditionally been framed. I review the 'war over the family' and consider whether there are in fact educational effects of changes in family life. I also look at the debates about maternal employment and their effects on children's education and their performance in school.

By way of conclusion, in chapter 11 I draw together the various complex strands of the argument about how social researchers and social reformers have together developed the agenda for strategic policy developments. I then broaden the analysis to consider the joint implications of family changes and education reforms for the future of children's lives and address the question as to whether there will be more or less social diversity and sexual difference by the year 2,000. I also address the issue of the implications of such reforms for 'educational standards' for all children or for children differentiated by race or gender. I ponder whether such trends will exacerbate social and sexual inequalities or reduce them. I also conclude by demonstrating the difficulties of such an analysis in the context of a limited perspective on policy and research. It necessarily constrains the opportunities for understanding the likely impacts of social and family-life changes for men and women's development.

2

The Family Policy Context: The War over the Family and Family-Life Changes, 1944–1992

Educate a man and you educate a person,
Educate a woman and you educate a family
Ruby Manikan, 1947

Most policy and associated research developments on parents and education are based on an unquestioned set of assumptions about gender and generational relationships both within the private family and in the wider public world of politics and employment. The above quotation illustrates the point that women are assumed to be responsible not only for caring for the family but also for the education of their children. Although this was written over 40 years ago, most reformers and social researchers still accept as unproblematic the nature and characteristics of families and their relations to the educational system. Indeed in some curious way, given the growing and explicit feminist critiques in the public arena, notions of families have either become less explicitly gendered than in the past or have continued with stereotyped notions of mothers and fathers. The term 'parent' has become something of an ungendered political slogan, used in policy notions such as 'parental' choice and 'parental' involvement or participation. It is assumed that all parents have the same relationship to their children's education, or at least to their more formal schooling.

In this chapter I shall set the scene for the subsequent discussion about how the relations between families and education have been framed in a particular way. I shall first look briefly at different perspectives, then at the policies that have developed in Britain since the Second World War about the relationships between families and public life, in particular about families with dependent children. I shall also briefly consider the growth of social policy analysis as a way of understanding developments in social policy, social welfare and the welfare state. I shall also review developments in studies of the family and the ways in which feminist perspectives have developed in the context but have not been used for policy appraisal. In order fully to set the scene for the review of the particular policy focus, in the final section of this chapter I will look at the evidence for changes in family life, focusing on demographic trends in marriage and divorce and patterns of maternal as well as paternal employment. This places in context the care and education of children and questions the extent of changes in family life which affect children's lives.

The limitations in perspectives on parents and education

What is interesting to note is that both family policies and associated social research have tended to develop in parallel with, rather than together with, educational policies. This is not because educational policy-makers did not problematise notions about family or gender. They were not questioned in family policy until relatively recently. However, feminist critiques developed rather earlier in relation to families and family life than they have in relation to education, or rather to the connections between families and education. As we shall see, this is probably because the majority of 'research' in the area of families and education is narrowly related to specific policy evaluations.

One of the first comprehensive reviews of the complexity of the evidence on the connection between social class, family life in its gendered forms and education was published as recently as 1987. We shall consider the evidence, and particularly Toomey's review (1989), in chapter 10. Until the late 1980s, most of the evidence, in Britain at least, has ignored the complexity of family life, and in particular the relations between mothers and fathers over children's scholastic achievements. Indeed, Toomey's conclusion that differences between families are more important than social class for children's educational achievements is both startling and important. This kind of evidence, which focuses upon mothers' occupational or employment status in terms of children's educational achievements can, however, be used both negatively and positively. For example, Chubb and Moe, two American educational researchers, have used this, as we shall also see in subsequent chapters, to develop essentially 'conservative' arguments for mothers' occupational activities, in the interests of children's educational success (1990). They do not, however, discuss this differential impact on boys' and girls' attainments.

Epstein (1990), reviewing research around families and education in the US, has also reached the conclusion that the two kinds of policy and scholarship have developed separately and in parallel rather than together. Her particular focus, however, is on how to integrate the two kinds of study to ensure an emphasis on improved relations or partnership in the interests of children's education. She writes:

All the years that children attend school, they also attend home. The simultaneous influence of schools and families on students is undeniable, but too often ignored in research and in practice. In research, social scientists who study one environment rarely give serious attention to another. Sociologists of the family rarely study how family practices affect student success in school, or how school practices affect family attitudes, interactions, and practices. Sociologists of education who study school and classroom organisations rarely examine how school practices affect home environments, or how family cultures, attitudes, and practices affect school practices and effects. (1990: 99)

These are important points which we shall discuss in more detail. What Epstein herself does not do is to consider the gendered nature of the practices and evidence in the sociologies of education and families.

Similarly in most of the recent and growing literature around families and education, the notions remain ungendered and unquestioned – although there is now more questioning of social class, if not of race or ethnicity. For the moment two examples suffice. Two recent collections by John Bastiani entitled *Parents and Teachers*, (1987, 1988) do not question the *gendered* characteristics of, or processes in, families. They do refer to the more generally radical critical social scientific literature. Similarly, his more prescriptive study, looking at home–school relations and entitled *Working with Parents: A Whole School Approach* (Bastiani 1989), does not question the differences between working with mothers or fathers. Alastair Macbeth, who has written widely on issues of parents and schools in Britain, especially Scotland, and also reviewed the European context, also has not questioned gendered parenthood or the gender or generational processes within families. This is despite an extremely thorough review of the issues in his most recent textbook entitled *Involving Parents: Effective Parent–Teacher Relations* (1989). Issues about gender in the characteristics and form of families remain absent from the prescriptive literature on parents and schools.

Curiously, however, this is also true of the literature which adopts a rather more critical perspective, even that produced by feminists. Most of the feminist literature in education does not address the question of the gendered nature of families, but has taken its focus from the rather more social-democratic or social-equality approach to questions of education. It has tended, on the whole, to concentrate on the issues of the social construction of gender or femininity through schooling and, as a corollary, on issues about how to achieve equal opportunities through education and in the labour market. To the extent that the contribution of education to occupational choice and social mobility has been questioned by feminists, it has been from a wider feminist perspective on the family rather than on education.

The now 'traditional' focus of feminist thinking has been on relationships between men and women. It is this approach that has dominated within the extensive feminist literature on education. For example, the very important and critical work of Dale Spender has looked at the ways in which women and girls have been treated relative to men throughout the educational system, focusing especially upon male power and dominance as the reasons for women's relatively poor treatment within the system. This theme of the ways in which the educational system itself produces and reproduces gendered people, together with the associations with the labour market or occupational system, has dominated feminist research. There is now a vast accumulated literature about the differential treatment of boys and girls, from different class and ethnic backgrounds, within and throughout the educational system. Perhaps this is best summarised by two collections by Arnot and Weiner (1987) and Weiner and Arnot (1987).

However, not all feminists have ignored the question of the gendered structuring of families and their relations to the educational system. My own concerns had originally been to investigate the ways in which state policies have attempted to maintain and reproduce particular gendered relationships between families and aspects of the educational system, but particularly schooling. However, I had not, hitherto, looked at the ways in which the evidence has been predicated on particular assumptions about gendered relationships within the family. A most influential feminist, noted for her development of a particular feminist methodology, Dorothy Smith, has drawn attention to these questions in an early article entitled 'A peculiar eclipsing: women's exclusion from man's culture', first published in 1975. This influential article, which has been republished, makes two important points, similar to those made recently by Epstein, but with the addition of a feminist perspective. Smith notes:

> The enormous literature on the relation of family socialization and educational attainment, in which the role of the mother takes on such a prominent part, can be seen also to have its distinctive biases. The treatment of mothering in this literature is in various ways evaluative, critical or instructive with respect to the practices and relations conducive to educational attainment or to the psychosocial well-being of children. Virtually the whole of this literature presupposes a one-way relation between school and family whereby family practices, organisation, and, in particular, mothering practices are seen as consequential for the child's behaviour at school. The phenomenon of school phobia as it is vulgarly described is one notorious example, whereby the protectiveness of mother is understood as creating a dependence in the child and hence the child's fearfulness at school . . .

Smith goes on to question why this has not been seriously addressed as an issue:

> Who has thought to take up the issue of these relations from the standpoint of women? Might we not then have studies concerned with the consequences of the school and the educational processes for how the child matures in the family and for the family itself? Where are those studies showing the disastrous consequences of the school for the families of immigrants, particularly non-English speaking immigrants . . . Where are the studies telling us anything about the consequences for family organisation of societal processes that 'subcontract' educational responsibilities for homework and so forth to the family and in particular to the mother? . . . What are the implications of this role for family relations, particularly relations between mothers and children?

She then adds the point that the majority of educational research has been conducted from the standpoint of men:

> In the field of education research itself, our assumptions are those seen from men's position in it. Turn to that classic of our times, Phillippe Aries's *Centuries of Child-hood*. Interrogate it seriously from the standpoint of women. Ask, should this book not be retitled *Centuries of Childhood of Men?* Or take Christopher Jencks's influential book entitled *Inequality*. Should this not be described as an examination of the educational system with respect to its implications for inequality among men? [The very terms in which inequality is conceived are based on men's occupations, men's typical patterns of career and advancement . . .]
> A work examining the educational system with respect to the inequality of women would be focused quite differently. It would, among other matters, be concerned with the educational system as systematically producing a differential of competence among women and men in almost every educational dimension, including that of physical development. It would focus on inequality between the sexes as a systematically organized product of the educational process. (1987: 24)

From these examples, Smith tries to reach a broader theory about women's exclusion from wider social processes. She claims it illustrates the 'outcomes of women's absence'. She also sees it not as 'accidental' but as 'a general organisational feature of our kind of society' (p. 22). Her analysis has had important repercussions for feminist research methodology. Oddly, it has not created a more systematic mapping of the presuppositions in educational research and the policy consequences of such 'absences'.

Other feminists writers have, more recently, begun the process of more detailed studies of the educational process. For instance, Walkerdine and Lucey (1989) have reanalysed a study of young children's learning both at home and at school. The study was originally conducted by Tizard and Hughes (1984) from a traditional social psychological perspective. Walkerdine and Lucey critically appraise that perspective and reach rather different conclusions about mothers' contributions to children's learning. We shall return to their findings in chapters 9 and 10.

Similarly, Gordon (1990) has studied the ways in which mothers who consider themselves to be feminists rear their children in the present climate. She looks at their relationships to schools and the educational system. She concludes that, although it is fraught with difficulties, such women take pleasure in trying to develop alternative styles of family life and child-rearing. However, these two studies are most unusual in taking the mothers' perspectives as central in the education and care of children.

Despite these new and critical perspectives, educational policy and research is still based on the assumption of an unchanging and unproblematic set of gendered relationships within the family. What are the origins of this set of presuppositions and how do they now accord with the nature of family life in contemporary advanced industrial societies? I shall attempt to answer both of these questions, relying on the evidence of changing family characteristics and circumstances particularly from the burgeoning critical literature. Much of this literature has drawn on official statistics and reports, but reinterpreting them by highlighting gender relationships. It begins to show the complex relationships between families and education, illustrating the extent to which schooling represents the intersection between families and education as a whole. It also highlights the fact that most of the work on families and family policy has continued to develop without considering formal education or informal family socialisation practices.

The family policy context

The assumptions that were built into social policy in Britain from the origins of the welfare state, and are articulated most clearly in the Beveridge report (1942), have not accorded with changing family circumstances (Land 1976; Pascall 1986; William 1989). The assumptions, which have been adopted by social-democratic policy-makers and social researchers alike, were of the privacy of the family for the purposes of the care, maintenance and upbringing of its members. The welfare state was not to take over these familial activities but was to provide social supports and services to maintain the family in its traditional nuclear form of two biological parents with dependent children (Zaretsky 1976).

The welfare state in Britain was developed by a partnership between Fabian or 'liberal' social reformers, and social scientists as researchers. They believed in the necessity of state intervention in economic and social life to sustain economic growth. However, the precise forms of intervention were to be developed in a partnership between policy-makers and social researchers, who would review and evaluate the specific and particular effects of these developments. But as Mishra (1984) has noted, in the formation of welfare states especially in Britain and the US, there was a 'bipartisan political consensus' over the necessity of state intervention to support such developments. Both political parties accepted and extended this consensus to the relationship of the family to the state (Moroney 1976; Land and Parker 1978).

As the 1950s and 1960s progressed, a controversy about the form and delivery of social services developed, in particular about the extent and nature of support for families. In Britain, as in the US, in the early 1960s 'social-democratic' researchers discovered or rediscovered poverty among families (Abel-Smith and Townsend 1965; Thernstrom 1967). A massive debate developed about the extent and nature of state support to families deemed to be in poverty, to which social researchers contributed. In the US, policies that were set in train in the aftermath of President Kennedy's assassination were entitled

'The War on Poverty' and the 'Great Society' legislation. In Britain, similar if more limited policy developments occurred, but with less fanfare. All these policies had differential impacts upon families and family life but their impacts on gender relationships, especially women's role and position as mothers, were rarely considered or contested. Indeed, to the extent that a bipartisan political consensus about family supports has continued into the 1980s, it has been about children's care and ungendered parental responsibilities. The Children Act 1989 in Britain addresses the twin questions of care for children in deprived circumstances and in the context of changes in family formation through divorce. However, no consideration was given in the legislation to questions of gender. We shall further consider these questions in the next chapter as they relate to educational policy and research developments.

It was only as a result of these social welfare and allied developments, such as the growth of mass political and social movements, that consideration was given to a more explicit review about women's position in family life. Piven and Cloward (1971, 1976) have discussed the role of such movements in policy developments, especially in the US. Coote and Campbell (1982), among others in Britain, have illustrated the development of the women's movement, and its demands for social policy changes particularly around family life.

The development of a more scholarly analysis of women's position in the family, especially in relation to public and social policies, only began in the early 1970s, as an outgrowth of the women's movement. Although two of the first 'demands' of the women's movement related to women's 'oppression' in the family and equal educational opportunities, these were still not put together in the burgeoning feminist critiques about women's relations to men, to early childcare and to employment opportunities as well as to the family.

A literature around women's changing and complex position in families began to develop, giving a critical perspective on family policies and their effects. It ranged from specific issues to do with social welfare and childcare, such as the Children Act 1989, to more complex issues to do with the social analysis of family life. Land (1976) was one of the first in Britain to point up the assumptions about the relations between the sexes built into the British welfare state and subsequent social policies, and the fact that they were erroneous assumptions. A sustained feminist critique of social policies developed (Dale and Foster 1986; Pascall 1986; Williams 1989).

In broader studies of the family, as well as of family policies, a feminist strand has also become important (Delphy and Leonard 1992), but much of the study of the family remains based on uncritical analyses of gendered relationships (Bernardes 1987, 1988). Moreover, the study of the family remains at least as controversial as the more policy-oriented issues of feminist social policy analysis. Indeed, the question of the future of families and women's role within them has been the subject of much critical feminist and other analysis and debate (Segal 1983, 1987; Wilson 1983; Phillips 1987; Sassoon 1987).

The assumptions that were built into the welfare state about a conventional nuclear family with two biological parents, the father the breadwinner and the mother the housewife and 'homemaker', have also been uncritically accepted by educational as well as social policy reformers, as we shall see in subsequent chapters. Yet the notion of the family has, over the last 50 years, become a major area of political dispute and one that has frequently been the subject of controversial social analysis. One of the best studies of the conflicts in the political arena in the US over the notion of the family is Berger and Berger's *The War over the Family* (1984). They set out to demonstrate how different political groups and parties have approached the question in the US. Their own view of the family ends by being the traditional 'liberal' approach, in which the privacy of the family, with an unquestioned sexual division of labour, is left untouched by public policies. The subtitle of their book is a clear indication of their stance: it is *Capturing the Middle Ground.*

Family changes and the family policy 'war'

In Britain there have been similar disputes over the notion of the family and over appropriate public and social policies either to sustain or reinforce particular family formations. Given the bipartisan political consensus on the role of state intervention to sustain economic growth and its relationship to families, there was relative agreement on maintaining the privacy of the family and traditional sexual relationships. There was a relatively mild intellectual dispute between academic advisers and policy-makers on the forms of social and income support to be provided to families. The disputes centred on the extent to which social services or income maintenance should be used to iron out differences between families in their socio-economic circumstances. The work of Peter Townsend as both a social scientist and a political critic was particularly influential here (especially Townsend 1979).

In the 1980s, right-wing politicians and their intellectual advisers began to dominate the debates about the family in Britain through a number of semi-academic publications, such as Ferdinand Mount's *The Subversive Family* (1982). At the time, Mount was a member of Prime Minister Thatcher's Family Policy Group, advising on policy development (David 1985). A number of 'think-tanks' such as the Centre for Policy Studies, the Institute for Social Affairs and the Institute for Economic Affairs, as well as the Adam Smith Institute, have also been interested in promoting a 'conservative' and traditional notion of the nuclear family, in particular as the basis for public and social policy developments. They have taken up the arguments by 'New Right' writers on the family in the United States. In particular, George Gilder's arguments that changes in family life had occasioned changes in welfare policies to the extent that 'men had been cuckolded by the welfare state' (cited in Eisenstein 1982) were taken up as the basis of criticism of welfare developments in Britain (David, 1986). Similarly and more recently, and with greater media attention in Britain at least, Charles Murray's work on the effects of social welfare on families and family formation, through his two studies *Losing Ground: American Social Policy 1950–1980* (1984) and *In Pursuit of Happiness and Good Government* (1989), have been used as the basis of right-wing arguments about family policy developments. Murray, too, has argued that changes in family formation and family life have rendered men 'uncivilised' and without purpose in life. These arguments have echoes in the arguments which formed the origins of the welfare state, at least in Britain, when there were major discussions about what the impact of family allowances might be (Land 1976).

Murray (1990) also developed arguments about 'the problem of the family' seeing it as a specific class and 'racial' issue. Again, his arguments have been used by the right in Britain to develop rather more punitive social policies, ignoring the systematic differences between the social class and racial structures in the US and Britain. Murray himself wrote a brief account of the similarities rather than differences in social developments around the 'family' for a specifically British audience (Murray 1990).

Although not articulated specifically in gender or generational terms, most of the arguments presented by the right have been about how problematic demographic trends in family formation have become. Although concerned about a range of changes in family life such as the increase in divorce and marital breakdown, the main target became lone-parent families, especially those in poverty, in which children are reared by lone mothers, with absent fathers. Thus from the perspective of the New Right 'the problem of the family' has become, in both theory and policy terms, one in which the traditional two-biological-parent household has been replaced by one in which mothers are alone, rendering fathers 'useless'. Although the arguments are presented as general arguments about the implications of changes in family life in terms of parenthood and child-rearing, they clearly have particular implications for parental roles and responsibilities in relation to education as well as childcare. Of course, mothers' traditional responsibilities as primarily involved in childcare and education, including involvement with school, cannot be as easily sustained in a changed family context, especially if other family policies remain the same. We shall return to discuss these issues in chapters 9 and 10.

Family-life changes

However, the question that must first be addressed is to what extent there have in fact been major changes in family life, including family formation, marital breakdown and divorce and mothers' paid occupational activities, since the origins of the welfare state in Britain in the 1940s. What are the statistical picture and the likely demographic trends which have become the subject of political dispute? By the end of the 1980s, there had been two major types of change since the 1940s in relation to families. One has been the changing occupational activities of women as wives and mothers; the other has been changes in the form of the family from what has been assumed to be the traditional two-natural-parent family. The key characteristics of families are no longer – if ever they really were – that mothers of dependent children are involved exclusively in their care and education at the same time as looking after household and husband. Rather, the majority of mothers of dependent children in Britain are involved in some form of paid employment, although characteristically on a part-time rather than full-time basis, with the extent of mothers' involvement in the paid employment tending to vary with the age and educational stage of the child or children as well as with the particular family-form of the household.

The ways in which families have changed over the last 50 years have been at least as dramatic as changes in the occupational activities of women as wives and/or mothers. Indeed, these two sets of changes may have partly gone together as well as having been affected by changes and developments in education and social policies. Increases in educational provision, especially for girls and women, have arguably had a major impact upon women's involvement in paid employment, even as wives and/or mothers. (This is a point to which I shall return in chapters 9 and 10.)

Certainly increases in educational provision for middle-class girls in the immediate aftermath of the Second World War increased their aspirations and expectations of involvement in public life as well as private family life. There are now numerous accounts, especially by feminists, of the ways in which such expectations and aspirations were shaped. In particular it is important to note the autobiographies of Wilson (1982) and Oakley (1983) as well as the more analytical accounts such as Wilson's *Only Half Way to Paradise* (1978), *Truth, Dare or Promise: Girls Growing Up in the Fifties* (1985), edited by Liz Heron, Mary Ingham's *Now We are 30*; *Fathers* by Ursula Owen, and work by Carolyn Steedman (1986) on her relationship with her mother as she was growing up. Ros Edwards (1991) has explored how women return to higher education as mature mother students, shaped by their own particular expectations of their roles in adult life.

Feminists have also considered how women's role within the family might be more appropriately understood and analysed. The growing literature of women's roles as 'carers' of families, inspired initially by work on women as mothers in families, has focused increasingly on more general issues about 'care', particularly in Britain. Perhaps most significant is the work by Janet Finch (1989) on women's family obligations, which excludes *all* the literature on dependent children and focuses entirely on adult rather than child dependents. A less theoretical and more practical study of women's role as carer is that by

Cherrill Hicks (1988) which compares and contrasts a number of case studies of women's roles as carer by looking at mothers of young dependent children with the care of sick, mentally handicapped and elderly relatives, trying to tease out communalities and contrasts in these various roles. Similarly Clare Ungerson has studied women's role as carer, largely focused upon adult dependents (1988).

Sassoon (1987) has drawn together a number of both cross-cultural and nation-specific studies of women's changing role in particular in relation to state welfare. In particular, one article in Sassoon's collection by Laura Balbo uses the term 'crazy quilts' to illustrate the complexity of women's lives as carers in relation both to the private family and public agencies, particularly on behalf of children.

Both Carol Gilligan and Nell Noddings in the US (as well as Cari Waerness from Norway in Sassoon's collection) try to develop more analytical concepts of caring in relation to women's roles, relying here more on the conventional assumption that women are first and foremost 'carers' of children. Noddings (1985) and Gilligan (1984) look at women's activities in relation to more moral issues rather than the 'work' *per se*. Noddings discusses women's moral development and their role in the moral education of children. Gilligan focuses on differences between men and women in how they approach the task of caring or being concerned about children's moral development.

More recently in Britain there have been a number of studies of mothers in relation to their particular activities in terms of caring for and bringing up children. Sharpe has carried out a number of studies of mothers – *Double Identity (1984); Falling for Love: Teenage Mothers Talking* (1986) – as have Oakley and Backett. Most of these studies focus on mothers' feelings and how they cope with domesticity, rather than on the 'work' of caring for children. Both Sharpe (1984) and Brannen and Moss (1988 and 1990) look at mothers' experiences of early childcare and paid employment. The title of Brannen and Moss' second book, *Managing Mothers* (1990), is most instructive. It is an account of how mothers' 'managed' the process of returning to paid employment, shortly after the birth of a child.

Ann Phoenix's study of young mothers (1991), all of whom are teenagers and many of whom are black, looks at how they cope with early childcare and, for a very small number, their own early departure from the educational system (a point to which I return in a later chapter on mothers in education in chapter 9). It also looks at their relationships with the fathers of their children.

What all of these studies serve to illustrate are the varieties and complexities of family life today in Britain and other advanced industrial societies. They flesh out the statistical picture which has been built up of the changing pattern of family life referred to above, and the fact that women as mothers are involved in paid employment from an early stage in a child's life; as well as the fact that a child's upbringing may take place in contexts other than the traditional family.

Changes in marriages as the context for children's varied family lives

In the first place, there have indeed been major changes in the structure and form of family life, as well as in the paid employment activities of mothers in a variety of types of family. The changes in family life in Britain in the 45 years since the Second World War have been very complex and are difficult to characterise, given that future trends are projected to be different again from those of the last 50 years. What does seem to be a very important feature of changes in family life over the last 50 years or so, particularly from the point of view of child-rearing and education, is the changing and variable rates of marriage and divorce or separation. This has also been true of other advanced industrial societies (CERI 1983).

Between the 1940s and the early 1980s there was a trend towards marriage as a major feature of family life. In Britain for example, in 1971, by the age of 50, 96% of women and 93% of men had married, whether one or more times. By 1987, these figures had reduced to 83% of women and 79% of men. This is partly because of the changing age at which men and women marry. However, these figures only serve to illustrate changes in the approach to the legal institution of marriage. Indications are that many couples now cohabit instead of marrying.

Similarly, there have been major conflicting trends in childbearing and child-rearing in different family contexts. Most women still become mothers, but the context in which they do so has changed. Over 80% of all women of child-bearing age are expected to have children in the next decade, but the age at which women have children is now on average older. From the 1940s to the 1980s there was an increase in the number of families formed in a marital situation; since the end of the 1980s, there is a trend towards more women choosing either remain childless or to have fewer children, and, among those who do decide to have children, for more to have them outside of wedlock. Thus, in 1989, the percentage of births outside marriage reached 27% of all births (*Social Trends 21* 1991: 43), having been a mere 5% in 1960, and 16% in 1986 (*Social Trends 20* 1990: 46). However, the majority of births out of wedlock are registered in the names of both parents, indicating a trend towards cohabitation or at least co-parenting rather than the assumed notion of more lone parenthood:

Most women have children, though families are on average becoming smaller . . . The percentage of women who had a child at all increased steadily from about 80% of those born in 1920 up to a peak of 90% of women born in 1945. For women born more recently the likelihood of remaining childless has increased and it is estimated that 17% of women born in 1955 will not have any children. Corresponding to the upward trend in the proportion of women remaining childless, the proportion of women projected to have two or more children now looks likely to fall. It is assumed that the proportion of women remaining childless will level off, os that just over 80% of women born in 1975 and later years are projected to have at least one child. (*Social Trends 21* 1991: 42)

There has, however, been a major trend towards marital changes in the last 30 years. The proportion of households containing a married couple has been decreasing (*Social Trends 21* 1991: 36), reflecting the falling birth rate from the mid 1960s (although this rate started to rise again in the 1980s). However, three-quarters of the population of Great Britain in 1989 still lived in families headed by a married couple. But the proportion of people living in a 'traditional' family – that is a married couple with dependent children – fell from 53% to 42% between 1961 and 1989. On the other hand, the proportion of people living as members of lone-parent families containing dependent children more than doubled, to reach 5.8% in 1989. More importantly, the proportion of all families with dependent children which are lone-parent families increased from 8% in 1971 to 17% in 1989, largely reflecting the rise in the incidence of births outside marriage (as noted above) and the incidence of divorce and/or separation. Over the 30-year period the proportion of families with dependent children headed by a lone mother has almost doubled, to 12.3%. In addition, the percentage of such lone mothers who are single or divorced has increase steadily over the last 20 years and, in 1990, comprised three-quarters of all lone mothers. Moreover, the majority of lone-parent families are in a sense 'initiated' by women: in 1988, 83% of divorces were initiated by women (Coote et al. 1990). But less than 4% of mothers of dependent children are single mothers. In terms of race, Brown (1984) as cited in Coote et al. (1990) found that 31% of West Indian households with children were headed by a single adult, 5% of Asian households and 10% of white households. There is, however, enormous regional variation in lone parenthood status. For example, in inner London in 1981, the proportion was almost 27% and in Glasgow and Liverpool 20%.

Children are thus now likely to be growing up in a variety of family situations. Indeed, the distinction is not just between lone parenthood and the traditional family. Although the rate of divorce has been increasing rapidly over the last 20% years, so has the rate of remarriage (Joshi 1989). Divorce is expected to occur in almost 40% of new marriages. In 1971 the rate of re-marriage involving at least one divorced partner was 21% while in 1987 it represented 36% (Coote et al. 1990). However, the rate of remarriage ending in divorce is also increasing. For example, Coote et al. observe that 'Couples in which only one of the parties has been previously married and where there are no step-children have the lowest risk, whilst those marriages where both husband and wife are remarrying and both have children from previous marriages have the highest risk' (1990: 15).

Children may therefore spend a part of their childhood in a traditional family or a lone-parent situation, and a part in a reconstituted household, with step-parents and siblings as well as half-siblings, etc. Indeed, in 1990 a quarter of all children were expected to see parental divorce before aged 16 (Haskey 1989). However, the scanty evidence indicates that, in 1985, 80% of children under 16 lived with both natural parents, of whom 78% were married and 2% cohabiting. The other 20% lived in a variety of situations, namely 10% with a lone mother, 7% with a natural mother married to a step-father, almost 2% a natural mother cohabiting with a step-father and almost 2% with either of a lone father, adoptive or foster parents or relatives or in a special home or school. In 1989 17% lived in lone-parent households (*Social Trends 21* 1991), the proportion having more than doubled since 1971. More important, two-thirds of lone parents live in poverty, compared to 10% of two-parent families.

Bradshaw and Millar in the first major sample survey of lone-parent families in the UK, found that:

> 64% of lone parents had been married and 37% were single. However, the patterns of relationships preceding and after lone parenthood are often very complex and the present marital status of the lone parent is not necessarily a good indication of the routes into lone parenthood. In particular 18% of single lone parents had cohabited before they became lone parents . . . and 15% of lone parents had been lone parents more than once. Only 2% of single lone parents had had their first child aged under 16 and only 12% of all single lone parents had planned to have a baby. (1991: 36)

At one point in time, therefore, the traditional natural family is clearly the dominant form, although alongside it a variety of different situations for child-rearing exist. And moreover, as noted above, there is added diversity regionally. Malcolm Wicks of the Family Policy Studies Centre summarised these trends as 'key family indicators' in a table presented to the Social Policy Association Conference (1991), and these are reproduced in table 2.1 in modified form to demonstrate patterns of both marriage and parenthood in terms of gender and the context of family change.

Changes in mothers' occupational activities and children's family lives

Not only are family structures now very complex, but mothers' activities in these contexts, in Britain especially, have also changed enormously over the last 50 years or so. Evidence about mothers' changing economic activity rates in Britain can be found in a variety of sources, as summarised by Coote et al. (1990: 17), and most recently by Wicks (1991). With Kiernan, Wicks wrote:

The proportion of married women going out to work has doubled from 30 per cent in 1951 to 60 per cent in 1987. Almost all the increase has been in part-time employment. In more than half of all couples with dependent children, both partners are in paid employment (Kiernan and Wicks 1990: 26).

Table 2.1   *Key family-life change indicators*

Key family indicators in the UK	Late 1950s/early 1970s	Late 1970s/early 1980s	Late 1980s
Marriage and divorce			
Total number of marriages	379,000 (1961)	398,000 (1979)	392,000 (1989)
Cohabitation – % of all women aged 18–49 years cohabiting	–	3% (1981)	8% (1988)
Number of divorces	27,000 (1961)	157,000 (1979)	164,000 (1989)
Projection: % of new marriages that will end in divorce	–	34% (1979/80)	37% (1987)
Parenthood			
% of births outside marriage	8% (1972)	12% (1980)	27% (1989)
% of children living with both natural parents	–	83% (1979)	78% (1985)
% of families with children headed by lone parents	8% (1971)	12% (1981)	17% (1989)
% of children under 16 with divorced parents	–	20% (1979/80)	24% (1988/89)
Parental employment			
% of married women in paid employment	30% (1951)	–	60% (1987)

Source: Adapted from M. Wicks, 1991, Key Family Indicators, Table 3 in his paper 'Social Politics 1979–1992: Families, Work and Welfare' to the Social Policy Association Annual Conference, University of Nottingham, 8 July.

This pattern is not dissimilar to that in other countries of the European Community (EC). More details, especially of the arrangements that parents make for pre-school children in day care, are to be found in a collection edited by Melhuish and Moss (1991). This discusses not only the statistical picture but also the policy implications. Peter Moss (1988 and 1990) has provided an excellent survey and summary of the evidence about mothers' employment and 'child care', covering all the countries of the EC. In the original evidence presented in 1988, he compares and contrasts the part-time, full-time and total employment rates in 1985 with the unemployment rates for mothers and fathers with children aged 0–9. This is also linked to the numbers of children within the family. In the first place, the proportion of fathers in full-time employment in Britain compared to other countries of the EC is very low – about 84–85%. All other countries, with the exception of Ireland with rates of 80%, have rates of well over 90%.

The rates of mothers' full-time employment in the UK are similarly lower than those of mothers in other countries of the EC, again with the exception of Ireland and also the Netherlands. The rates are between 29 and 45%. However, the rates for part-time employment are higher than in most other countries of the EC with the exception of Denmark. As might be expected, employment rate for women vary considerably according to the number of children (Moss 1988). The drop is more appreciable in the UK than in many other countries of the EC. Employment activity rates also vary by age of child and regionally. In the study that contributed the British evidence to Moss' final summary, Bronwen Cohen (1988) has shown the variations according to age of youngest child and region. Taking her data from the unpublished 1985 Labour Force survey, she found that, for Great Britain as a whole, 28% of mothers whose youngest child was under 5 were in paid employment, while for those whose youngest child was between 5 and 10 it was almost 58% and for those 11–16, 69%. For all mothers with children (including those with children in education up to the age of 18) the figure was almost 50%.

Cohen also found that there was variation not only by age and region but also between ethnic minorities. West Indian/Guyanese women with pre-school dependent children are found to have a higher rate of employment activity than other women in this category, while Pakistani/Bangladeshi women have a very low rate of employment activity (1988: 12).

In the subsequent final study Moss (1990) shows the changes in 'maternal' employment, of women with children under 10, between 1985 and 1988. His table is reproduced here as table 2.2 entitled Parental employment, 1988. In this short period of three years there was an increase of 7.5% in maternal full-time employment and 6% in maternal part-time employment in the United Kingdom. In 1988 46% of mothers of children under 10 worked full-time and 32% part-time. A further 8% were unemployed. The 1988 figures for the United Kingdom are, very similar to the average for the whole European Community,

Table 2.2 Parental employment, 1988

Country	% employed women with child under 10		% employed men with child under 10		% employed women aged 20–30, no children		change in % employed women with child under 10, 1985–88		% unemployed women with child under 10	% unemployed men with child under 10
Germany	38%	(21%)	94%	(1%)	75%	(15%)	+2.6%	(+2.5%)	6%	3%
France	56%	(16%)	93%	(1%)	75%	(11%)	+1.3%	(+1.9%)	10%	5%
Italy	42%	(5%)	95%	(2%)	55%	(4%)	+3.6%	(+0.7%)	8%	3%
Netherlands	32%	(27%)	91%	(9%)	68%	(30%)	+8.2%	(+7.7%)	8%	5%
Belgium	54%	(16%)	92%	(1%)	68%	(13%)	+2.8%	(+2.4%)	12%	5%
Luxembourg	38%	(10%)	98%	(–)	69%	(5%)	+3.7%	(+0.6%)	2%	1%
United Kingdom	46%	(32%)	88%	(1%)	83%	(20%)	+7.5%	(+6%)	8%	8%
Ireland	23%	(7%)	79%	(1%)	67%	(6%)	+5.1%	(+1.5%)	8%	17%
Denmark	79%	(32%)	95%	(2%)	79%	(6%)	+2.6%	(−1.5%)	8%	3%
Greece	41%	(5%)	95%	(1%)	52%	(3%)	+3.8%	(−0.2%)	6%	3%
Portugal	62%	(4%)	95%	(1%)	69%	(6%)	No information		6%	2%
Spain	28%	(4%)	89%	(1%)	44%	(5%)	No information		10%	8%
European Community	44%	(17%)	92%	(2%)	71%	(13%)	No information		8%	5%

Figures in brackets = % employed part-time

Source: P. Moss, *Children in the European Communities 1985–1990*, Commission of the European Communities, No. 31, August 1990, p. 6.

being 44% and 17% respectively and 8% unemployed. By contrast, the figures for paternal employment in the United Kingdom of 88% full-time and 1% part-time ar rather lower than the EC average of 92% and 2%. The figure for paternal unemployment in the UK of 8% is higher than in the EC as a whole at 5%. Moss also documents the ways in which families and households have changed among countries of the EC and attempts to link these changes to changes in employment rates. He states:

> The proportion of one parent households was 12% for households with a child aged 0–4 and child age 5–9, the highest level in the Community (excluding Denmark). Lone mothers were substantially less likely than all mothers to be employed, with an employment rate of 18% (19% lower) for lone mothers with children aged 0–4 and 37% (16% lower) for lone mothers with children aged 5–9; this difference was mainly due to lower levels of part-time employment among lone mothers. Lone mothers had higher unemployment rates than all mothers – 10% for lone mothers with children aged 0–4 (compared to 9% for all mothers) and 11% for lone mothers with children aged 5–9 (compared to 7%). (1990: 34)

Moss' data for Britain were again drawn from the studies by Cohen, who found major differences in rates of employment among lone mothers depending upon the age of the child and familial status of the lone mothers (1988: 12). The age of the child had a considerable impact, since only 17% of lone mothers with a youngest child under 5 worked either full or part-time. For those with a youngest child over 5, the rate was about 50% divided relatively evenly between full- and part-time work. Single mothers were less likely than divorced, separated or widowed mothers to be involved in paid employment whether full or part-time. Only 24% of single mothers of children of all ages worked, while the comparable figure for divorced was 45% and widowed 48%. 39% of separated mothers worked.

As Cohen remarks: 'The hours that women work are significantly affected by parenthood' (p. 12). She shows that those lone mothers in paid employment, however, are more likely to work full-time than married mothers; as she states, this is likely to be attributable to the system in Britain of income support. This has been endorsed by the more recent official survey of lone parenthood by Bradshaw and Millar (1991):

> Among the lone mothers 23% were employed full-time (here defined as more than 24 hours per week) and 17% were employed part-time. Among the lone fathers 46% were employed full-time and 6% part-time. Both the men and the women had higher than average rates of registered unemployment . . . The women most likely to be economically active were older women, ex-married, with school-aged children, some educational or vocational qualifications, living in owner-occupied housing and receiving some maintenance. An analysis of the factors affecting the probability of full-time employment found that the most important factors were predicted wage rates, not having young children and child care availability. (1991: 96)

However, Bradshaw and Millar point out that this latter group is very distinctive, and constitutes a group who also may not have to rely on income support. They show that 'as many as 85% of the women received income support at some time since becoming a lone mother' (p. 97). In that respect, as is also the case for married mothers, the question of childcare is also very important with respect to their paid work: 'A third of the women on income support said that difficulties with child care were the main or most important reason they were not working. The main problem identified was cost, and that working would not be worth-while because of the cost of child care' (p. 96).

Indeed, it is this issue of the effects of policies of income support on lone mothers that the right-wing critics of the changes in the family have been at pains to point out. Given that systems of income support now predispose lone mothers *not* to be involved in the labour force or to have to work full-time in order to make ends meet, right-wing critics now argue for different systems of income support. On the whole, they have argued to make it more difficult for lone mothers to manage the care and upbringing of children alone, forcing them to stay in marriages (or presumably, now, cohabiting relationships) rather than be dependent upon state income support.

Left-wing commentators on the family and on family policy have been slower to develop arguments about how to deal with these massive changes in family life. Most of the traditional left-wing commentarys (for example, Townsend's major studies of poverty and the work of the Child Poverty Action Group) were concerned not with gender or sexual inequalities but with socio-economic differences. Similarly, in the US, left-wing concerns until recently have focused on social rather than sexual inequalities in family life.

However, even these left-wing arguments have tended to be about how to equalise between families on the basis of their socio-economic circumstances, rather than marital or familial status. Most recently however, Coote et al. (1990) have begun to present the evidence and arguments about how to develop social policies that will enable women as mothers to participate in both family life and paid employment on an equal basis with men. However, their arguments still hinge on assumptions about women's primary role being that of mother and 'carer' rather than equally involved with men in both family life and paid employment. Moss, too, has developed arguments about the necessity of childcare facilities which are publicly funded to enable women to participate equally in both paid employment and family life. Moss lists a whole range of facilities and services which, if implemented, would contribute to wider measures of equality of opportunity between the sexes. Hopefully too they would contribute to allowing for choice amongst families of a variety of different statuses. Together with Melhuish, Moss has also discussed more detailed comparative evidence from a range of advanced industrial societies (1991).

Conclusions

The aim of this chapter has been to illustrate, on the one hand, the simplicity of the notion of family which is embedded in social and educational policy and the research evidence on which it is based, and, on the other hand, the complexity of family life and the changes in family life that have taken place since the formation of the British welfare state 50 years ago. I have shown how the idea of the family in both policy and research developments remained that of the traditional two-parent unclear family, with father as breadwinner and mother as homemaker. This idea was used in family and educational policy development and the research studies on which they were based. I have shown how critical and especially feminist perspectives began, in the 1970s, to illustrate the inadequacy and limitations of these notions.

I have also shown how changes in family life provoked a policy 'war' about the evidence and policy solutions, and have reviewed the evidence in terms of the changing marital and parental contexts of children's lives and the question of parental, especially maternal, employment. I have also briefly addressed the ways in which both left and right policy-makers consider how to deal with these questions.

I turn now, in chapter 3, to look first at the ways in which the educational policy context has developed around particular assumptions of parents and family life. I shall then, in chapter 4, look at the ways in which, more recently, this policy emphasis has shifted to a concern not with ironing out socio-economic differences between families but with involving parents as *consumers* in the educational process. In both contexts, the notion of family has remained narrow and ungendered and has ignored shifts in family life. I shall investigate the various types of research studies around the relations between parents and education and the research findings which have been spawned by these policy developments. I shall move on to look at the evidence for the two-way processes at work between families, especially parents in their gendered roles, and education, and then return to a consideration of the impact and potential effects of changes in family life on education.

3

The Education Policy Context:
The Idea of 'Meritocracy', 1944–1976

Introduction

This chapter considers the ways in which the relations between parents and education were developed through the education policy context in the 30-year period from about the end of the Second World War. The next chapter will focus on the subsequent social and educational reforms from 1976 to the present. I shall consider the social-democratic developments in British policy and also those in the US. I could also have looked at the influences and effects of other industrial societies, such as Sweden or Australia. In the formation of this particular policy context, as I hope to illustrate, the US was by far the most dominant influence. Silver (1990) has nicely illustrated the interplay between Britain and the US in the formation of these policy processes. In looking at the more recent stages of education reforms, I intend to consider other countries. I shall also concentrate on the ways in which social scientists, as researchers, became involved in the policy processes of formation and implementation as well as evaluation and review.

There is now an enormous literature about this period of educational and social policy development. It has been researched and evaluated by a variety of social scientists and historians, from social policy analysts to political scientists to sociologists and educationalists and so on. What has been rather absent from these varied and various accounts has been a feminist perspective on these particular developments, although there has been some consideration of aspects of the issues from a gender perspective. The theoretical perspectives have also varied in their accounts of the changes and processes and there is certainly little agreement on quite how to evaluate the impacts of these social and educational reforms. However, there is more agreement about the form and characteristics of the policy developments, if not their actual and intended effects or outcomes.

I have found Phillip Brown's (1990) notion of three 'waves' in the socio-historical development of British education particularly useful for distinguishing between the periods from the point of view of parents and education. Although his analysis is, as he himself states, tentative, particularly in respect of the aims and effects of the contemporary 'wave', the idea of attempting to classify policy developments is useful. He relies not just on the values underpinning the political perspectives that were dominant during the periods under review but tries to tease out the particular ideology of the policy under evaluation. He is interested in the ways in which different ideologies have underpinned forms of educational selections. As he argues:

> The 'first wave' is characterised by the development of mass schooling in the nineteenth century. It was intended to confirm rather than transcend existing social divisions . . . Therefore this . . . highlights the fact that schooling during the 'first wave' was structured on the basis of ascription for one's predetermined future social, occupational and domestic roles . . .
> The 'second wave' involved an ideological shift in organising principle, from an education determined by an accident of birth (ascription) to one based upon one's age, aptitude and ability (achievement). In a 'meritocratic' system of education (Young, 1961), all must be given an equal opportunity of gaining access to jobs concomitant with their abilities. However, the meritocracy never promised equality, only that inequalities would be distributed more fairly. (1990: 67–9)

I want to look more closely at how this 'ideology of meritocracy' was translated into policy initiatives and practice and by whom, attempting to provide more detail than Brown has done.

Within this 'second wave' of socio-historical development around the idea of 'meritocracy', I think it is possible to distinguish three stages in its implementation. Silver (1990: 190–4) identifies the first stage as the concern in the 1950s with secondary schooling and social class, the second stage, in the late 1960s, with primary and early childhood education. Given his particular interest here in the concept of the 'socially disadvantaged child' he does not add further stages. In this chapter, I will only be concerned with these two, leaving their elaboration in research, until chapter 5. Hewison (1985b) provides an account of how the particular forms of 'parental involvement' developed out of this second stage of early childhood education. Hurt (1985b) adds a third stage: that of the development towards parents being given a role in management of schooling. This will also be considered in more depth in subsequent chapters, especially in chapters 6 and 7.

As Silver in particular acknowledges, these various processes 'borrowed' extensively from American experience and practice; the obverse of the US borrowing from Britain is not so much over the role of parents as over the form and nature of the curriculum. Silver writes: 'It is important to note that from the late 1960s, in particular, Britain and the United States exchanged messages about the education of the disadvantaged child in various ways, though often with a degree of hesitation and resistance . . .' (1990: 199). He has also commented more generally on 'Britain's process of educational exchange' (1990: 149). He continues:

> Britain has given and taken, and Britain itself has received, adapted and resisted –
> for example . . . the American or Swedish variants of the common school, and
> ideas and ideals of pre-school or compensatory education. The whole of this
> international traffic has been periodically busy, always complex. (p. 149)

He has also commented about this in particular, adding that:

> . . . the crucial policy issue of the 1950s and 1960s therefore became the Second-
> ary Comprehensive School. Lady Simon, in *Three Schools or One?* (1948) brought
> the American high school into the British debate . . . Admiral Rickover, in what
> became a 'back to basics' involvement, took the message of the high quality of the
> British grammar school to the United States, just as the American comprehensive
> high school was becoming a thread in the pressure for change in Britain. (1990:
> 158)

In fact, the 'liberal-democratic' educational reforms which were the way in which the 'ideology of meritocracy' became translated into policy and practice eventually came under pressure for change in the late 1960s and early 1970s. I shall also consider the ways in which there developed a 'conservative backlash' to the reforms in Britain and the US, which eventually took the form of what Brown calls the 'third wave', the 'ideology of parentocracy'. I shall review the particular issues about secondary comprehensive education which became the central issue of that backlash, before turning to consider, in chapter 4, the 'third wave', with its central focus on parents' role in education from the point of view of being 'consumers'.

The origins of the 'ideology of meritocracy'

The Second World War marked a major watershed for the development of social and educational policy in Britain. The policy developments and the evidence used to sustain those social and educational reforms went hand in hand. Both were based upon what have been called Fabian notions: the idea that social progress could be achieved through gradual state intervention, using social scientific evidence as a basis. Many commentators have pointed to the origins of the social sciences as academic disciplines, in Britain at least, in the throes of the Second World War, although the main influences on such developments go back over the previous four decades.

In other industrial countries – particularly the US – the origins of socio-logy certainly predate the Second World War and come from rather different theoretical and ideological origins. However, the concern with public policy by academic social scientists developed after the Second World War, too, with the ascendance of a more liberal polity. As in Britain this involvement of academic social scientists was relatively slow to develop. In the US it reached its ascendance in the 1960s and was particularly associated with social and educational reforms.

The peculiarly British concern with the 'creation' of the welfare state was a concern to achieve equality of opportunity through state intervention. The period of its development has also been referred to as a period of social reconstruction after the Second World War. The particular concern was with attempts to reduce social class distinctions and to allow for individual and personal development on the basis of *merit*, regardless of family socio-economic circumstances and parental privilege. Social services were to be developed to ensure the means for full participation in social and economic life, covering therefore the creation of a National Health Service (NHS), massive changes in social services for children and in housing and employment policies as well as extensions to the education service.

As Gray et al. have noted (1982), there were two strands to the 'debates' at that time – what they call an evaluative or moral strand and an explanatory strand – about how such developments could be achieved. They too point to the intimate relationships between social research and political practice. They also develop their approach from that of Kogan (1975), who has argued that for the 20 years from the Second World War there was what he has called a 'shared identity' between the two.

There has indeed been an enormous amount of research around the developments from the Second World War, whether about the creation of the welfare state or about educational policy developments *per se*. In the last 12 years, under 'Thatcherism', there has been a growth in the revisions of the accounts about social reform in the direction of social progress and economic growth. I do not want to rehearse here all of the arguments of this voluminous literature, save to pinpoint the ways in which both the social reforms and the associated social research were centred around attempts either to 'equalise' between families or to reduce disparities in access to participation in economic and social life on the basis of family circumstances.

However, the notion of 'family' that lay at the root of these policy developments was never clearly articulated and was often used as the 'best' indicator of other social factors, in particular social class and/or social status. The political (or policy) intention never seemed to be to vitiate all types of socio-economic differences between families, but merely to ensure that they did not weigh heavily on individual opportunities for employment or public participation, or individual social and occupational mobility. As noted in chapters 1 and 2, although the notions of family and parents appeared genderless, the key issues addressed in these early policy developments were between individual male members of families, although never explicitly articulated as focusing on boys' prospects for social and/or occupational mobility.

In Britain, until the Second World War, the educational system was closely linked to what was later seen as the entrenched system of social class. Indeed, Tawney, a noted socialist, wrote in the 1930s that this was 'the hereditary curse of the Englishman' (Tawney 1931). He influenced the development of social research, especially at the Fabian-established London School of Economics, into social and occupational mobility, both theoretically and also in terms of the prospects for policy changes. This in particular was developed by Glass (1961) as a major field of inquiry into social mobility.

Social psychologists, however, had an earlier influence on the developments in educational policy which were oriented to reducing class differences and attaining a more 'meritocratic' educational system. Cyril Burt, for example, was very influential in the inter-war years in developing psychological ability tests based upon American developments (Silver 1990: 191). These began to be used by local authorities to distinguish pupils' abilities in order to allocate to appropriate secondary schools on the basis of academic merit and ability rather than purely on the parents' ability to pay. Indeed, it was the evidence that there were objective means of assessing pupils' academic merits that led to the particular framing of educational policies towards the end of the Second World War.

The political objective of equality of opportunity which underpinned the various social reforms contemplated and developed during the war was developed especially for education in the first instance and lay at the basis of the educational reforms devised during the Second World War by a coalition government. Indeed, the principle of equality of educational opportunity was shared by both political parties, although the interpretations and meaning of it in precise policy-implementation terms may have differed between Conservatives and Labour. The Conservatives were the dominant party in the framing of the legislation: Labour were the party in power, after the Second World War, when it came to detailing the process of implementation. Mishra (1984) and others have pointed to what became known as a 'bipartisan political consensus' over the development of the welfare state in this early period. This was true not only of Britain but also of the US and other advanced industrial societies.

However, Britain has always seen itself as having taken the lead in this respect. The wider aims of social reconstruction lay behind the specifics of the policies, as articulated in numerous reports written during the war. The 1944 Education Act took on board most of these discussions, but remained rather distanced from the specifics. For example, the legislation created compulsory 'free' secondary education for all children from 11 to 14, later to be 15 (1948), with 16 promised for the 1950s. (This did not materialise until the 1970s.) However, the types of secondary education to be provided were not specified in the legislation, except for differences between state-maintained and voluntary controlled or aided schools provided partly by the religious authorities.

Opportunities for parents to continue to send their children to private, fee-paying schools or to educate children otherwise than at school were also not removed by the legislation (Walford 1990). However, all parents gained the opportunity, through the Act to have their 'children educated according to their wishes' and in accordance with 'their ages, aptitudes and abilities'. The legislation itself did not specify or even clarify what this phrase might mean. It was left open to the local authorities to devise new schemes of secondary education, although a clarifying circular proposed a tri- or bi-partite system of secondary schools, based upon the legacy of schools coming under the LEA mantle.

The aim clearly was to ensure that children's chances of educational and occupational opportunities should be in accordance with their academic merits, rather than their parents' socio-economic circumstances. The corollary especially of helping children from poor home circumstances was not considered at this juncture, except through modest methods to provide financial help. Schemes such as scholarships, especially for pupils of poor parents at particular schools such as the direct-grant schools, or for help into higher education, were increased. Curiously at this juncture, broader schemes of help for educational maintenance in the state system of education, particularly at the level of further education, were barely considered. (Also there were only slight revisions to the system of scholarships as a form of access to higher education, i.e., the universities, at that stage.)

The main thrust of the legislation was to ensure a modicum of similarity across the range of schools and to open up the opportunities for some kind of secondary education for all children from the age of 11. This was never meant to imply that all children should have access to the same kinds of education; rather than tests of ability would enable schools and LEAs to distinguish different levels of ability.

As McPherson and Raab have noted in their excellent, if rather discursive, account of the history of education in Scotland by comparison with England and Wales:

One may . . . extend to Scotland Salter and Tapper's conclusion that 'the almost universal employment of intelligence testing in the secondary school selection process *after* 1945 was a direct consequence of how the 1944 Education Act was implemented rather than any dramatic change in the character of capitalism as a result of the war years' (Salter and Tapper 1981: 146 emphasis in the original). What is more dubious is that the intention in Scotland was to 'protect' the senior secondary or grammar school from mainly lower class incursions. This is the motive that Salter and Tapper discern in England (*ibid*, chapter 7).
    . . . Nevertheless, it could be argued that reference to the consequences of testing, and reference to the motives of its originators, is to miss the point that the mental testing movement legitimated the bipartite policy by giving it scientific respectability. (1988: 369)

The policy developed under the 1944 Education Act thus tried to reduce, but not completely vitiate, parental privilege in access to education, but allowed for parental 'choice' across a range of different types of school, whether state or private schools. Thus there were opportunities for parents to choose secondary schools which were partly funded by the state but provided in 'partnership' with religious authorities, such as the voluntary aided or controlled schools, completely private schools, or those with both a test of ability and a test of parental means – the direct-grant schools.

In Scotland this system was slightly different since there was a wider range of state-provided schools, but as McPherson and Raab point out:

> Senior secondary expansion meant that inequalities of provision . . . grew starker; and also that more parents were touched by the failure of their borderline children to gain access to this privileged provision. The demand for equality of opportunity for access to privilege began to harden into a stronger demand namely for equality of treatment as such. (1988: 370)

In this context, there developed concerns about the effectiveness of the particular policies oriented to achieving the goal of equality of educational opportunity. Initially the main focus of social or educational research was on the effects of policies to reduce parental privilege on the basis of individuals or groups, even social classes, in terms of access to types of secondary school. Questions were also raised about the nature of elite education, and access to private as opposed to forms of state education on the basis of social status or socio-economic circumstances.

However, over the next 30 to 40 years this embryonic research tradition has blossomed into major fields of enquiry, creating at least two types of social science discipline – that of the sociology of education and, secondly, the sociology of social and educational policy. Both developed out of the Fabian tradition of a mix of social progress and social enquiry, initially developed by the Webbs in the beginning of the twentieth century (David 1990). They themselves became models for the development of a peculiarly British social scientific tradition, which mixed involvement in the policy process and social policy evaluation. However, it was not until after the Second World War that this process really began to develop into a fully-fledged field of social scientific endeavour. It was after the war, with the election of a Labour government, that Fabians properly became involved both in the processes of policy development and policy evaluation. The implementation of a 'full' welfare state, which had begun during the Second World War, was really made more effective by the post-war Labour government. Nevertheless, both political parties shared the 'ideals' or 'ideology' of a welfare state, comprised of a new partnership between families and the 'state' in the provision of social welfare, including education. In fact, education was the first of the welfare policies to be developed.

Similarly, education policies were some of the first to be carefully scrutinised and evaluated by social scientific researchers, working in this 'new' Fabian tradition. All the initial developments in this mix of policy implementation and scrutiny were commenced at the London School of Economics. Since then, social researchers and analysts have shifted their emphases over time from a concern with the direct effectiveness of particular policy prescriptions to looking more carefully at the effects of both policy and practice or social processes. Thus social research endeavour has blossomed into complex and major fields of enquiry, from looking at educational policies and processes to the inter-relationships with family processes and systems. The notions of family–education interactions and policies have, over time, been transformed.

The initial research endeavours to chart the effectiveness of particular educational reforms reached relatively cautious conclusions, and did not conclude that educational reform would necessarily be capable of vitiating completely the social class differences, using family socio-economic circumstances as an indicator of social class, that had pertained in Britain up until the war period.

Two types of social research developed in the immediate post-war period: one was concerned with investigations of previous policies and the other with the development of policies in the context of the new principles of equality of educational opportunity. This latter type of research had a particular emphasis on the role of education in relation to social and occupational mobility, either on a group/social class basis or on an individual basis. Both, however, were concerned with the effects of educational reforms on opening up opportunities to wider groups or individuals in society and trying to reduce the effects of education in elite schools on access to higher levels of education and occupational opportunities.

The overarching ideology of the period was that intellectual merit and academic ability were more important than social status or family background in helping to develop and then sustain economic growth and social progress, through individuals' involvement in particular occupations in the labour market. However, the particular policies developed to these ends would be important to monitor and evaluate.

Both Olive Banks and Asher Tropp were the initial and critical social researchers in evaluating the effects of previous policies and practices around such educational developments. Banks carried out careful investigations of the developments of secondary education from the turn of the century up to late 1940s, while Tropp looked at the developments, from its early beginnings in the nineteenth century through to the 1940s, of school-teaching as a profession. Both pointed to the continuing effects on the wider society of a class-based system of education. Banks, however, was particularly pessimistic:

This attempt to use the secondary schools as a means to 'unite instead of divide the nation' raises in an interesting way the whole problem of the relationship between the education system and the social structure . . . much recent educational policy has underestimated the influence of the social and occupational structure on the development of the secondary schools . . . the popularity which the grammar schools have always enjoyed in the eyes of parents is derived ultimately from their social role. . . . (1955: 8)

She then reached the conclusion that:

While the precise relationship between the school and society is still not understood, it is reasonably clear that the history of English secondary education has been profoundly influenced by its role in selection for social mobility. As a result, purely educational reforms have foundered whenever they have set themselves against the selective function of the schools. (1955: 248)

Banks both pointed to the 'conservative' nature of schools in terms of their continuing links with a social class system and the fact of modest developments with respect to social mobility, albeit not from across the range of the social classes. Indeed, her pessimism rested on the fact that even modest proposals to reduce class or parental privilege were doomed if they did not fit with the existing notions of modest social reform rather than major shifts in social and occupational mobility.

Similarly, Tropp demonstrated how the system of school-teaching remained tied to a fairly entrenched social class system, despite dramatic expansions and developments in the educational system from the middle of the nineteenth century through to the 1950s.

Halsey and Floud, the two other major innovative liberal or Fabian sociologists of education in the early post-war period and also working in a similar social research environment, set themselves a slightly different research agenda. Instead of reviewing the effects of past educational policy and practice, they began to investigate the contemporary relationships between social class, social structure and the educational system. Their frame of reference was the potential of education for achieving social mobility, developing their work from the pioneering studies of social mobility by David Glass at the LSE.

In one study, with Martin, they looked at the links between social class and educational opportunity, defining social class in terms of parents' (but especially father's) occupational status. They pointed to the modest effects of changes in educational opportunity on both individual and group prospects for social and/or occupational mobility (Floud, Halsey and Martin 1956).

This led them to a concern to investigate the broader issues of the relationships between the social structure and the economic system, in particular in relation to the widening and diversification of the labour market. They also began to develop arguments about how important the educational system was in mediating such relationships. They saw the prospects for improvements in the economy in terms of the expansion of educational opportunities, provided to children on the basis of academic merit rather than family background. They developed this argument not only for Britain, but also drew from their knowledge of and research findings about the expansion of educational opportunities in countries such as the US (Halsey, Floud and Anderson, eds, 1961). This approach to educational reforms and their relationships to the wider society continued to influence the growth and development of sociology as well as more official, policy-oriented social research. During the 1950s, arguments were also developed by educationalists about the most effective means of reducing parental privilege in education, and achieving the expansion of educational opportunities regardless of parental or social class background.

For example, Robin Pedley, a Professor of Education, developed a very eloquent case for what was now becoming known as the comprehensive school rather than the bi- or multi-lateral school. His argument was based upon evidence drawn from the US, among other countries, for what they called the 'common' school, a school open to all in the local community regardless of parental circumstances or differences in academic ability. In other words, it was an argument for what subsequently became known as social mixing as well as mixed ability. It was also the beginnings of the argument for community schools, although these, too, had been started in the inter-war period, in particular in terms of the developments in London's schools.

Secondly, as this kind of social research about what Gray et al. (1982) have called 'social reconstructions' began to grow apace, so too did more official concern with the particular effects of governmental educational policies. In particular, the kinds of changes in secondary education aimed at through the 1944 Education Act were not as effective as the intentions of the legislators. A problem, seen as a 'wastage of talent', began to be identified along with that of what was called the 'untapped pool of ability'. In other words, it was increasingly recognised that policies to reduce social or family differences in educational opportunities were not being achieved by the particular reforms of schools. The reforms, through the creation of bi- or tri-partite schools, for different classes of ability or social classes, maintained rather than reduced social inequalities. Gray et al. (1982) have also noted how this problem of 'wastage' was identified about the same time in Scotland.

During the 1950s, social research on these issues not only began to develop in the academy but was also developed by quasi-official governmental agencies, comprising in part social scientists. They built upon a rich social tradition in Britain, developed in the nineteenth century, of trying carefully to document the effects of particular governmental educational policies. In the past, this tradition had been developed into official methods of social investigation. In this post-war period, those methods were becoming increasingly social scientific and reliant upon an accumulating body of knowledge about methods of social enquiry. The details of this process have been discussed in *The State, the Family and Education* (David 1980). By the end of the 1950s, social researchers had begun to raise a number of related questions about the impact and effects of educational policies, oriented to widening opportunities for children regardless of their parental backgrounds. There were two sets of concerns about: how to widen access, but still remain within the educational opportunities 'paradigm': how to open up further educational opportunities and how to ensure that education remained tied to widening economic opportunities (see David 1980).

The paradigm, in other words, was very narrow – how to get the best out of young people in terms of their intellectual abilities and not have to do anything with changing their home circumstances – although Gray et al. have pointed out, with the benefit of hindsight, that there was an assumption that education led not only to economic and social improvements but also to social change, including an impact again on the family.

Similarly, the Centre for Contemporary Cultural Studies (CCCS) (1981) has pointed to the complex process of policy developments associated with both policy-makers and social researchers. However, although official reports, commissioned by Conservative governments, raised the issues, it was a Labour government in opposition that focused on how to develop the details. From the late 1950s, there were beginnings of change in the ways in which educational policies were conceived and formulated. As noted variously by Saran (1973), David (1980), James (1980), CCCS (1981) and Gray et al. (1982), policy formulation took account of the reviews of social researchers, both those involved officially in the processes of policy inquiry and those working independently. In the late 1950s and early 1960s there was indeed a spate of official and academic or independent inquiries into aspects of secondary education. All were concerned with the extent to which policies were achieving the aim of equality of educational opportunity, essentially by providing education appropriate to the abilities and needs of a range of students and pupils, without regard to their parental home circumstances. It was increasingly recognised that there remained what became known as an 'untapped pool of ability' that official policies seemed unable to 'exploit'. This notion was considered in several official and unofficial reports.

Consideration was therefore given to how to tap this 'pool of ability' by means of more extensive educational policies. Three areas of policy were considered. First, policy-makers and social researchers focused upon issues to do with changes in secondary education and its links with both further and higher education and the labour market. Secondly, issues to do with primary education and access to early childhood educational opportunities were raised. Throughout this process of reconsideration, the question of how to try to develop educational opportunities for children and students on the basis of merit rather than parental home circumstances remained paramount. However, within that, the emphasis had shifted from consideration only of access to educational opportunities to how to deal with obstacles within the educational process, such as issues to do with social and economic disadvantages. In other words, increasing consideration was given to factors such as poverty and poor material home circumstances that might inhibit children from participating on an equal basis in education and in access to labour market opportunities.

The beginnings of the breakdown of the party political consensus

As regards secondary education, several official committees of enquiry put forward proposals from which reforms were developed. Under a Labour government from 1964 to 1970, a variety of policy changes were proposed and implemented. In particular, the notion of abandoning academic selection to secondary education in favour of comprehensive education was pursued. However, the pace of change was quite slow, as the Labour government had only a slender majority and remained unsure as to the Conservative support for such measures. Indeed, reforms of comprehensive education created a major party political controversy, leading eventually to the breakdown of the party political consensus over state intervention in education. Initially comprehensive education was suggested by the growing evidence from research that forms of academic selection at age 11 did not necessarily reach all the children capable of benefiting from an academic education. In fact, evidence increasingly showed that children in secondary education were still 'educable' and capable of benefiting from academic education. However, arguments were also developed to demonstrate that comprehensive schools did not necessarily continue adequately to develop academic capabilities.

It was not only arguments about academic standards and access to such educational opportunities that eventually led to the breakdown of the party political consensus. It was also arguments about the extent to which particular forms of access to privileged education should continue which led to the major particular controversies. The Labour government attempted to allow for 'parental involvement' in the processes of educational decision-making over comprehensive reorganisation through a series of amending pieces of legislation (see in particular Saran (1973) for accounts of this). However, it was their policies towards private schools and voluntary schools that began to make the issues more controversial. For example, the two committees of inquiry on the public schools also raised issues that later led to charges of 'egalitarianism' as being in contradistinction to a policy of equality of opportunity.

Similarly, policy changes with respect to further and higher education also led to such charges. During the 1960s, the Labour government, building upon the policies developed by a Conservative administration to expand educational opportunities in higher education, aroused further controversy. In this case, rather curiously, policies were developed that ran counter to those in secondary education whereby they had attempted to reduce forms of stratification. In higher education, the Labour government developed the binary policy which created two sets of educational institutions which were intended to suit different types of student and labour markets – the polytechnics and the universities. However, it was the very expansion of this elite level of education that led to the subsequent party political controversies about the necessity of educational expansion to meet the needs of a more educated labour force.

The policy of secondary school reorganisation commenced in 1965 but took over ten years to be implemented fully because of the controversies it provoked. Those LEAs which began a wholesale removal of academic selection to state-maintained grammar schools met with considerable parental resistance (James 1980). However, more resistance to the LEA-wide changes was found in Conservative than in Labour-held authorities. Indeed, under a Conservative administration from 1970 to 1974, with Mrs Thatcher as Secretary of State for Education, the policy was revoked. However, between 1974 and 1979 the Labour government pressed ahead with firmer policies in the form of legislation: specifically the 1976 Educational Act. During this period of time, as Benn and Simon (1971) noted, changes in fact proceeded apace. However there was a noticeable backlash.

As stronger policies developed around equality of educational opportunity, such as comprehensive education and the expansion of higher-education opportunities, the increasing voices of dissent from the right were expressed. By the late 1960s, these views found more group expression in the, albeit still minority, publication of the Black Papers by a right-wing academic pressure group. The pamphlets were given the ambiguous name of Black Papers which gave a hint of possible British officialdom given that statutory publications are called White or Green papers. The first Black Paper was published in 1969, edited by two right-wing academics (Cox and Dyson). It contained a series of brief articles bemoaning the various education developments under a Labour administration from primary to comprehensive to higher education. It provided the first relatively sustained critique of educational policies which were seen as leading inexorably to uniformity and mediocrity as opposed to quality and higher educational standards. Indeed, the unifying aim of these right-wing educationalists was that of 'excellence in education' or 'standards of excellence', as opposed to what was now dubbed by Angus Maude, one of the contributors of the first Black Paper, as 'the egalitarian threat' (Cox and Dyson, 1969a).

The principle of equality of educational opportunity had, in 1944, been accepted by both right- and left-wing administrations. In detailing of this principle, over the next 30 years, there were many party political disagreements, and research evidence was amassed on both sides of the political spectrum to illustrate the problems and controversies with its implementation. It was, however, under the two Labour administrations from 1964 to 1970 that the right-wing opposition to the ways in which equality of opportunity was being developed as an educational policy began to grow. A clear 'socialist' strategy, articulated by Crosland, the then Secretary of State for Education, with a group of left-wing educationalists and social researchers, provided the occasion for the divergences (Wright 1977; CCCS 1981).

The right-wing arguments revolved around the notion that 'more meant worse': the expansion of educational opportunities inevitably meant a 'decline in the academic standards' and a 'growth of mediocrity' rather than a meritocracy. The Black Paperites argued that there should be choice for parents among schools and that changes should not be implemented in school organisation or where traditional types of selective schooling had not been proven inadequate. By 1977 five Black Papers had been published, each providing evidence from a range of educationalists, from teachers to head teachers to academics, of the problems with the left-wing policies on primary and secondary education as well as higher education. It is a measure of the growing strength of these so-called 'Conservative educationalists' (Knight 1989: 3) that they were able to continue to publish what were initially recherché 'research' pamphlets.

Nevertheless, the views of these pamphleteers did not greatly influence the development of education policy during the four years of Conservative administration at the beginning of the 1970s. The government remained committed to the principle, and the practice, of equality of educational opportunity as a means of maintaining economic growth. In particular, a White Paper entitled *Education: A Framework for Expansion* was published in 1972, including the aim to expand opportunities in both nursery schools and higher education (David 1980).

It was in the next period of Labour administrations, during which there were successive economic crises, that the more right-wing arguments of the need to link education more effectively to the needs of the economy, in order to raise standards rather than provide equality of opportunity, began to gain currency. For example, in 1976 the Labour Prime Minister, James Callaghan, launched 'a great debate on education' specifically to consider how to restructure the educational process so that it tied education and training more clearly to the needs of industry and the economy.

Expanding educational opportunities without regard to parental circumstances was no longer seen as a consonant with economic growth. The Labour government focused on ensuring that parents played a role in this process of restructuring, arguing that there was a clear parallel between state and parental needs. Callaghan prefaced his introduction to the debate with these comments: 'What a wise parent would wish for their children, so the state must wish for all its children' (CCCS 1981: 220). In that respect, Callaghan considered the most important issue not that of equal opportunities but of preparing for the world of work. But this did not mean involving parents in the discussions about the question of links between education and work:

> In that context, parental 'interests' were to be represented through the rational organisation, by the state, of the school to work transition, and the matching of

the appropriate skills and aptitudes to the needs of the labour market. Schooling and its social purposes were therefore to be politically subordinated to the perceived needs of a capitalist economy in the throes of crisis. A restructuring was required because of the *failure* of schools to fulfil the older social democratic equation that investment in the education would produced economic benefits. (CCCS 1981: 220).

In other words, the Labour government was beginning to renege on its commitment to the principle of equality of educational opportunity and the policies that it, and previous Labour and Tory administrations, had pursued. These policies were seen to have failed to produce economic growth. The argument that the state should invest in human capital or potential on the basis of academic ability, rather parental background, was beginning to be questioned. Instead the government began to consider ways of developing and improving educational standards in school, pressured by more right-wing arguments. To this end a common core curriculum for all state schools was proposed to be taught throughout primary and secondary schools. However, although this proposal was not implemented it provided the starting-point for subsequent, more right-wing, debates (David 1980).

So, too, did the setting up of a committee of inquiry into the 'Government and management of schools' in 1977. The Taylor committee eventually proposed the development of a system of representative parent and teacher school governors along with community representatives. It was the recommendations of this committee that subsequently formed the basis of Labour's Education Bill in the late 1970s, which began the process of transforming the role parents in education decisions. However, despite the opportunities to provide a more collective role for parents in the process of educational decision-making, it was the more individualistic role that has later been seized upon and elaborated by the right (Woods 1988).

Developments in parental involvement and early childhood education

Although the major political controversies were sparked by these two educational measures in the first instance, it is the development of policies for primary and early childhood education that have had a longer-term controversial impact upon education policy developments and the transformation towards the 'ideology of parentocracy' rather than that of meritocracy. It is also the case that the involvement of social scientists in the policy process and the development of educational policies has been greatest in this particular area of reform. This has perhaps led to the longer-term impact upon both policy developments and transformations.

In both political and sociological writing, the common move . . . has been to start with equality of opportunity and move thence to equality . . . arguments about 'equality', appear even in the most utilitarian arguments about economic growth . . . there was . . . a considerable slight of hand . . . in the tendency in the sociology of educational to claim a socialist pedigree . . . the 'old' sociology of education belong(s) to a long tradition of English middle class reform and social investigation . . . the parallel between the long-standing concern with popular morality and behaviour and the sociologist's interest in 'educability' is (likewise) very close . . . . (CCCS 1991: 96; 99)

The American heritage

In the first instance, however, policy developments around primary and early childhood education were slow to develop and were borrowed almost exclusively from the United States, and almost entirely derivative of them. In the 1950s in the US concern about the access to educational opportunities of particular minority groups in the population began to receive public attention. The initial issues were to do with the question of race and the system of educational 'apartheid' or segregation that had developed in the previous 50 years. Gunnar Myrdal, a Swedish social scientist, had become involved in investigating these issues and had begun the process of highlighting major inequalities. These have recently been discussed in a new study of Myrdal's American policy developments (Jackson 1990).

Moreover in the early post-war period the civil rights movement began to campaign for changes in the treatment of black people, particularly in the southern states. A major *cause célèbre* was the case of a black family whose child had been excluded from the nearest school on the grounds of colour. The case was eventually heard in the US Supreme Court and became known as Brown versus the School Board of Topeka in Kansas, in 1954. This case was the first in which social scientific evidence was presented to sustain arguments about the inequities of segregated education, in what was known as an *amicus curiae* brief. The effect of the landmark decision in the US Supreme Court was to led educational desegregation in the southern states, albeit at a slow and rather controversial pace. It also eventually led to what later became known as educational integration in the northern state where the issues were rather different (see especially here Glazer (1973) and also Orfield (1978)).

A wider issue that was raised from the campaigns of the civil rights movement and the legal case itself was the question of educational opportunities for children from various social groups, and the evidence on which educational separation or integration should be sustained and based. By the end of the 1950s, arguments were being developed for wider measures of equality of educational opportunity for racial and ethnic minority groups. In the presidential election of 1960, such issues became major items of importance. President Kennedy was eventually elected on a platform to develop and provide equal educational opportunities. He also aimed to promote a wider participative society sustaining liberal goals of equal opportunities in employment and social as well as economic activities.

To this end a number of community-action and social programmes were developed in the early 1960s (Marris and Rein 1966). However, Kennedy's assassination in November 1963 hastened the process of social reform around liberal measures. Under the new President, Lyndon Johnson, a whole panoply of social measures were developed around equal opportunities. In particular, there were measures to deal with civil rights and the involvement of poor people in wider social programmes. The main focus, however, was on educational measures. As President Johnson announced in his War on Poverty and Great Society legislation: 'The answer to all our national problems is one word and that word is *education.*'

The educational strategies pursued were very wide-ranging indeed, covering vocational and training measures for teenagers and adolescents, educational desegregation and integration, and measures to deal with early childhood education and the involvement of parents in the processes of educational decision-making and delivery. However, the social programmes developed were often attendant upon the work of social scientists. During this time social scientists became heavily involved in the processes of educational research and policy proposals and prescription. In particular, legislation in the US started the involvement of social scientists in policy formulation and evaluation. The Economic Opportunity Act of 1964, along with the Civil Rights Act of 1964, set up an investigation of equal educational opportunities.

The research was commissioned from James Coleman, then a professor of sociology at Johns Hopkins University. The report that he wrote and which was published within two years of being commissioned marks the high point of social scientists' involvement in the policy of formulation and designation. The report was entitled *On Equality of Educational Opportunity* (1966). It documented the fates of over 500,000 students and their teachers in a very thoroughgoing analysis of their educational achievements and the reasons for such differential group effects. The two major findings were that children from racial or ethnic minority backgrounds achieved considerably more in mixed-race settings than those who were in one-race groups, with the exception of white children. It also found that children's educational performances were likely to be greatly enhanced by involvement in early childhood education before the start of compulsory schooling.

These two sets of findings inevitably led to policy developments and to the spawning of further research to confirm or deny the initial findings. The policy developments were all in what later became known as 'compensatory education'. Policies to provide support for children from families in poor circumstances, which had disadvantaged their children from receiving educational opportunities, were quickly set in train. Educational programmes were devised, such as Headstart for children from poor and socially disadvantaged families in the summer before the start of schooling. Financial equity programmes were also planned, especially to provide differential resources to areas of poverty. Two principles were enunciated for these kinds of social policies: one was to provide additional help to those children deemed to be from poor home circumstances, and the other was to achieve 'maximum feasible participation'. In this second set of programmes new social institutions were devised for the delivery of social and educational policies, rather than remaining reliant upon the traditional 'democratic' systems of local government. Indeed, new community groups and organisations were invited to constitute themselves as organisations to apply for government funding, based more on the sense of local and neighbourhood groups. Funding was to be distributed on the basis of an evaluation of their viability and efficacy in relation to community and parental participation and control.

British strategies for parents and education

British policy-makers and researchers were quick to borrow from this array of liberal social-welfare developments in the US. However, the focus in Britain was less on education than appeared to be the case in the US. An official report was commissioned to inquire into aspects of the state of British education. Here the central advisory council for education, chaired by Lady Plowden, was asked to investigate *primary* education. It too looked into the questions of how to deal with the 'family deficit' notion of access to educational opportunities. It too came up with the ideas of early childhood education and parental participation as well as positive discrimination in resources to poor areas, enabling poor families to have access to better educational facilities.

Hewison ((1985b) has written:

> Probably the most important turning point in postwar thinking about the role of parents in education was the publication of the Plowden Report in 1967 . . .
>   Although home background was recognised as an important influence on school achievement, the development of policies relating to parents was not seen as a high priority . . .
>   The appearance of the Plowden Report brought about major changes . . . Drawing on existing and specially commissioned research . . . Plowden . . . re-emphasized the importance of home background, and concluded further that difference in home background explained more of the variation in children's school achievements than did differences in educational provision.
>   The Plowden Report was a turning point because it made recommendations for the future as well as trying to analyse the past . . . A variety of recommendations were made about the strategies which might be adopted for raising the standards of educational achievement in EPAs. One of these was that efforts should be made to involve parents to a greater extent than previously in their children's education . . . attempts were made to 'compensate' children for the inadequacy

of their language backgrounds by providing them with additional 'enriched' language experiences in pre-school or school. (Hewison 1985: 41–3)

In the first instance, a wide programme of early childhood education was not pursued; rather, a special policy, through the Urban Aid programme of providing resources for inner-city areas, was developed (Higgins 1978). In the early 1970s, under a Tory government in which Mrs Thatcher was the Education Secretary, a policy of nursery education was formulated though never fully implemented.

However, the policy of positive discrimination was developed into a major programme of 'educational priority areas' (EPAs), entailing at one and the same time a massive programme of social evaluation by social scientists recruited especially for the purpose of such public policy evaluations. Social research of an independent kind was also developing on similar lines. As in the US, this marked the high point of social scientists' involvement with the policy process of formulation and evaluation. It began a major process of social research now known as action-research. In the first instance, the concern was with the evaluation of the appropriateness of particular strategies to involve parents in the educational process, designed to improve the education of their own children. A variety of different local strategies was designed and developed, from schemes of involving parents within schools to schemes of education home visitors to help transform the home settings into more educational contexts. All the schemes, however, assumed that parental behaviour and attitudes could be altered by these kinds of methods of social intervention.

The one major critique of such schemes of intervention was mounted by Basil Bernstein, who argued that such social and educational interventions could not 'compensate' for the more deeply structured social inequalities in society. His sociological research began to investigate more deeply the causes of the kinds of inequalities which led to differential educational performance and outcomes. Although his critique was seen as a serious limitation on these public policy strategies, such strategies continued to be pursued and evaluated for their effectiveness especially in dealing with family disadvantages in relation to schooling.

The Plowden committee had proposed a number of different strategies in relation to both families and schools, many of which were pursued in the next 10 to 20 years. Although a major focus was on 'parental involvement' in the educational process, other issues were changes in the primary school curriculum and educational processes themselves. These were pursued with equal vigour in the 1970s. However, a wide-ranging review of these various approaches was commissioned by the *Oxford Review of Education* (ORE) for the twentieth anniversary of the Plowden committee's publication. The general consensus of this very disparate group of social scientific evaluators, all of whom had been involved in their different ways in the origins of the Plowden committee's recommendations – either as supporters or critics – was that the schemes to link home and school more effectively were more successful than methods to transform the curriculum or the educational process (Plowden 1987).

Indeed, making schooling more effective through the relationships with families became a major public policy issue of the 1970s. Not only were particular schemes to link home and school pursued more vigorously, but so too were more general schemes to develop the 'democratic' processes of educational decision-making. Again borrowing from the strategies developed in the US known as community control or participation, schemes were developed to try to get the political processes to be more effective. Until the 1960s, the partnership for educational decision-making had essentially been that of central and local government together with educationalists. Parents were not involved as parents in the collective decision-making processes, except insofar as they were political representatives. They were allowed some individual choices in the educational process, as regards their own children's schooling.

Hurt has written:

> From 1944 onwards all primary schools . . . as well as all secondary schools had to have managing or governing bodies . . . What, however, is clear is that local education authorities over the next 20 years attached little importance to the question of parental representation . . . As the Plowden Report observed in 1967, 'The whole subject of school management requires reconsideration' . . .
>
> Two surveys made in the mid-1970s by the National Association of Governors & Managers broadly endorse the findings of the Plowden Report . . . of 104 local education authorities surveyed in 1975 less than one quarter had more than one parent governor or bodies associated with primary, secondary and special schools . . .
>
> The same survey shows how recent was the growth of parent governors. . . . (1985b: 32–4)

However, one way of attempting to make education generally more effective, it was argued, was to involve parents in the wider issues of decision-making. In the 1960s, a number of minor changes were made to ensure that a parental voice was heard in decision about changes to individual schools, particularly in the process of reorganising secondary education on comprehensive lines. It was on this basis that further strategies were pursued to try to get a more coherent and consistent approach to parental participation.

In the 1970s, further consideration was given to the involvement of parents and other community representatives. The Labour government set up a committee of inquiry to consider the means of such involvement for each educational institution. The Taylor committee did then recommend that each school have its own system of government or management rather than only being tied in to local government. These governing bodies, as they were to become known, would be representative not only of the political balance of local government, but also of the local parental body, the community and the teachers. Legislation was to be developed to set in train these new proposals which departed considerably from past practice. However, this was eventually effected by a Conservative administration, not that of a socialist government.

Conclusions

The educational policies that were pursued from the Second World War to the mid to late 1970s were all focused around the political ideology of equality of opportunity: the idea of meritocracy. This ideology and principle was shared by the political parties of both the left and right. It was assumed that state intervention in social and educational provision was necessary to sustain and contribute to economic growth. This notion was based upon economic and social theories developed in the 1930s and specifically associated with Keynes.

However, the translation of those theories into political practices and policies over the subsequent 30 years led to major political controversies. This was particularly true in the area of education, where agreement on the principle tended to be only in relation to access to equal educational opportunities. The development of social-democratic or liberal schemes not only to limit parental privilege but also to try to reduce family deficiencies in relation to schooling led to major political controversies. In particular, the strategies to reorganise secondary education on comprehensive rather than selective lines began to arouse political controversy, especially over parental rights and academic standards. This led into a different debate about the role of parents in education.

Similarly, the developments of parental involvement in education particularly for socially disadvantaged children, growing out of the Plowden committee's recommendations, led to a further questioning of both the aims and objectives, and the effects for parents and children. As Hewison has further commented:

> Since 1975 the desirability of parent involvement has been accepted in principle, but not in practice . . . No mass movement in the direction of greater involvement has occurred; and the interesting innovations . . . have given the unfortunate impression of 'preaching to the converted', rather than offering compelling evidence to the unconverted. (1985b: 46)

By the mid 1970s, the bipartisan political consensus over educational policy and the ideology of meritocracy had begun to dissipate, in particular because of the strategies of implementation, especially those involving a role for parents. They had been devised by a partnership of educational and social reformers and researchers. They had shared a perspective on education contributing to social and economic growth and the fact of a partnership between the traditional family and the state over education. Those 'social-democratic' reformers and researchers agreed on the principles and the practices of equal opportunities. Right-wing reformers also agreed on the principle of a *role* for parents but it was to be a different one: as consumers of education. I turn now to look at the revised political ideas.

4

The Education Policy Context:
The Idea of 'Parentocracy', 1976–1992

Introduction

In this chapter I look at how the relationships between parents and education
were altered through changes in the policy context from a social-democratic to
a right-wing political position. The focus is on the 'education reforms' which
were set in train by the New Right as a reaction to the developments that had
occurred during the previous period of 'liberal-democratic' reforms. The political reactions to the previous policies of trying to achieve equality of educational
opportunity through attempts either to reduce differences between children on
the basis of their *parental* circumstances of privilege or poverty were not,
however, based upon any serious social scientific review of the evidence.
Indeed, despite the deep involvement of social scientists in both the policy
prescriptions and policy evaluations, as we noted in the last chapter, little
evidence had yet been adduced to 'prove' the effectiveness of strategies oriented
towards equal opportunities. As we shall see in subsequent chapters, the
evidence was never more than equivocal (Halsey et al. 1980).

The political movement to the right has occurred not only in Britain but also
in the US and other advanced industrial nations. Silver comments that:

> As the 1970s moved on, however, attention in both countries was directed by
> economic and social events to other educational objectives. The 'civic' missions of
> concern with poverty and disadvantage were increasingly replaced in the late
> 1970s especially by the 'economic' or 'business' missions of successful inter-
> national competition, and the training of appropriately skilled manpower for
> new technologies and a changing world of work. The policy priority, in both
> Britain and the US, turned to 'standards', 'excellence', and accompanying moves
> towards more vocational curricula and increased testing . . .

> In terms of research, it is interesting that in the 1980s new directions not only bypassed the focus on disadvantage, but explicitly appeared to eclipse it . . . (1990: 199)

A number of other writers, but especially Guthrie and Pierce (1990), have also investigated the comparisons and contrasts between education reform in Britain and the US, focusing on the implications of economic developments. They have pointed out the extent to which the right-wing movements for education reform have been developing in all advanced industrial societies:

> . . . changes in technology, international competition, and markets are forcing industrialized nations to adopt new policies to remain competitive . . . in the United States and Europe . . . concern about Asian economic competition is creating a major review of public and private economic strategy.
>
> Much of the blame for both America's and the British deteriorating economic position had been placed on each nation's respective education system . . .

Guthrie and Pierce go on to argue that: The education reform movements in the United States, Britain and many other industrialised nations . . . have accepted the challenging goal of elevating national education performance; even if they do not always have complete agreement regarding means for doing so. (1990: 184–5)

However, Clark and Astuto (1989: 3) point out the extent to which the 'language' of education reform is similar, even if the methods of application vary because of differing political and economic contexts. In particular, the right-wing movements emphasize *parental choice*, as a basis for pursuing academic excellence, standards of performance, ability, institutional competition and deregulation over equity, needs, access, social and welfare concerns, regulations and enforcement. Boyd (1991) has also talked of 'a new lexicon' which consists of the five Ds – disestablishment, deregulation, decentralization, de-emphasis and diminution – and the three Cs – core content, moral character and choice of school. This represents a shift from social equality to quality and excellence in education, based upon a different view of the role of parents.

Brown (1990) has also observed that these shifts have been occurring in an international context, but he confines much of his analysis, as we noted in the previous chapter, to the socio-historical developments in British education. He states:

> We are entering a 'third wave' . . . which is neither part of a final drive towards the 'meritocracy,' nor the result of a socialist victory for educational reform. To date, the 'third wave' has been characterised by the rise of the educational parentocracy, where a child's education is increasingly dependent upon the wealth and wishes of parents, rather than the ability and efforts of pupils . . . the ideology of parentocracy . . . involves a major programme of educational privatization under the slogans of 'parental choice,' 'educational standards' and the 'free market'. (1990: 66–7)

In this chapter, I shall briefly review the origins of the movement to the right, especially for its influence on parents and educational policy, then consider the detailed policy developments in Britain and contrast them with the ways in which such developments have been occurring in the US. The question of the effects of such education reforms on families, both parents and children, will be left for chapters that follow.

What is important to note is that social scientists were involved to a much lesser extent in the development of policy proposals and prescriptions under the New Right than they had been during the era of social democracy. The kinds of social scientists who were involved in the processes of developing policy tended to be economists and political scientists rather than social policy analysts and sociologists. Nevertheless, social scientists continued to provide policy evaluations and analysis, and have become critical observers rather than being involved in policy creation. There has been an even greater accumulation of social scientific research and evidence about the emergence of the New Right and its 'education reforms' than about the previous period. That may, however, merely bear witness to the spread and significance of social scientific approaches and political endeavours. What remains lacking in this area are any sustained feminist critiques, with focus specifically on education reform. There has, of course, been a proliferation of feminist perspectives on other areas of social life and state policies.

Origins of the educational right

The origins of the movement to the right in both Britain and the US are to be found in the politics and policies of the 1960s and 1970s. As we have already seen, there was a 'liberal-democratic' political consensus on the need for some measure of social and educational provision and support to both families and industry to sustain economic growth after the Second World War (Mishra 1984). There were political disagreements between the major political parties about the means of ensuring a healthy mixed economy, but left and right alike agreed that at least minimal state intervention was necessary to ensure the smooth running of the economy, and that there should also be educational provision to support economic growth, through an emphasis on ability and merit, regardless of parental circumstance. This social-democratic political consensus reached its apogee in the 1960s, first in the US, later in Great Britain.

However, the expansion of educational and economic opportunities aimed at reducing differences in socio-economic and family circumstances began to come under criticism from right-wing political pressure groups in the late 1960s and early 1970s. There had always been a strand of right-wing or conservative thinking that had been committed to both 'excellence in education' and the promotion of academic standards, rather than to equality of opportunity regardless of home background. The policies of the social-democratic administrations were therefore criticised for being too rapid and too extensive in terms of social class equality. It was argued by the right that they would lead to a reduction in educational standards and create educational mediocrity.

Shifts rightward in Britain

In Britain, a group of right-wing academics and political commentators began to give voice to these concerns in a series of what were initially somewhat recherché pamphlets. The pamphlets were given the ambiguous name of the Black Papers. Five different pamphlets were published between 1969 and 1977, all dedicated to the same themes of 'more means worse' and 'the egalitarian threat'. In the 1975 pamphlet, a ten-point set of Black Paper Basics was produced which included these four points:

> If the non-competitive ethos of progressive education is allowed to dominate our schools, we shall produce a generation unable to maintain our standards of living when opposed by fierce rivalry from overseas competitors.

> It is the quality of teachers which matters, rather than their numbers or their equipment. We have sacrificed quality for numbers, and the result has been a lowering of standards. We need high-quality, higher-paid teachers in the classroom, not as counsellors or administrators.

> Schools are for schooling, not social engineering . . .

> You can have equality or equality of opportunity; you cannot have both. Equality will mean the holding back (or the new deprivation) of the brighter children. (Cox and Boyson 1975: 1)

However, these criticisms remained very much fringe or marginal right-wing political concerns in the 1970s. In Britain, they had relatively little influence on the development of social and educational policies, despite the fact that between 1970 and 1974 there was a Conservative government in power (Dale 1989: 106). It remained committed to some equal measures of social and educational provision to maintain economic growth. Mrs Thatcher was the author of the official White Paper, in late 1972, entitled *Education: A Framework for Expansion*. It included attempts to expand nursery education and to achieve some limited kinds of socio-economic equality, by aiming at a social mix of family backgrounds (David 1980).

However, the international oil crisis of 1974 put paid to many of these plans. In the first place, the Tory government fell as a result of serious economic mismanagement and was replaced by a Labour government with a slender majority. Although the Labour party remained committed to the principle of equality of opportunity and the expansion of equal opportunities in education on the basis of social class or home backgrounds, this became more difficult to achieve given the recurring economic crises. In 1976, James Callaghan replaced Harold Wilson as Labour's prime minister and immediately targeted education as a cause for concern. By the mid 1970s, right-wing pressure groups were growing in strength and number, and were beginning to influence to the parameters of the political debate. Three years later, Stuart Hall, an academic, claimed in a paper entitled *The Great Moving Right Show* that 'the Tories had gained territory without taking power' (1979). This was a reference to how influential the right had become over the terms of the educational agenda.

'The Great Debate on Education' was launched by Callaghan in 1977 specifically to consider how to restructure the educational process so that it tied education and training more clearly to the needs of industry and economy. Expanding educational opportunities was no longer seen as simply consonant with economic growth. Nevertheless, the Labour government was concerned to ensure that parents played a role in this process of restructuring on the grounds that there was a clear parallel between parental and state needs, as noted in the previous chapter.

This policy debate was narrowly conceived and did not range over all aspects of education. Despite the Labour government's commitment to equal opportunities through other social or public policies such as those on race relations and sex discrimination, these were ignored in the debate. 'The question of racism was not confronted', according to the authors of *Unpopular Education*, nor was that of sexism (CCCS 1981: 222). The outcome of the debate was an official government Green Paper, a discussion document as a prelude to legislation. 'Gone were the references to any egalitarian ambitions for schooling' was the additional comment of the same authors of *Unpopular Education* (p. 225). The paper focused on how children should be prepared for work through schools and other forms of training, in further education or 'on the job'. To the extent that equal opportunities could be said to entail the same education for all, the proposal for a core or a common core curriculum of all schools could be seen to be a continuation of this process. The 'core' was to consist of three basic subjects to be taught, throughout schooling, to all children; namely English, Maths and Science with Technology. These proposals, however, remained but proposals and were not translated into policy. Yet, they have provided the starting-point for subsequent and more explicitly right-wing debates.

By the end of the 1970s British educational policy was no longer officially debated in terms of its ability to aid in the process of, and achieve, equal opportunities on the basis of reducing differences in socio-economic family backgrounds. This was despite the creation of two quasi-non-governmental bodies (quangos) charged with monitoring those processes for minority ethnic groups and on the grounds of sex. These two bodies were the Commission for Racial Equality (CRE) created in 1976 and the Equal Opportunities

Commission (EOC) created in 1975. These two bodies did include equal educational opportunities as part of their brief. Moreover, education required special quasi-judicial processes in both cases (Gregory 1987). Yet these never influenced the educational debate, except to the extent that a special governmental inquiry was set up to investigate the education of West Indian children in the late 1970s, largely as a result of pressure-group activities. The scene was set for a rightward move as education was increasingly blamed for the economic ills of the nation. The increasingly influential right-wing arguments were that children were not educated with the skills and habits necessary for the 'world of work' and that the educational system was too distant from the needs of the economy.

Parallel moves in the US

A similar process had occurred in the US over a similar period of time. When Richard Nixon became President in 1968, it had been assumed that this signalled a move to the right. However, during Nixon's period of office social programmes, including education, continued to enjoy some expansion. As in Britain, there were plans further to extend early childhood education through the Comprehensive Child Development Act. However, Nixon vetoed this plan, seeing it as committing the vast moral authority of the nation to socialistic measures. He favoured instead a Family Assistance Plan aimed at giving a basic minimum income to families. Although his measure was never fully implemented, it was seen as 'Nixon's Good Deed' (Burke and Burke 1974).

Under President Carter, spending on social reforms still continued to rise and plans to expand both education and training continued apace. The Comprehensive Employment and Training Act of 1976, for example, opened up a range of new training initiatives, designed to extend educational opportunities, as did the Education of All Handicapped Children Act of 1975, which attempted to ensure equal protection under the law for all citizens. There were also measures to reduce inequalities in educational opportunities for racial minorities and women.

Nevertheless in the 1970s the right, in the form of 'single issue' political pressure groups, was also becoming vocal in the US. Their arguments took three forms – one was critical of increased social spending and its impact on the fiscal behaviour of the states and another was critical of the kinds of educational expenditure which were still designed to achieve some measure of educational equity. A third argument raised the question of the content of schooling in terms of the kinds of subjects taught and books used, from moral and religious standpoints. These ideas were expressed both by individuals and by groups on the right. There was, however, no one coherent set of right-wing educational critiques. These ranged from those of the New Right religious groups, such as the Moral Majority, to those of the neo-conservatives who were less concerned with the content of educational programs and more with limited social spending (Peele 1986), to yet others concerned with declining academic standards and growing 'mediocrity' (Bunzel 1985).

Rethinking education reforms

In Britain, too, the various right-wing critiques initially were not coherently articulated. Dale has argued that, in Britain, the Labour government's policies in the 1970s were

> . . . a watershed in the post-War history of education . . . because the settlement enshrined in the 1944 Act was showing increasing signs of strain and breakdown . . . the nature of the problems facing the education system have (sic) changed so much that only the construction of a new settlement has been adequate to enable an effective response. (1989: 105)

He goes on to argue that the response of the right was disjointed and complex, not straightforward and coherent. It involved a process of recasting the ideologies underpinning education and then restructuring the system, all taking place over a lengthy period of time from the mid 1970s to the late 1980s (1989: 105–21).

Dale identifies five different strands of Conservative thought that could be teased out of this attempt to revise and develop a New Right ideology, with various impacts upon educational policies and developments. He refers to them as 'the industrial trainers', 'the old Tories', 'the populists', 'the moral entrepreneurs' and the 'privatizers' (1989: 80–9). He then asks 'what distillate of these five ingredients constitutes Thatcherism in education?' His argument is that the crucial factor that eventually, in the 1980s, created a coherent philosophy and policy was 'Mrs Thatcher's own personal political stand' (p. 89). He states:

> Thatcherite education policy might be seen as not so much anti-statist as anti-universalist and anti-social democratic. While the State is to be rolled back – or at least cut back – that is to be done selectively. Thatcherism is very much in favour of selectiveness, of allowing the natural differences between people to grow, both as a reward to the talented and successful, the intellectually and morally deserving, and as a spur to the less well-endowed, successful or responsible, to make the most of what they have. The spur is signally absent from a universalistic, social democratic welfare state. (p. 90)

It remains to be seen quite what influence Thatcherism as analytically distinct from the other notions of the New Right, had on the development of education reform.

By the end of the 1970s, the New Right or neo-conservatives were in the ascendance in both the US and Britain. In both, they blamed the political parties who had agreed to the 'bipartisan political consensus' on state intervention in social and educational policies for causing their country's serious economic decline and lack of international competitiveness (Guthrie and Pierce 1990: 179). Both Thatcher (in May 1979) and Reagan (in November 1980) gained political office, in part, because of this critique of the failure of social-democratic policies, targeting education among other issues. Both pursued similar objectives in the ensuing process of educational and social reform, but within different political contexts and constellations of power. The balance between economic and financial controls or educational standards and the pursuit of educational excellence differed both in terms of time and the strength of the arguments. Nevertheless, by the end of the decade, both administrations had come to similar points in the transformation of their education systems from a commitment to equal opportunities to an emphasis on consumer or parental choice, seen as a way of raising academic standards.

Thatcherism and education reform in Britain

In Britain, Thatcher came to power in May 1979 with a new right-wing platform, blaming social-democratic ideologies for Britain's economic failings. The aim of the New Right government was to reverse Britain's economic decline with new monetarist economic policies and reduced social intervention. Educational policies which aimed at equal opportunities were seen as part of the problem, too. However, the first Thatcher administration did not focus its energies on education reform directly; rather it dealt with it, according to Bull and Glendenning, by stealth (1983: 53–8). It aimed to reduce spending on education, through various local fiscal controls and the reform of local government expenditure.

The three major pieces of educational legislation were all fairly limited in their scope. The first, passed in 1979, reversed the central government requirement that local education authorities (LEAs) reorganise their secondary schools on comprehensive lines. However, in the 14-year period of this policy, the majority of LEAs had already reorganised most of their secondary schools and were loath to undo what had been a costly and difficult process of educational change. However, the effects of the new Education Act were to produce some selective education in a few areas.

The second piece of legislation, the 1980 Education Act, borrowed extensively from the Labour government's draft legislation and a committee of inquiry into how schools should be governed especially in terms of the role of parents. The major aim of the legislation, therefore, was to make schools more open and accountable to the public and particularly parents. In this sense, the Labour government had anticipated the new right-wing mood, by its focus on the questions of accountability to parents.

The legislation, therefore, required schools and LEAs to make public both their 'planned admission levels' or entry numbers and their educational strategies and results. In other words, all schools had to produce both a prospectus and annual report on their achievements, especially in the area of examination results. It was argued that this would lead to parental pressure for improvement in educational standards. Indeed, parents apparently were given more rights, in three separate regards, through this legislation; first to choose schools, called parental preference; second to *complain* about procedures on an individual basis and third to be involved, through parental representation, on school governing bodies. The ultimate sanction of the former procedure was through the (national) ombudsman. Parent governors came to be one of four types of governor in the first level of school management. However, the role of school governing bodies remained quite limited, and they were not a strong influence in the process of educational decision-making.

This piece of educational legislation, like its successors in 1981 for Scotland and for special education in England and Wales, was short on specification of curricular issues and more concerned with parental choice, rights and relationships in education. The third piece of legislation, the 1981 Education Act, was concerned to implement a report on children with special educational needs. It required all LEAs to produce a statement of need for each child's parents and to attempt to integrate all such children into mainstream educational provision. Here it was essentially concerned with the dual issues of parental rights and limited educational expenditures.

One of the main measures implemented from the 1980 Education Act signalled the shape of things to come (Dale 1989). It concerned the redirection of educational expenditure across different types of schools. In the Education Act 1980, the government announced a modest diversion in public expenditure from state schools to individual children of academic ability who passed a selective test to an independent secondary school: if the child's parents were of low income, the state would pay the cost of the fees to the school. This reintroduced a form of selective academic education. In the past, a small number of schools participated in a similar scheme then known as direct grants. This assisted places scheme widened the range and number of private independent schools which were eligible to participate. It also provided an additional indirect subsidy to the private schools, apart from their charitable tax status. Since 1980, the scheme has grown and blossomed (Edwards, Fitz and Whitty 1989). We shall have occasion to review its impact and effects in subsequent chapters.

The second part of the Conservative policy, launched after Thatcher's re-election in May 1983, was the definite attempt to transform the welfare state by putting in place the idea of a market for social and educational provision, with parental/consumer choice its chief selling-point. Stuart Hall argued in 1983 that this process began to happen in the early 1980s:

> The right have temporarily defined the terms and won the struggle because they are willing to engage. For a brief period in the 1960s and 1970s the involvement of parents with the school was the left's most democratic trump card. The dismantling of this into 'parental choice' and its expropriation by the right is one of their most significant victories. They stole an idea designed to increase popular power in education and transformed it into the idea of an education supermarket. (Hall 1983: 1)

By this stage it was no longer simply consumerism, but enabling parents as consumers to demand higher educational or academic standards. These ideas were presaged in the Conservative manifesto for the election in which the then Secretary of State for Education, Sir Keith Joseph, argued for 'the pursuit of excellence'. This theme took the direction of developing quality, rather than equality, in schools through schemes which attempted to differentiate both between teachers and between pupils. For instance, proposals for merit pay for teachers were mooted and new forms of assessment, through pupil profiles and records of achievement, were initiated. These, and changes in the system of examination to a composite examination at age 16, were intended to placate not only parents as consumers but also industrialists and employers, as were the introduction of new technical and vocational courses and qualifications.

However, although attempts were made to transform school curricula, these were not easily implemented because of the financial stringencies applied to schools at the same time. Thus teachers were continuously involved in action over their pay and conditions for a two-year period. During this time, the government also tried, through legislation, to set limits to school curricular debates and to alter the decision-making processes. In this respect, the 1986 Education Act signalled the beginnings of the new, more coherent approach. It set limits to the kinds of subjects taught in schools, such as political and peace studies, aspects of multiculturalism and sex education. In other words, attempts were made to distinguish between education and indoctrination, on lines similar to those set out by a new group of right-wing pamphleteers (Scruton et al. 1987). Parents were given to withdraw their children if they did not feel that sex education was taught in the school according to the traditional family-centred approach.

Parents were also afforded a more significant role in the running of schools, through revision to the system of governing bodies. Following the publication in 1984 of the Green Paper, *Parental Influence at School*, a lively debate ensued about the balance between parental and professional influences in the management of schools (Cullingford 1985: ix). The Green Paper

... revealed the political will to use parents as customers who make clear demands on the education system, as clients who need to be satisfied. The Green paper assumed that parents wish to be involved in the running of schools and that such involvement would lead to the raising of standards ... In spelling out the conviction that schools should serve parents ... [it] did, however, constantly endorse the notion that school should have 'a life of its own' ... It is concerned that the school ... in being responsive to the demands of parents, should not be interfered with by too much professional expertise ... but that it should serve the clear expectations of parents for their children. .... (Cullingford 1985: 3)

It differed from the kinds of proposals developed by the Taylor committee in the central focus on parents, rather than a balance between parents, community and professionals. This paper greatly influenced the development of the legislation which gave parents a majority vote, and required the publication of annual reports from schools, and the holding of a school annual parents' meeting on business lines. This signalled the shifting lines in the reconstruction of an ideology.

A new ERA: education reform by the right?

It was another year and another general election before 'the Thatcherite project' (to borrow Dale's phrase) in education came to full fruition in the form of one comprehensive piece of right-wing legislation (Young 1991). It has been asked whether it required eight years to change the public ideological commitment from equality to quality in education. Did it also require eight years to transform the political and economic infra-structure to such an extent as to ensure the success of the educational legislation? Given the government's thorough-going commitment to a right-wing ideology, it is likely that this was the case. The then Secretary of State of Education, Baker, introducing the new proposed legislation, stated how the bill was informed by the central tenets of Conservative education policy: 'I would sum up the bill's 169 pages in three words: standards, freedom and choice' (quoted in Hansard 1987, December column: 780). He added that

... this bill will create a new framework, which will raise standards, extend choice and produce a batter-educated Britain ... We must give the consumers of education a central part in decision-making. That means freeing schools and colleges to deliver the standards that parents and employers want ... (pp.771–2)

The DES also elaborated these reforms, arguing that they would:

... galvanize parental involvement in schools. Parents will have more choice. They will have a greater variety of schools to choose from. We will create new types of schools. Parents will be far better placed to know what their children are being taught and what they are learning . . . And [they] will introduce competition into the public provision of education. This competition will introduce a new dynamic into our school system which will stimulate better standards all round. (Flude and Hammer 1990: 10)

The bill eventually became the Education Reform Act, known as ERA. It was heralded by Baker as creating a 'new era'. Indeed, the Act was unique in the history of British educational legislation in many senses: it covered both schools and higher education; it created parental choices; it allowed educational institutions to be removed from state financial control with impunity (David 1989).

The key issue claimed by the government in the ERA was that of '*choice*': choice for parents over a range of different types of school and the creation of new ones (Johnson 1990; Walford 1990). The right's overt aim with these changes was to produce better educational standards, based upon individual parents' demands. First, parents could choose schools in the LEA based upon information supplied about courses, curricula and examination results. Schools would no longer be able artificially to limit the number of children admitted (as previously specified by the Education Act of 1980), but were to provide open enrolment. Secondly, parents of children currently in a school were offered a chance, through the school governing body, on which there was to be a majority of parent governors, to vote through a secret ballot to take the school out of local authority control. The school would then become a 'grant-maintained' school, supported by central rather than local government; but based upon the per capita amount of money the local authority had to spend upon the school. The grant would be taken from the local authority's revenues through the community charge and central government financial support to local authorities (Fitz and Halpin 1990). Thirdly, parents of children of secondary school age could choose schools financed variously by special business sponsorship and central government, namely the city technology colleges (Walford and Miller 1991). Fourthly, parents would also be able to choose private schools, entirely independent of the local authority, which could offer places to children whose parents do not have the financial means to afford the fees. The assisted places scheme was, from the 1980 Education Act, considerably widened to cover the majority of traditional independent and public schools (Edwards, Fitz and Whitty 1989). In other words, the aim of the central government, in this educational policy, was to move the locus of decision-making about schools away from the state, but most especially local government, and back to individual parents, or the private family.

Part of the concern of the Tory government has been with the monopoly power of local authorities over decision-making in education, in particular that of ILEA, the Inner London Education Authority: hence the change to allow parents to get some schools to 'opt out' of local authority control and become grant-maintained schools. Even those schools which remained within the ambit of local authorities were to be less circumscribed by local government controls than hitherto. First they were given more powers to determine how to finance the schools, through the scheme of local financial delegation now known as local management of schools (LMS). Local authorities are required to determine, through a centrally prescribed formula, the average per capita spending on education in their area and to delegate to individual schools such finances as necessary to spend on their own complement of teachers and educational resources.

Thus local authorities were reduced to being more of a financial conduit than a decision-maker over the determination of educational resources. This power would also be eroded if proposals to reform the community charge by removing educational expenditure from local to central control were enacted. However, for a time they also retained modest powers of inspection or advice. By the summer of 1992 the Education (Schools) Act 1992 had removed these powers. In other words, the key feature of the legislation was the financial autonomy of each educational institution. Moreover, each LEA was itself to be more controlled by external forces, through parallel moves to alter the funding of local government and central government's control of that. Thus it was intended that each educational institution become subject to the vagaries of the market and parental consumer choice.

Educational institutions were afforded the freedom to raise funds and control their expenditures within clear financial parameters, the explicit aim being to ensure that consumer demand by parents would determine the schools' styles of spending and power. This aim was clearly stated by a right-wing pressure group, the Hillgate Group, in their initial commentary on the proposed legislation:

> The aim, we believe, is to offer an independent education to all, by granting to all parents the power, at present enjoyed only by the wealthy, to choose the best available education for their children. This aim can be accomplished only by offering schools the opportunity to liberate themselves from Local Authority control . . .
> It is . . . necessary . . . to be prepared to defend merit, standards and achievements, against those who promote mediocrity in the name of 'social justice' . . . the deterioration in British education has arisen partly because schools have been treated as instruments for equalizing, rather than instructing, children. Merit, competition and self-esteem have been devalued or repudiated. . . . (1987: 1–2)

A second key issue in the legislation was the designation of 'standards' through the specification, for schools, of a national curriculum and related specific assessment tasks or targets, as well as forms of age-related testing. Since the Second World War, there had been no agreed set of subjects to be taught to school-children, except those enjoined by external examinations. Yet there was a consensus on what that core knowledge would entail, already clearly articulated by the Labour government in the mid 1970s. The legislation amplified the core to require ten compulsory subjects, including the three foundation disciplines of Maths, English and Science, together with seven others, namely a modern foreign language (not required in primary schools), technology, history, geography, art, music and physical education, plus the one previously compulsory subject of religious education. Precisely what would be covered was to be determined by a National Curriculum Council, working groups in the key subject areas, and a Schools Examination and Assessment Council, together with specific task groups on assessment and testing.

The subjects specified in the National Curriculum represented a very traditional view of education. This could be imputed even by the concept of 'national', with standards related to a traditional academic curriculum. This was clearly stated in the Hillgate Group's commentary:

> They can succeed . . . only if the curriculum introduced by them is truly national. The attainment targets for history should ensure a solid foundation in British and European history, and should involve no concessions to the philosophy of the 'global' curriculum currently advocated by the multi-culturalists. Teachers of English must be obliged to impart a proper understanding of English grammar and of the written word together with some knowledge of the true monuments of our literature. (1987: 9)

The traditional approach was further elaborated through specification of the kinds of modern languages considered appropriate, namely French, German, Spanish and Italian rather than either European or non-European languages related to minority ethnic groups in Britain, such as the Greek, Turkish or various Asian groups. Indeed, minority languages were specifically excluded. Bilingual education was encouraged only for Welsh speakers. In a previous government-sponsored inquiry into multicultural education, eventually published in 1985 after lengthy controversy, bilingual education in the languages of minority Asian groups especially had been rejected even in early childhood education as 'linguistically impoverishing' (Swann 1985). This point was repeated, by the Hillgate Group, despite their general attack on the Swann report entitled *Education for All*.

The intention of the government, in the National Curriculum, was to inculcate a specifically British set of standards, related to an academic curriculum judged relevant to the more able children. The clear implication was that difference and diversity would be extolled rather than diminished. But no concessions were to be made to children from family circumstances where such quintessentially British experiences had been unknown before the experience of schooling. Rather they were expected to adapt to a specifically British form of education, valuing only traditional English subjects and knowledge, rather than appreciating the diversity and richness of the varied cultures from which British citizens are now drawn. The 'British' approach was further implied by changes in the legislation to ensure that religious education, and daily religious assembly, including the daily act of worship, were specifically Christian, because this was seen as the main religion of the country.

By the end of the 1980s, the educational system of England and Wales had been reformed so that it bore only a little resemblance to that created after the Second World War through the 1944 Education Act. The reforms had set in place educational institutions competing with each other for finances and for consumers or customers as parents and/or students, similar only in the requirement that the subjects taught within the institutions conform to the National Curriculum with its nationalistic emphasis. In all other respects, the institutions were likely to develop differently depending upon their clientele, their abilities ad susceptibilities. Indeed, some LEAs had already begun to develop magnet schools, focusing on particular subjects within the required National Curriculum, in order to build up particular competencies, such as skills in science and technology. Many schools had begun the process of balloting parents on whether to become grant-maintained schools (Fitz and Halpin 1991). Indeed by 1991 over 50 such schools had already begun (Fitz 1991, personal communication). A number of city technology colleges had been established (the establishment of the first has been carefully documented by Walford and Miller 1991). Local management of the schools that remained within the LEA ambit had also begun with a vengeance (Ball 1990b).

However, the balance between these schemes for parental choice and power and central control remained uneasy during the first three years of implementation. But there were probably more changes to the initial National Curriculum through the changes in the National Curriculum Council and its associated Schools Examination and Assessment Council than to the former schemes to devolve power to the individual educational institutions. In other words, the tendency has been in the direction of parental choices rather than the specification of educational standards at a national level.

There have also been further developments in the clear specification of a parental role in education, since John Major replaced Mrs Thatcher as Prime Minister in late 1990. He developed the idea of the Citizen's Charter which would include education prominently on the agenda. By September 1991, a special Parent's Charter for Education had also been published. In that respect, parental rights to information about schools and their own children's progress and results in the context of wider performance would be mandatory. Moreover, parental governors would be given an even wider role in school decision-making through budgetary control and choice of inspection. On the other hand, testing would be simplified in order to produce national league tables of educational achievements, regardless of the school's socio-economic context, especially through national examination result. These notions were translated into an Education (Schools) Act which received royal assent in the spring of

1992. In essence, this afforded even more powers to parents and individual educational institutions, at the expense of nationwide educational standards, which had been achieved through the inspections of Her Majesty's Inspectorate. The aim has been further to extend parental choice of schools by creating a 'market' in educational provision. In the summer of 1992, a White Paper was published, proposing yet further schemes of parental choice and the abolition of local control of schools through LEAs.

Similarly, in this kind of context, the Labour party have begun to consider how better or develop parent–school relations, in a much broader framework than a specification of rights. Recently, the ideas from some European countries of compacts or a 'home–school' concordat have been mooted (Tomlinson 1991). By the beginning of the 1990s, the whole approach to parent–school relations had shifted from one about how to ensure some measures of equity to how to ensure parental rights and responsibilities in order for individual parents to be able to influence each child's educational success in formal examination situations.

Education reform in the US

In the US, the same objectives of education reform have been pursued as in Britain. Indeed, it could be argued that Britain followed rather than led the US. Historically speaking, however, some of the actual US policy reforms occurred at a slightly later stage. Indeed, the complexities of the American political system, interwoven with the legal system, meant that national educational reforms were achieved by different means. Until the 1960s, the federal government had played a very limited part in educational provision, responsibility being largely at the state and school-district levels. However, a federal involvement in educational provision became part of the liberal agenda of the 1960s, particularly giving power to the federal Department of Health, Education and Welfare, to achieve some measures of fiscal or financial equity in educational provision by the individual states, and school districts. Reagan's ascendance to power, like Thatcher's, involved a critique of educational policies aimed at achieving equity and equality. One of Reagan's first aims was to reduce that federal role and to abolish the relatively new federal Department of Education. These goals were not easily achieved and the federal role continued, albeit in a different mode from that initially aimed at. It shifted to a concern to deal with public disquiet about the future of the nation's schools, especially the secondary schools and their curricula. As Altbach notes:

> The 1970s were not a happy time for public education in the United States ... As the 1970s came to a close, it was clear that the schools had not solved America's social problems. In retrospect, they could not have been expected to do so. They did as well as most other social institutions – the church and local government

are two examples – but problems of social equality and racial harmony proved difficult to solve . . . Education had previously been seen as a panacea for social ills; now the schools were abandoned as a means of social change. (1985: 17)

In the 1980s, there have also been several 'waves' of educational reform to deal with the perceived problems of schools failing to maintain US competitiveness. Guthrie and Pierce identified at least two waves but state that:

> The United States altered its education system in a far less comprehensive manner than the United Kingdom . . . even though many national influences came to bear upon US education reform, actual statutory and regulatory changes had to proceed on a state-by-state basis. (1990: 191)

However, to the extent that it is possible to generalize, the first major wave focused on curriculum, the second on raising standards through parental choice and the third, in the Bush administration, on national goals (Boyd 1991).

In the first place, the Reagan administration, like that of Thatcher, used massive cuts in public expenditure to try to reorient the school system. As Altbach also notes, 'these cuts were particularly difficult, since many programs mandated by the federal government had to be maintained regardless of federal funding' (1985: 17). Federal legislation also continued to require many recent developments similar to those in Britain, such as 'the mainstreaming of handicapped students' by integrating them into regular classrooms with other students.

Secondly, Reagan's Secretary of Education appointed a national commission made up of America's corporate as well as educational elite to inquire into the question of 'Excellence in Education'. Its report, entitled *A Nation At Risk* and published in 1983, had a dramatic impact. It was followed by a spate of other reports from different agencies, a few research-based studies and wide public debate and discussion:

> President Reagan, accurately sensing public sentiment about education, rapidly associated his administration with the report and its recommendations. A wave of reform interest spread rapidly . . . Public officials and political aspirants were quick to board the education reform band wagon. (Guthrie and Pierce 1990: 196)

Altogether about a dozen major reports were produced, all with different approaches but essentially arguing for changes in schools and, given the notion that 'the nation [was] at risk', for a back-to-basics approach (Kelly 1985: 31). As Altbach noted:

> There is unison on the need to improve standards, stress science and ensure that students are 'computer literate'. In general, there is a concern for the role of education in equipping America for participation in a cut-throat global economic war. (1985: 20)

In addition, there were recommendations, as in Britain, for foreign-language instruction, relating the school curriculum to the perceived needs of industry and the improvement of the quality of teachers through merit pay. Such was the range of recommendations from these diverse but primarily business sources that it too was named a 'great education debate'. But as Kelly has noted,

> It is indeed telling that the National Commission on Excellence appointed by Ronald Reagan's Secretary of Education addressed its findings to parents and individual citizens and not to the Congress or the federal government and its agencies. The National Commission on Excellence, if anything, absolved the federal government of any responsibility beyond a moral one, for educating the nation's young people. Rather it shifted the responsibility to parents, business and the local community . . . These reports reflected a rethinking of not only the federal role in education, but also the role of any level of government in education . . . School reform is . . . a matter for individual schools, and not a matter for any level of government or the business community. (1985: 39–40)

In other words, the role of government and the courts in ensuring some measure of social justice and quality of educational opportunity for minorities, women and handicapped people had been reduced and reoriented.

The reports themselves produced a spate of responses. One conservative writer argued, in support of the first report's recommendations:

> In our time the public interest groups connected with education are so powerful that they can stop real reform . . . Let us hope this will not be so, let us hope that the fifty state legislatures will take an easier path to reform. Let them ignore grandiose schemes to rebuild our public school system. Ask them for no new programs. Merely urge them to unleash the resources and power of citizens, teachers and principals, to rebuild a diverse and locally rooted set of public schools. Then, and only then, will Americans have educational institutions that can do what must be done: provide quality education to our children, who will carry on our glorious experience in self governance. (Hawkins 1985: 45)

Indeed, these 'conservative' arguments about a reduced federal role – despite the counter-arguments also raised by the right, for a curriculum to reflect the needs of modern industry and technology to improve America's competitive edge – won out by the mid 1980s. Margaret Goertz, summarising the education politics of the 1980s, has argued that:

> During the Reagan years, the federal government sought to influence education policy with moral suasion rather than federal aid; to emphasize demonstration over intervention; and to decentralize the administration of federal programs. As the 1980s unfolded, abandonment of education by the federal government created a leadership as well as a financial vacuum . . . the 1980s reform was dominated by business leaders and elected public officials. (1989: 5)

She goes on to note that

> ... the absence of a broad consensus about the purpose of education led to a patchwork of state education programs to meet the demands of different and competing interests. (p. 5)

She also notes that it was 'unique' in the politics of state education that education interest groups played a 'relatively unimportant role . . . in the formulation of new state policies'. Guthrie and Pierce also note that there was a patchwork development:

> The United States, with a far more decentralized set of governmental arrangements for education, has proceeded in a crazy-quilt, *ad hoc* state by state manner. (1990: 197)

They add that the 'second wave' reforms addressed more difficult reform proposals such as

> ... the fundamental content of courses to be taught in schools, the structure of school- level decision-making – the balance of authority between teachers, administrators and parents and positive and negative sanctions intended to enhance the performance of schools and school district. (p. 197)

They also comment that these included parental choice solutions in Minnesota, and nationwide schemes to enhance teacher professionalism. In 1986, the Carnegie Corporation issued another important report, entitled *A Nation Prepared*, focusing more on efforts to increase teacher professionalism, restructure schools and develop forms of school site management (Boyd 1991).

President Reagan and his Secretary of Education, Terrance Bell, also began, in the second administration in 1985, to argue 'strongly in favour of business support of education to compensate for federal spending cuts particularly in the areas of vocational and adult education' (Useem 1988: 21). Ray and Mickelson have commented that:

> By 1987, more than 300 business-initiated studies about the quality and content of education, and suggestions for reform had been completed (Business Roundtable 1988) . . . Drawing on the corporate model in its recommendations for school reform, Kearns and Doyle's (1988) book *Winning the Brain Race: A Bold Plan To Make Our Schools Competitive* captured the strong socialization and restructuring themes of business leaders' current attempts. (1989: 122)

The process was one of government reducing its role to be replaced by business leaders. But as Ray and Mickelson go on to suggest:

> Towards the end of the 1980s, corporate leaders still directed their attention at the 'restructuring' of the educational system (Perry, 1988, Kearns and Doyle, 1988)

but placed increasingly heavy emphasis on low-income and minority students. At the national level it is clear that the concerns of business leaders about education are directly linked with the productivity crisis, the growing inability of US business to maintain global market leadership, and, most recently, a domestic labour shortage which is forcing businesses to hire workers previously labelled unemployable. (1989: 122)

However, the process of educational reform in the US was very different from that in Britain. Given the evidence and ideas underpinning the voluminous national reports in the early to mid 1980s, the approach was one of continuing to reduce the federal and state role in educational provision, rather than of using central government, as in Britain, to insist on reduced spending. So very little legislation, compared to Britain, was attendant upon the spate of recommendations.

Indeed, the approach of the moral right in the US in the early 1980s may have been an object lesson for the neo-conservatives and the corporate and business elites (David 1986). There were two relatively unsuccessful attempts to reorient aspects of the school curriculum through the Family Protection Act in the early 1980s, which was described by the *Congressional Quarterly* as a 'tidy wish list for the New Right' (David 1986). The two key issues here were to control the content of school textbooks in terms of their delineation of sex roles and the nature of sex education. At the same time, the right also attempted to introduce school prayer and religious education into hitherto secular schools. However, all these issues were dealt with only cursorily by the federal government. The proposed legislation included the possibility of tuition tax credits for private schools, which was subsequently taken up in a number of states. Nevertheless, the legislation did not provide the new framework initially hoped for it.

So the dominant approach in the US in the 1980s under Reagan became that of fiscal restraint and moral persuasion rather than federal legal edict. This process has been followed through by President Bush:

> The first Bush budget in education called for new initiatives in education that would cost some $450 million the bulk of which Congress would have to find in existing programs. The majority of the funds were earmarked for awards to excellent schools, alternative systems of certification for educational personnel, educational tax credits for low income families, the Drug Free Schools and Communities Act, the Youth Entering Service program, and magnet schools (with a special admonition that funds not be used to foster desegregation). Almost without exception, the new programs emphasize institutional competition to de-emphasize the monopoly of the public schools, e.g., magnet schools, excellent schools, tax credits, alternative certification routes. The President is not only comfortable with the political stance of conservatism and devolution, but with the educational stance of the Reagan administration structurally, substantively, and effectively. (Clark and Astuto 1989: 16)

Indeed, President Bush's policies could be considered as the 'third wave of education reform'. As Guthrie and Pierce note:

Models for a national curriculum have been proposed, but adoption of such an idea has never previously been given serious consideration. However, in a virtually unprecedented Governors' 'Summit' meeting in September of 1989, President Bush first raised the idea of 'national standards' or 'national goals' for American schools. In his January 1990 State of the Union address, Bush proceeded further by specifying seven national goals. (Guthrie and Pierce 1990: 187)

Boyd also noted how these goals were not dissimilar to those specified in Britain, for a national curriculum, at the same time as implementing devolution in administration. By the end of the 1980s, decentralization and the reduction in the federal role appeared to have been relatively well achieved. On the other hand, the process of setting national standards had also begun.

Conclusions

In both Britain and the US, by the beginning of the 1990s, the right-wing goal of educational reform seems to have been accomplished, although by very different means. In Britain, the central government has played a key role in attempts to diversify the school system through parental-choice schemes to the extent that there no longer appears to be anything that could be graced with the term 'system'. In the US, it is the reduction in the federal role that has occasioned such decentralization to states and school districts, or schools themselves. Both countries have, in effect, created a range of types of school not wholly reliant on public funds and support. Moreover, in the US, the recommendations for a more defined school curriculum have not been implemented by legislation; rather, individual schools – private or public, parent-run or religious – have been encouraged to foster their own initiatives and developments. Most recently, however, Bush has set out a national framework. Originally the American approach was by marked contrast with Britain, where the main emphasis has been on the detailed specification of a national curriculum not only for state schools, but also for those which choose to opt out of the LEA system. The National Curriculum was also seen as recommendations for the private, independent schools.

In Britain in the 1980s and early 1990s, the shift to the right has meant an emphasis in policy on diversity and difference, rather than the raising of educational standards. As the 1980s wore on and, especially as the ERA has been developed, school diversification to grant-maintained schools, city technology colleges and magnet schools has been pursued in preference to the National Curriculum. In other words, the aims of the right in their educational reforms have been to widen social differences between schools and therefore social inequalities. They may recreate major disparities between children on basis of their parental socio-economic circumstances. Although there were major attempts from the 1950s to the 1970s to reduce socio-economic disparities between families through educational policies, all the social research has indicated the difficulties of so doing. We shall turn to this in the next chapter. Indeed, even British state schools or public education in the US continued to reproduce social inequalities despite differential resources. Policies aimed at diversity rather than equality are likely to build upon these socio-economic differences rather than reduce them.

In the US, the term 'risk' was used originally to illustrate the problems of American international competitiveness. But as Clark and Astuto have pointed out:

> The space between concern and risk is broad . . . The risk lies with poor children who may have meagre home support structures, are lagging far behind in school achievement, may be homeless, are often hungry, ill and can see little chance for a decent job . . . if you are a young Black parent-to-be in our nation's Capital, you can anticipate that your child will have one chance in forty of dying before or within one year after its scheduled birth date (US Conference of Mayors 1988: 53). That is 21/2 times the national average. If the child survives, chances are one to three that s/he will live its childhood in poverty (*ibid*: 23). The chances are 50/50 that the child will not finish high school (State Education Performance 1989) and nearly 50/50 that, if this is the case, the youngsters will be unemployed (Council of the Great City Schools: 22). . . . (1989: 16)

The risks of poverty, especially for minority children, increased at alarming rates in the US in the 1980s and, without federal intervention to reverse the trends, may be poised to continue. The Commission on Minority Participation in Education and American Life noted that by the year 2,000, 16 per cent (21.8 million persons) of the US labour force will be non-white and one-third of all school-age children will be minorities. Yet right-wing politicians and their policy analysts have not attended to the potential consequences of these demographic shifts. Rather they have continued to try to develop diversity, ostensibly to raise standards. Indeed, most recently two such policy analysts, Chubb and Moe (1990) have argued that the waves of education reform have not gone far enough in creating markets in education. They advocate more such markets. I will consider these arguments in more detail in chapter 8.

Education reforms as currently specified by the right in Britain and the US will contribute to trends towards diversity and difference, rather than equal educational opportunities. Such right-wing education reforms have already begun to produce a new era, which is far from committed to equal rights and opportunities. The policies of the 1990s, are predicated on individual competition, consumerism and educational inequalities. The new era may result in greater bifurcation of society into rich and poor. The Conservative policies of individuality, competitiveness and consumerism have already begun to create a patchwork of educational institutions in Britain. Chances for a good education will depend on parental socio-economic circumstances, area of residence, ability to make demands upon individual schools, as well as intellectual ability and the desire to be educated (Adler et al. 1989).

We turn now to look at the varieties of research evidence and evaluation, to understand the impact and effects of these various policies and ideologies on parents and education. First, we will review the impact of the social-democratic education policy context on parents' roles in schools and then we will turn to the impact of the shifts to the right and consider the evidence, accumulated particularly in the 1980s, of the effectiveness of policies of choice and consumerism, especially for raising educational standards.

5

Parents and Education: The Social-Democratic Reformer–Researcher Partnership over Equal Opportunities

Introduction

As we have seen in chapter 3, the relationship between parents and their children's education was the subject of major policy concern throughout the period from the Second World War to the late 1970s, and beyond. The issue of parents' role in education has continued to tax policy-makers in the 'new era', despite the fact that the New Right administrations have a different vision of parental rights and responsibilities. The New Right, as we saw in chapter 4, has been concerned to allow parents the freedom to make their own decisions and choices about their children's education. The period of so-called social–democratic or 'liberal' politics was one in which there was more of a concern to reduce differences between children on the basis of their parents' socio-economic circumstances, whether of privilege or poverty. It was a period characterized by the political concern to allow for equality of educational opportunity on the basis of children's academic merit or ability, rather than socio-economic home backgrounds.

However, this political concern was not translated into one strategy for dealing with inequalities between children on the basis of their parental circumstances. Rather there were several strategies that were developed on the basis of the complexity of the research evidence that was accumulated. Eventually, however, these were 'distilled' into strategies for early childhood and primary education around the notion of 'parental involvement', on the one hand, and on the other hand, for secondary, further and higher education around notions of equal access and equal outcomes, regardless of parent's social class. However, as both Hewison (1985) and Mortimore and Mortimore (1984) mention, there was no coherent policy in Britain about the role of parents in education until after the Plowden report in 1967. In the US a more coherent policy predated this. Finally, strategies were developed to broaden parents' role in education, ranging from those about individual parental relationships with the individual child's school to those about more collective parental involvement or participation in children's schooling. Given that this latter type of strategy did not focus on the issue of equitable educational performance or achievement but rather on the question of political and democratic rights, I shall review the ways in which this was developed separately, in chapter 6.

In this chapter, I want to look at the evidence on which reforms were developed, particularly in the context of policy concerns about equal opportunities in education regardless of parental circumstances. This in itself is complex because of the ways in which reformers and social researchers were closely involved in developing both the theories and the practices. As we have already seen in chapter 3, the social sciences developed academic areas of study in close association with the developments in 'social-democratic' educational policies. Many of the most pre-eminent sociologists (especially of education), both in Britain and the US, were involved both in policy-oriented research and as government advisers as well as in developing the more fundamental and theoretical aspects of the subject. For example, A. H. Halsey in Britain was influential in providing policy evaluations, such as the action-research into educational priority areas (EPAs) and in providing more fundamental analyses of the relationships between parents and education (Halsey (ed.) 1972; Halsey, Heath and Ridge 1980). He had also been one of the main originators of the research in Britain which focused on relationships between families and education and became the sociology of education (Floud, Halsey and Martin 1956; Halsey, Floud and Anderson, (eds) 1961). Similarly, in the US, J. S. Coleman, who had been a sociologist at the University of Chicago and was responsible for studies of adolescents in American high schools (1964), became the director of the largest (ever) officially-sponsored social scientific investigation which had major implications for educational policy and the role of parents (US Dept of Health, Education and Welfare 1966). He has also continued to develop more fundamental theoretical sociological inquiries on families and education (Coleman, Hoffer and Kilgore 1982). Unlike Halsey, who has continued to advocate developing forms of the parental relationship, especially around involvement in education, Coleman became critical of his previously 'liberal' policies and began to advocate more right-wing policy solutions, especially notions of parental or family choice in education (Coleman et al. (eds) 1977).

In this chapter, I shall review the ways in which social scientific knowledge was accumulated in both Britain and the US which bore on the policy proposals and prescriptions about parents' relationships to their children's education and which tried to go beyond the policy solutions. Indeed, although the policy issues were presented in relatively simple and clear terms, the research evidence that was collected demonstrated that the issues were far from simple. As Banks noted in her careful review of the evidence:

> Perhaps the most important of the several reasons that underlie all the problems in this area of study is the enormous complexity of the concept of home environment or home background. Not only are there many different aspects of family life which appear to be important, but these are themselves frequently hard to pin down into suitably operational terms. (1976: 68)

The main 'problem' for social researchers, whether working in an official capacity for governmental bodies or in a more academic setting, was how to develop the concepts of parents, family or home into broader notions of social class, based upon the available evidence of material or economic home circumstances which was at times combined with ideas about values, attitudes and aspirations.

Nevertheless, policy-makers in both Britain and the US did develop clear strategies for parental involvement in early childhood and primary education with the ostensible aim of reducing social and educational disadvantages on the basis of home environments or home backgrounds. Similarly, they also tried to develop educational policies with respect to secondary or higher education that allowed for both equal access and equal educational attainments regardless of family circumstances. In Britain, this strategy was largely one of comprehensive schooling in place of selective tri-partite education, and consisting of secondary grammar and secondary modern schools. In the US, the strategy was one of educational integration rather than segregation, through 'busing'. In other words, the former concentrated on issues about social class; the latter on issues to do with racial or ethnic origins as indicators of forms of social or economic disadvantage or poverty. Both these strategies were the occasion, as we have already seen in the previous two chapters, for a right-wing backlash which eventually led to a concern more with parental rights than with educational 'equity' or equality.

Educational research and reform: the emerging partnership over equal opportunities

Throughout the 'social-democratic' or 'liberal' period, the aim of social researchers was to try better to understand the complexity of home and school relations, in order to improve upon educational provision and ensure a more 'meritocratic' society. The development of most social scientific research was narrowly oriented to this policy goal of equality of educational opportunity and the operationalisation of notions of social and economic class in research terms, consonant with policy formulation and implementation. Although Michael Young parodied the aims in his *The Rise of the Meritocracy* (1960), they were taken very seriously by this research, and policy-oriented, community. However, the ways in which family, home or parents were used in research instruments was narrow and largely focused on questions of material or socio-economic definitions of disadvantage or social class. Although in the American context race or national origin was to some extent a consideration about how to determine poverty or social and educational disadvantage, it was not a significant consideration in the British context. Virtually no consideration was given in either Britain or the US to the gendered nature of parenting or the gender structure of families, despite the fact that many of the eventual policy prescriptions around 'parental involvement' centred upon parental roles at home as well as in the school as volunteers or 'helpers' (David 1985).

The development of a feminist perspective in the social sciences originally came out of a socialist, Marxist or liberal set of concerns. In education, feminist perspectives focused largely upon issues to do with equal opportunities for pupils or students within schools (Banks 1982). What is fascinating is the lack of attention paid by most feminist researchers to the interplay between equal opportunities on the basis of the gender of pupils and their parents. More recently this has become more of a concern both in social research and in policy analysis. However, given the fact that this did not emerge until the 1970s and 1980s, it has barely been incorporated into the body of knowledge about parents and education.

The early work of Dorothy Smith (1987), based in Canada, as we noted in chapter 2, provides something of an exception. However, although she has been influential in the development of feminist methodology, her work has not influenced the mainstream of the social sciences. Moreover, her work is so fundamental that it goes well beyond the usual concerns within the social sciences. In particular, Smith points to the effects of education on families, parents as well as children, rather than adopting the conventional approach of the effects of parents on children's education; whether on performance, attainment or opportunities.

Smith's work is also grounded in a Marxist or socialist perspective. This has been an influential development within studies of education, providing a serious and sustained critique of the more 'liberal' or 'social-democratic' theories largely associated with policy proposals and developments. Indeed, by the end of the period under review – the so-called 'wave of the ideology of meritocracy' – although there was an immense body of research evidence about the relationships between parents and education, home and school, etc., much of it focused not on the potentialities for social change but rather on the facts of social and economic reproduction. In other words, the socialist or Marxist perspectives viewed the goal of equality of educational opportunity pessimistically. They saw that there were limits to the role of education in bringing about either social or economic changes, in reducing social class differences in family circumstances. Rather they claimed that education was chiefly aimed at reproducing the social and economic structures of society (Bowles and Gintis 1976; Apple, 1979). This meant reproducing the social relations between social classes found in the economic system through the educational system.

Many of the Marxian theories of social and economic reproduction through education, such as those of Bowles and Gintis (1976) and Apple (1979) in the US, were developed specifically as an antidote to the rather 'dismal' theories about the origins and prospects of social change through education. In particular, Bowles and Gintis' work came to be seen as an instant 'classic', especially as a response to the study by Jencks and his colleagues, entitled *Inequality: A Reassessment of the Effects of Family and Schooling in America*, which had been published in the US in 1972. In fact, Gintis was one of the co-authors of *Inequality* and his reanalysis with Bowles is something of an auto-critique. Gintis was concerned with the inconsequential findings of the Jencks' study that children's educational achievements and chances for economic or social mobility in adulthood were based on 'serendipity' or 'luck' rather than a social structuring on the basis of family background. He therefore set about a further reconsideration.

Bowles and Gintis demonstrated that there was a 'parallelism' or 'correspondence' between the structures of social and economic life and the social relations in education. Rather than children's chances of occupational or economic success in adult life being based upon chance or 'luck', Bowles and Gintis argued that they were based upon social and economic relations. Schools reproduced the pre-existent social relations between families in the economic system, through their social organisation and social relations. This kind of theory was dubbed by many critics as a form of Marxist functionalism, and was seen as a very pessimistic theory given the absence of any notion of the potential for social or educational change.

Jencks' reanalysis of the Coleman report was itself also seen as very pessimistic, in that it appeared to offer little by way of policy solution or prescription. Rather it was seen to offer a hostage to 'conservative' political forces since it did not provide any easy policy remedies. Indeed, when it was published, amid considerable media fanfare, some 'liberal' policy analysts feared that it would provide the opportunity for cuts in public expenditure on the American public schools since it suggested that 'schools make no difference' to children's economic success in adulthood. In fact, its publication coincided with a political period of lessening emphasis on achieving social changes and equity through education. Although the reductions in public expenditure on education did not occur, there were also no appreciable additions to educational expenditures, to achieve equity or equal opportunities.

Moreover, *Inequality* as a piece of social and educational research marked the high-point in American studies of the relationships between families and education. Since that time, educational research has re-oriented its focus to more detailed policy-oriented studies of parental involvement or issues in educational equity concerned with sex or racial origin, or concerned with more structural analysis. Some researchers, however, have tried to show in a less functionalist way than Bowles and Gintis that 'schools can make a difference'.

Indeed, in *The Inequality Controversy* a number of authors tried to point up the key findings of the report (Levine and Bane (eds) 1975). Godfrey Hodgson was probably the main proponent of the view that schools can make a difference to the educational fates of children (Levine and Bane 1975: 22–45).

Inequality, the study by Jencks and his colleagues including Acland, was critically important for three reasons. First it brought together the mass of social research evidence around families and schools, from studies of early childhood education and social intervention to studies of high school (or secondary school) effects. It consolidated and summarized the vast amount of research that had been accumulated in the US around the effects of early childhood interventions, such as the Headstart schemes. Second, it also, by way of comparison and contrast, analysed the data collected in Britain for the Plowden report, work which had been conducted by Acland for his doctoral thesis (1972) and also disseminated in other contexts. The main body of the evidence, however, was the attempt to reanalyse the data collected for the Coleman report. But its concerns with the data were very specific – to assess the role that families played in children's educational and economic achievements. They were not particularly concerned with whether parental involvement, of the kind suggested in the US by those interested in child development, might have added differential social effects. I will return to this later.

The third reason for the importance of the study is the way in which it influenced the development of social and educational research not only in the US, to which we have already referred, but also in Britain. Two studies in Britain were attempts to consider the issues about the effects of expanding educational opportunities on children's economic fates and social life. One study, by Rutter and his colleagues, based on an analysis of secondary schools in the Inner London Education Authority, deliberately pursued similar themes to those studied by Jencks (Rutter et al. 1979). However, the study was more interested in the detailed effects of particular school policies and educational variables than in the longer-term prospects for economic and occupational success. Indeed, through a complex statistical analysis of a multitude of school-based variables, Rutter and his colleagues found that schools did have appreciably different effects on their children's educational attainments and achievements. They argued that schooling, given the length of time that children spent there, was more important to children's success than merely to their happiness. They also argued that different school regimes – the school ethos – could have a differential effect on children's educational performance, given comparable home or parental backgrounds. In other words, schools could and did make a difference to children's educational outcomes and subsequent economic life.

The effects of this study in Britain were controversial. There were disputes about the forms of the statistical analysis, just as there had been about the type of social analysis in the Jencks study. There were also disputes about the detail and importance of the findings; in particular, the disputes centred upon the nature of what constituted the differential effects of schooling. In what ways could schools, in fact, alter children's social and economic prospects? Could they transform children's social class origins into different adult outcomes or did they merely adjust economic fates within social class groupings? Given the relatively homogeneous class sample in London's state schools, the argument that Rutter and his colleagues presented was largely one of alterations within social class. Nevertheless, the importance of this study was to transform educational and social research and restore it to its former position of being able to contribute to policy debates. In other words, Rutter and his colleagues showed in a careful and detailed way that it was possible to alter school variables and resources so that they could have an effect on children's educational performance. This study opened up the possibilities for more detailed studies of particular forms of 'school effectiveness' on children from different parental or family backgrounds. In the 1980s, these studies have been quite extensive (see especially Reynolds (ed.) 1985).

The main study to emerge out of this 'new' approach to the analysis of the role of schooling in children's lives is that by Smith and Tomlinson (1989). In a detailed study of 20 multiracial secondary comprehensive schools, Smith and Tomlinson were able to show differential social effects on children's educational performance. They showed, in particular, that particular types of school 'ethos' and management could have an impact upon the success of children from minority ethnic group backgrounds as well as the traditionally socially disadvantaged homes. They argued that schooling was more important than type of family background in children's educational attainments. We shall return to discuss this in chapter 8, in the context of further developments in policy-oriented research which draw on home–school relations.

The other major study which attempted to assess the effects of schooling and family in Britain was one conducted under the auspices of the Oxford Mobility Studies. This project was extremely wide-ranging in looking at a variety of social and educational factors to account for social and occupational mobility. Its chief focus was on attempts to operationalise notions of social class and thereby account for changes in the social structure of Britain (Goldthorpe 1980). One of the many social analyses in this research project was the study conducted by Halsey, together with Heath and Ridge. As the authors themselves state, 'We have set ourselves a question . . . which in its most general and deceptively simple form is whether education can change society' (1980: 1). However, they go to argue that this question was modified by the context in which they asked and analysed it:

> We ask it particularly of England and Wales in the twentieth century, having at our disposal summary familial and educational biographies collected from a sample of *10,000 men* living in these two countries in 1972. We ask it still more

particularly of the period since the Second World War and the Education Act of 1944. . . . (1980: 1) (emphasis added)

Although the focus of the data and their analyses are British, they compare the theoretical and methodological approaches with those in America and also the studies in France by Bourdieu (1974, 1977) and Boudon (1973). However, it is important to note that this study, unlike the others already referred to, is even narrower in its remit. It is a study of the social, occupational and educational fates of a sample of *men*. This issue, indeed, became the subject of much academic controversy not merely to do with the educational analysis but also Goldthorpe's allied analysis of social class. The debate about how to understand social class, without the inclusion of women's 'class' position either as mothers or as subjects, has since raged in the academic journals, particularly in *Sociology*, the journal of the British Sociological Association.

Nevertheless, Halsey, Heath and Ridge's conclusions are important to the understanding of the significance of family, class and education, albeit that they are limited in their generalisability. In particular, the issue of whether education can change society must perforce be limited in this context to whether it can change particular sections or components of society, in relation to occupations or jobs in the labour market, with a particular masculine orientation. The separate assessment of that question as regards women has yet to be conducted, as has that of the joint impacts of gendered parenting on gendered adult lives.

Halsey, Heath and Ridge state by way of conclusion:

> Our fundamental theoretical concern has been with the question of whether education can change the class character of childhood. A strong strand in liberal traditions of political and social thought it (sic) that it can . . . But against the optimism of the liberal educational reformers has to be set the pessimism of the Left and the Right. On the Left writers such as Bourdieu have argued that the educational system serves merely to reproduce the distribution of cultural capital . . . A parallel argument comes from the Right . . .
>
> Eighty per cent of boys at the technical schools and two-thirds of those at the grammar schools came from homes with no tradition of formal academic schooling . . . Even at the apex of the educational system, 88 per cent of the boys at University came from families in which neither parent was a graduate, and 41 per cent from homes in which neither parent had been to selective schools. The state system of education, therefore, gave 'superior' education to vast numbers of boys from 'uneducated' homes. (1980: 198–9)

Moreover, Halsey, Heath and Ridge argue that they used a variety of factors to assess 'the determinants of educational attainment', from 'material circumstances' to 'family climate'. All had the same effect, namely that 'cultural capital influences selection for secondary school but thereafter its importance is minimal'(1980:200). They go on to add that

> ... class differentials widen at each run up the educational ladder ... there was a persistent class difference in survival rates, and inequalities thus increased ... *For those who survive*, inequalities of opportunity are much reduced, although not entirely eliminated ... In summary, school inequalities of opportunity have been remarkably stable over the forty years ... Throughout, the service class has had roughly three times the chance of the working class of getting some kind of selective secondary schooling. Only at 16 has there been any significant reduction in relative class chances, but even here the absolute gains have been greater for the service class. (1980: 204–5)

Halsey, Heath and Ridge then try to apply their conclusions to the questions of the future of education and social policy:

> ... our retrospect might be held to have demonstrated that expanding a traditional structure of opportunities guaranteed failure to equalise. Those who want equality of outcome between classes might then gloomily extrapolate from the past and conclude that this ideal is beyond the reach of public policy. Such an inference would be false. (1980: 216)

Curiously, they then go on to argue, more optimistically, that public policy could still be effective:

> The growth and spread of educational qualifications bears witness to a larger and deeper pool of educability than some policy-makers ever envisaged, and the actual history of rising norms of educational attainment discredits both the Black paper pessimism of the political right and the parallel despondency of those who predicted from the political left that working class children were doomed to be incapable of grasping any opportunities apparently offered to them by educational expansion ... So now, for the first time in our history we stand on the threshold of a period where a sustained policy of expansion could at last attain what for so long has escaped the intentions of reform. The fall in the size of the school population will make equality of opportunity easier to achieve, but educational retrenchment will just as surely postpone it ... The least we can say is that the egalitarian potential of expansion has yet to be fully exploited ... Even so, the economy may reasonably be expected to afford higher average material standards of life for children, parents, and teachers than were contemplated by those who framed either the 1902 or the 1944 Education Act. (1980: 216–19)

However, Halsey, Heath and Ridge's analyses were published in 1980, a year after a Conservative government had been voted into office. As we have noted in the previous chapter, this government was not committed to the goals of equality of educational opportunity, defined in terms of equal social class outcomes at the higher levels of education. Indeed, they were also not strongly committed to somewhat 'weaker' definitions such as equal access to higher levels of schooling. They were more concerned with issues to do with parental rights and responsibilities than the ironing-out of socio-economic differences on the basis of parental backgrounds. We shall return to this.

As Jencks et al. had done for the US, so Halsey, Heath and Ridge had tried to do for Britain; which was, to summarise and classify all the available evidence about the relationships between family and schooling as applied to the British context. As we have seen, however, the form of the summary was to focus specifically on the issue of whether education could alter the 'class character of childhood'. This used social class as a summary for different types of family defined either in terms of material circumstances or 'culture' including a range of values, aspirations and attitudes. However, not all the findings of other studies can be so neatly filled in to this kind of framework, since their orientation may not be towards one particular kind of approach, namely the use of education alongside other social policies in attempts to try to change the nature of society. In any event, as I hope this detailed commentary on the Oxford Mobility Studies has shown, the particular forms of social change expected were relatively modest, and even in this context were difficult to accomplish. They showed not only the difficulties in finding especially appropriate educational policies but also those in breaking down the complexity of family variables.

Bernstein's critique of education research for education reforms

Bernstein's work has ranged over the complexity of these issues. Starting with a concern about class differences in schooling, Bernstein developed theories about, first, different types of family and their links to child-rearing patterns in social class terms. He constructed indices of maternal communication and control which influenced the ways in which mothers educated their children. Secondly, he theorized about the differences between the linguistic codes used in working-class and middle-class homes and those of the school. He initially referred to them as public and formal language, later revising these terms to restricted and elaborated codes. He argued that because of the differences between the codes in school and working-class homes, children from the latter were less likely to do well than those children from homes where the codes were more consonant. This kind of research was of fundamental importance in developing analyses of the specific kinds of *home* influences on educational achievements and outcomes. It also became an overarching influence on more policy-oriented studies about how to transform socially disadvantaged children from poor home backgrounds to make them more 'educable'.

Bernstein's work, however, did not stop at this kind of significance for policy-related work. He continued to develop his theories about the form and nature of education and the transmission of knowledge. This kind of theoretical development has been critical to our deeper understanding of the structures and processes at work both in schools and in families and in their inter-relationships. However, because of its theoretical complexity and sophistication, it has been much harder to use in terms of public policy. Indeed, Bernstein has been at pains, in any event, to distance himself from the simplistic applications of his theories to policy prescriptions. Nevertheless he has not distanced himself from providing particular critical evaluations of types of policy and proposals. For example, he has argued strongly against the notion of 'compensatory education' such as forms of pre-school education or positive discrimination through the educational priority area projects, saying that 'education cannot compensate for society' (1968).

His theories about types of pedagogy and in particular his analysis of the origins and impacts of 'invisible pedagogies' has been very important to our understanding of developments and conflicts within the middle classes, especially for women as mothers and as teachers in infant schools. He has shown precisely how these allow for further differences between types of middle and working-class families and children, according here a central and crucial role to mothers in their ways of transmitting knowledge and being an agent of cultural reproduction (Bernstein 1974).

Educational research and reforms around socially disadvantaged children

The process of developing an analysis of home–school relations took a considerable length of time and was very complex. Silver has provided a most useful history of this process, with an emphasis on the ways in which the concept of 'socially disadvantaged children' emerged and was used especially in educational policy and practice as well as research. He writes:

> School–home relationships across time as they affected children's position within school structures, and their attainment levels there, began to become public issues in the second half of the 1950s, and centrally so in the 1960s.
>
> The most prominent sociological work of the 1950s and 1960s focused on the relationship between class and educational structure, not on the precise workings of schools and the nature of children's experience there . . .
>
> It was the Plowden Committee, reporting on *Children and Their Primary Schools* in 1967, that effectively brought the concept of the socially disadvantaged child firmly on to the educational agenda. The widely read and discussed report changed this agenda in several ways. For the first time since the war, it turned some of the priority attention away from the secondary school. In doing so it placed a new emphasis on the educational experience of the younger child . . . Secondly, it accepted the evidence on continuing poverty and . . . emphasized environmental sources of early school failure . . . from . . . the American experience . . . Thirdly, the Committee commissioned a range of research . . . of . . . the confused area of the precedence of class or parental attitude . . . and . . . addressed issues of the schooling of immigrants and racial minorities. Fourthly, it proposed policies which would directly affect the school experience of children . . . The Plowden discussion sharpened a focus on earlier pre-school and primary school forms of social and educational disadvantage. (1990: 194–5)

Silver's account shows just how sharp the shift was, in policy terms, between the concentration on secondary-school children and that on early childhood and primary education. Nevertheless, as we have seen, social researchers continued, for at least the next decade, to consider issues from the point of view of secondary-school children.

At the same time, also drawing on American experience, debate and research, social researchers turned their attention to early childhood education. Here the focus was more on the concept of educational or social 'disadvantage' than it had been in the research on secondary schools. It also turned on questions that became known as the 'deficit model' as to whether such children were different from middle-class children and in what the explanation lay – the family or schooling itself. Research in Britain drew heavily on the American experience. As Silver notes:

> The American educational literature of the 1960s, reflecting research . . . is massively concerned with issues which related to improving the educational experience and performance of the disadvantaged child . . . 'Disadvantaged' became one of the most familiar words in titles of books on education . . . There is an emphasis on the deficiencies of the poor home and environment, and since a significant percentage of the targeted population was black, it was castigated as racist by some critics. (1990: 198)

But the concern in the US shifted away from the disadvantaged child in the 1970s almost as rapidly as it had embraced it. Attention became focused on 'effective schooling' rather than 'ineffective homes' (Tomlinson 1984: 15). Silver makes the rather cynical comment that:

> Whether the focus was on the child, the family, class, the school, policy or other socio-economic realities, from the 1960s through to the late 1980s, there were considerable zig-zags of attention, and widening ripples of interest in the schooling of either the disadvantaged, or of the education of younger children – with an eye to the strategies of success with the disadvantaged. In the American context, it has been suggested that in the history of schooling generally educational practice has been determined by economic, political and social considerations more than by what is good pedagogy to employ with children – with early childhood as an exception, which only lost its 'innocence' in the 1960s when it was pushed into the economic, political and social spotlight. (1990: 200)

In Britain, despite a later start, concern with poverty and disadvantaged children in education continued to be an interest to social researchers throughout the 1970s. As in the US, there was a mixture of interest in terms of research and practice and many of the studies were highly prescriptive in orientation, drawing on the seminal kinds of 'action-research' that Plowden had set in motion. As Tizard et al. (1981) surmised, explanations about under-achievement as a result of social disadvantage all stressed the need for changes in the family, and more parental involvement in schooling.

Plowden had, indeed, argued that 'one of the essentials for educational advance is a closer partnership between the two parties to every child's education'. In the 1970s, four types of action-research were developed, all around ways of altering the relationships between parents and school: first, intervention in early learning and mother–child interaction; second, easing the first transition to pre-school or school; third, developing parent involvement programmes in school, and fourth, involving parents in their children's learning at home, in particular by helping their children to read (Mortimore and Mortimore 1984). In fact, of course, all these projects focused on 'mother–child' interactions and maternal involvement with the school, rather than on un-gendered parental involvement. The question of the success of these various pieces of action-research has also been raised. To some extent these projects have become part of the particular practice of schools rather than the subject for separate social analysis and evaluation. Moreover, many of their developments coincided with policy shifts and transformations so that the evidence contributed not to any further research but to what became a revised conventional wisdom about schooling. Indeed, by the end of the 1970s, despite the massive investment and development of these schemes, policy had shifted somewhat away from this as a central concern.

However, this issue of the 'cycles of disadvantage' or deprivation received some further policy attention and much of the accumulated research and literature was gathered together in Mortimore and Blackstone (1980) and Rutter and Madge (1976). Tomlinson (1983, 1984) has also tried to summarise the accumulated evidence with particualar reference to ethnic minorities in schools, over at least two decades. She draws a conclusion that:

> Family, cultural and home differences, and 'deficiencies' have all been suggested as factors affecting the educational performance of both West Indian and Asian pupils, but the 'deficiencies' of Asian homes, low socio-economic status, language problems, cultural segregation and so on, have not been presented in a negative or intractable way as West Indian home and family background. It is not surprising that some West Indian parents are now suspicious of explanations locating poorer educational performance primarily in the home . . .
> But home–school relations have never figured as a priority in the education system generally, and home–school relations with ethnic minority parents appear at the moment to be far from satisfactory. If minority pupils are to succeed in education, schools and teachers should presumably be as informed as possible about their pupils, and seek to help and inform parents more than they have done in the past. (1983: 133)

In *Home and School in Multicultural Britain*, Tomlinson (1984) attempts a much more extensive review and analysis of the research evidence and findings. She considers a range of issues, from the socio-economic backgrounds of minority parents to their views of education, teachers' views and issues in home–school cooperation. She summarises the evidence as follows:

In the literature on home–school relations minority homes are invisible, are conceptualised as 'problems', or are subsumed under . . . the 'disadvantaged' . . . The stereotype of the 'disadvantaged' parent, who is in need of organisation by professionals and whose children are in need of 'compensation' for their back-ground, is inappropriate when applied to minority communities. Indeed, the model adds further stigmatisation to groups already at a disadvantage in society . . . Models of disadvantage may also be ethno-centric . . . Despite the undoubted social and material disadvantages to be found in urban areas, minority parents do not consider themselves to be part of a disadvantaged group, forming as Myrdal once wrote of the American pool, an 'inert and despairing social residue' (Myrdal 1964). (Tomlinson 1984: 118)

She also addresses a second theme – that of the mismatch of expectations between teachers and minority parents:

Minority parents have become increasingly anxious that schools did not seem able to equip their children with the required qualifications and skills to compete 'equally' with white children. This anxiety has been particularly acute for West Indian parents . . . [and] has come to dominate home–school relations in West Indian communities . . . the basis of this mismatch of expectations may lie more in the structure and functions of the education system than in any parental failure or teacher obtuseness. (1984: 119)

She then goes on to consider wider policy issues, including the questions of whether schools should allow for cultural diversity or the pursuit of equal opportunities. Her starting point is, however, that minority cultural values and traditions should have equal status to those in the so-called 'majority' society. She also considers improved practice around 'home–school' relations, suggest-ing more formal arrangements such as that designated by Macbeth (1983) as the 'family–school concordat'. Tomlinson's view is that 'relationships be-tween homes and schools are not a minor issue, they are crucial to the success of a multi-cultural society' (1984: 123).

However, Tomlinson's view remains rooted in an equality-of-opportunity approach, the idea that educational policy and practice can provide successful schooling for all. With the benefit of hindsight, the social scientific research which gathered momentum in the three decades from the 1950s has been less successful at achieving such equal opportunities than was originally hoped for it. In 1987, the Oxford Review of Education published a special issue, *The Plowden Report Twenty Years On*, focusing on both the subsequent political and administrative history and the research in and on schools. In it, Halsey and Sylva summarised the immediate policy effects and the development of a policy-related research agenda. They learnt, through the EPA and CDP research,

. . . that educational reform had not in the past and was unlikely in the future ever to bring about an egalitarian society. We learnt in other words the complexity of social policy for a rich, fair and educated society. We learned the limitations of unaided school reform (Halsey and Sylva 1987: 7).

Sylva also noted the limitations of the effectiveness of Plowden in guiding research that itself had substantial effects on classroom practice. However, she states:

> In summarizing this discussion of the classroom side to Plowden, we are left with two widely agreed observations; that the Plowden ideal has never been fully implemented in Britain . . . On the other hand . . . there is little evidence of falling levels of achievement; in fact Gammage argues that, if anything, there has been a rise in reading standards. Furthermore, the emphasis on parental involvement and the importance of pre-school education has become so much part of the accepted litany that we forget how new it seemed just two decades ago. (Sylva 1987: 10)

Most important, however, was George Smith's evaluation of the action-research strategy embodied in the educational priority areas (EPAs). He argued that the strategy faltered and tailed off by the end of the 1970s because of the failure to take account of particular research evidence and adapt to changing social conditions and values. In particular, the problem could be located in the increasingly divergent views on the causes of poverty from the more structured to what might be called 'social pathology'. The notion of EPAs became indissolubly linked to individual pathology rather than structural causes. More to the point, the choice of an area strategy developed the 'ecological fallacy' – namely that individual social disadvantage is not neatly clustered in a small number of areas, but is spread thinly over a large number of areas. As criticism of that developed there was also a subtle shift in policy and practice to the idea of 'educational disadvantage'. Smith, therefore, pondered whether from the vantage point of 1987, the strategy may be revived:

> The fierce clash between the individual or family based explanations and the more structural explanations of social disadvantage, particularly the charge that educational intervention somehow implicitly 'blamed the victim' . . . has now died down . . . A structural explanation on irs own has difficulty in accounting for the existence of successful individuals from a highly disadvantaged background. And an explanation that focuses on early socialisation in the home, followed by efforts to boost performance at school, cannot handle the frequent finding that children from disadvantaged backgrounds tend to achieve less well in terms of qualifications and staying-on rates than their peers of equivalent ability from more favoured backgrounds (Essen and Wedge, 1982; Cox 1982, 1983). A complete account would include complementary elements from both the structural individual or family based explanations. (G. Smith 1987: 35)

Smith therefore argued for a revival of the strategy on the basis of both the fact that any disadvantaged area selected contains a wide range of ability and potential and that neglect leads to despair.

Lady Plowden also offered an important review from her own self-professed 'non professional' position. She asked:

> Where has there been active progress? Certainly in the understanding of the importance of there being an active relationship between schools and parents . . . We did not invent the importance of parents – it was already in the air and acknowledged, but we strongly emphasized how vital it was . . .
>
> We know that it is the quality of the interest in the home taken in the education of the child or children of the family which lays the foundation for educational success. Unless the teachers in the schools can value the parents and give them confidence in their relationship with the school progress will be slow. (Plowden 1987: 121–2)

She also acknowledged developments particularly in the pre-school provision through playgroups as well as nursery schools, enabling mothers' participation and involvement. But she was saddened by the difficulties for minority ethnic group children and asked finally 'was the gulf between home and school and different codes of behaviour too difficult to bridge? (Plowden, 1987: 124)

Conclusions

In conclusion, the three decades of social scientific research linked to 'liberal' or 'social-democratic' education reforms in both Britain and the US spawned an enormous amount of literature all around the themes of parents and education. On the one hand, the simple policy aim of equality of educational opportunity was shown to be very complex to implement. Both American and British research showed the difficulty of operationalising the idea of home backgrounds, socio-economic circumstances or social class. It also demonstrated that there was no simple relationship between family or social class and educational opportunities. A rich social scientific body of knowledge developed in this context, which aided education reforms and yet distanced itself from the specifics.

On the other hand, especially for early childhood education, a closer partnership between researchers and reformers developed. Indeed, particular kinds of evaluative research of policies were created in this context. Nevertheless, the simple aim of achieving equality of opportunity by reducing social and economic home disadvantages was also found to be more complex than originally had been assumed. It did, however, open up the possibility of developing home–school relations as a basis for reducing social and economic disadvantages in family circumstances. This became the accepted wisdom of reformers and researchers alike by the late 1970s.

By the end of the period a great deal more was known of the complexities of the social and educational processes that underpinned policy changes and reforms. However, the main development out of this massive research work was the closer links between parents and schools with the aim, if not of more successful educational achievements on the basis of ability and merit, of more 'effective schooling'. We will return to the further elaboration of this in chapter 8, having reviewed other initiatives in parents' relations with education.

6

A Parental 'Voice' in Education as Community, or Consumer, Involvement?

Introduction

This chapter reviews the ways in which parents have become involved in education, in the context of changing policies about community participation or consumer involvement. This has more recently been seen as the notion of a 'parental voice' or a parental role in educational decision-making (Hirshman 1970; Westoby 1988). In the previous chapter, we noted the ways social researchers contributed to policy around the aim of equality of educational opportunity. As the period progressed in the 1960s, social researchers began to develop a body of knowledge which not only evaluated reforms but began to influence strategic political developments.

From the point of view of this account, the critical strategies proposed jointly by 'social-democratic' reformers and social researchers were those about the role of parents as both individuals and part of the local community. Social scientific evidence about the relations between family and education influenced the extent to which parents' roles could be altered in terms of their involvement in children's schooling. Crittenden (1988) has developed a broad philosophical analysis of these relationships covering evidence from the US, Britain, Europe and Australia. But he, too, ignores the questions of gender or race despite his broad perspective.

During the 1950s and 1960s, most of the policy debates focused upon individual parents and their influences upon their own children. As we have already seen, a strand of the researcher and reformer debates was concerned about the ways in which parental backgrounds of material poverty disadvantaged their children. Parental involvement in pre-school services, or early childhood education and primary schools, was viewed as a remedy to compensate for the disadvantages of a deprived socio-economic family background. However, it was gradually becoming the accepted wisdom of researchers and reformers alike that parental involvement, *per se*, was a way of improving home–school relations. This developed into a more intricate and lively social scientific debate in the late 1970s and 1980s, which we shall have occasion to review in chapter 8.

Another strand of the debate, however, was the notion that the parental role entailed more than involvement in an individual child's education. Indeed, this notion that parental participation in schooling could and should be broader than merely individual involvement either at home or at school became part of a lively political debate in the 1960s. However, this idea shifted in the 1980s back to that of individual involvement as consumers. We shall consider these contrasting debates and evidence in this chapter, focusing on a wide range of differing kinds of evidence and policy evaluation. For once, some of the evidence addresses the question of the effects of the gender and race of parents on strategies. However, most of it remains located in the contrasting policy debates about community or consumer involvement.

Parental participation as political

Beattie (1985) has carefully reviewed the ways in which the debates about parental participation in educational decision-making developed not only in England and Wales, but in three other countries in Western Europe. In a very thorough study entitled *Professional Parents: Parent Participation in Four West European Countries*, he has compared and contrasted the origins and developments of the debates. His argument is that the issues about parental participation originated in the wider political debates about increased citizen participation in decision-making during the 1960s. There was a concern, too, that democracy should be extended beyond the formal periodic election of some type of political assembly, into forms of workplace democracy. In reviewing the literature, Beattie, as a political scientist, draws on Carole Pateman's British study entitled *Participation and Democratic Theory* (1970) and that of J. Roland Pennock in the US entitled *Democratic Political Theory* (1979). Both tried to demonstrate that the arguments for citizen political participation drew on critiques of the workings of liberal democracy and attempts to make it both more responsive and legitimate in the eyes of political participants.

Beattie himself sets out to test two competing theories about the emergence of parental participation; first the reformist notion of democratic involvement, and second, in contrast, the notion of the ruling elite attempting to create legitimation for its policies in the context of more general crisis theory. Beattie tests these two contrasting notions in his four country-based case studies.

Beattie's case study of England and Wales contrasts sharply with those of France, Italy and Germany, in particular in terms of the origins of the debates. He argues that

... in England and Wales participation did not first present itself as a political demand. It was not an urgent response to crisis, as in France, nor a conscious attempt to root state institutions in the popular consciousness, as in Germany. No doubt 'participation' was part of the general intellectual baggage of thinking people in the late sixties; there is some evidence of that in the deliberations, of the Maud commission on local government, or of the Weaver report which introduced an element of lecturer and student participation into the management of colleges of education ... such shifts were evidence only of a general climate of opinion which was more likely to result in a revaluing of the teacher's contribution to school management; the involvement of parents in the running of schools required a rather different leap of the imagination and a commitment to working out practicable structures. (1985: 179–80)

Beattie argues that the links between parental participation and sociological interpretations of the educational process were provided by the Plowden report in 1967. However, they did not have much 'purchase in reality' (1985: 181). He goes on to argue:

All this activity remained in what we might almost call the Mason-Isaacs-Plowden tradition. Although less patronising and earnest than Charlotte Mason and her helpers, the theory of 'virtuous circles' assumed agreement on what constituted 'virtue': the basic aims of schools were consensual. The possibility of politicization on, say, the Italian model was there, and the presence of parents might pose awkward questions to the teachers ... There is little evidence that parents themselves were moving into the political area. (1985: 181)

But because of other political developments and changes, for about ten years from 1965 there was a 'threefold impact on the parent movement' (1985: 184). This meant that by the end of the period there was greater pressure on government – both central and local – to involve parents more closely in the running of schools. But Beattie argues that the initiative came much more from the 'machinery of the state' than the parents themselves. Indeed, Beattie concludes that

... instead we find a parent movement whose interest in collective or pressure-group activity remained negligible because of a fixation on individualistic interpretations of the parental role vis-a-vis the school, and which had little real impact on the style and character of formal parent participation when it was eventually introduced by ruling elites (1985: 212–13)

His own reviews centred on the development of the role of parent governors in the 1980s, an issue to which we will return.

Arguments about citizen participation also developed in the US. It was later that Britain began to borrow the arguments, and develop a research agenda around the issues of parental participation (Higgins 1978). In the US, as we have noted in chapter 3, issues about revised forms of political participation were also not confined to the schools debate but focused generally on ways to involve the local community or parents in decisions about a range of public and social services. To some extent new forms of community participation were seen as the antidote to the traditional bureaucratic local government structures.

The research evidence accumulated in the US around these questions, however, did focus particularly on schooling, as well as other developments in social services. Moynihan, for example, wrote a rather provocative review of the impact of new forms of community participation, associated with policy initiatives in social and educational services. He entitled the review *Maximum Feasible Misunderstanding*, (1970) to contrast with the political slogan for community development schemes, 'Maximum Feasible Participation'. His account demonstrated some of the difficulties of trying to get a new form of community participation as an alternative to democratic forms of local government.

An immense amount of social research was accumulated about particular educational schemes, both for early childhood education and for schools themselves. In addition, a strand of educational research which became known as revisionist educational history noted the problems with the traditional structures for the effective delivery of education. Of particular importance was Katz's study called *Class, Bureaucracy and the Schools* (1971) and the work of Cremin (1961), as well as Tyack's now classic study *The One Best System*, (1974). The community participation or community control debates built upon the evidence about the bureaucratic constraints over the operation of local democracy, particularly in the cities.

In the late 1960s and early 1970s, the political debates in the major cities of the US, especially in the north-east, focused upon how to revise traditional bureaucratic systems of control of schooling to allow for more community or citizen participation. On the one hand, the debate was generally about how to allow for community control on a par with that exercised in the suburban areas and small towns (Gittell and Berube 1967; Fein 1971). On the other hand, it focused particularly on community participation of blacks in the cities, and their exclusion from particular forms of community control (Altschuler 1967; Levin 1970; Cronin 1973). Much of the debate had been fuelled by both the New York teachers' strike in 1968 and the implementation of community demonstration projects (Ravitch 1976; Berube and Gittell 1969).

The model for these disputes and debates was local or community participation in decision-making to ensure equality of opportunity in education. It was assumed that community or parental participation inevitably led to better education and, particularly, educational achievements, because of the apparent successes of suburban school boards. Indeed, it is only in the 1980s, through the New Right in the US, that the notion of democratic control of schools through local communities, and specially elected school boards, has been called into question (Bunzel 1985; Clark and Astuto 1989; Chubb and Moe 1990; Guthrie and Pierce 1990).

As a result of the political action in the 1960s, revised systems of community control in the very large cities were created to allow for more parental participation on individual school boards. Parents became involved in running the schools of their own children, selecting teachers and disciplining pupils (Gittell and Berube 1967; Cronin 1973; Ravitch 1976). These schemes were subsequently evaluated for their effectiveness in allowing for a greater community or parental role in political decision-making, on the assumption of developing educational equity. Community was often used as the term in the US for particular social groups of parents, especially black parents. Throughout the 1960s and 1970s a vast research literature developed (David 1975, 1976).

Another strand to the debate raised at that time was about parental participation as *consumers* rather than as citizens, although it was not then as central as it has since become. In 1970, Hirshman wrote what has become a seminal text about the effects of different methods of criticism on organisations. He argued that the effects of people choosing either not to belong to or to leave organisations, especially those in a highly competitive environment, could be detrimental to the survival of the organisation, or its capacity to recuperate. On the other hand, participants who were given an effective 'voice' or role in decision-making in an organisation had an influence on how well it could operate. Hirshman's theoretical argument could be applied to any organisation. He used as one example state versus private education in the US, showing that more participation within an organisation such as a school or school system was more likely to be effective than 'exit' – leaving the school or system for an alternative one. His political theory, which modified traditional economic theories of competition, has been used and applied, in research studies, to a range of different types of organisation. This has caused him to reconsider and develop his theories (1981). They, too, have had an effect both in Britain and the US on the debates and research about consumer participation, especially British debates on education (Woods 1988; Westoby 1990).

The early research that developed both in the US and subsequently in Britain tended to be within the area of political science and policy analysis, rather than that of sociological or psychological theories of the impact of strategies on child development or children's educational performance. In the US, Paul Peterson's studies of political participation in educational decision-making became influential. Arnstein's (1969) model of citizen participation as 'ladder' towards the highest level of participation was used as a basis for considering the extent to which different types of political participation were effective.

In Britain, Parkinson's studies of educational decision-making attempted to replicate these. Third-world educators such as Freire (1972), interested in the broad concepts of community development, were also influential. They all had an impact both on the action-research projects spawned from both the Plowden Committee's report on educational priority area studies, and on the community development projects of the late 1960s. Much of this work has been nicely reviewed by Edwards and Batley (1978). However, the question of the role of parents or families in the ideas about community, citizen or political partici-pation was usually addressed only tangentially. As with the early American case studies or reviews, parents were subsumed under the broad heading of community or citizens. There were a small number of exceptions in the work of projects for the educational priority area (EPA) studies such as the Yorkshire project (Smith and Smith 1973). Midwinter (1980) also argued for community education to include parental involvement in the running of schools.

Yet the political and social research on parental participation in the 1970s tended to be rather sporadic and focused largely on evaluations of case studies of particular projects, rather than evaluations of the effective implementation of new schemes of participation. At the same time, arguments about political and democratic rights of participation in the effective delivery of social and educational services had developed to the extent that they appeared to be incontrovertible. By the mid 1970s, as a result, a departmental committee of inquiry was established in Britain under the chairmanship of Taylor, to consider the question of the more effective 'government and management of schools' as noted in chapter 3. Its report, entitled *A New Partnership for Our Schools*, (Taylor 1977) was thin on research evidence but strong on policy recommendations, including the notion that parents *as* parents should be entitled to a place in the government or management of individual schools. Bacon's (1978) study of governing boards, and particularly the innovative scheme in Sheffield, pro-vided the first of a series of analyses of parental participation in individual school decision-making and accountability. Beattie (1985) has provided a broad analysis of the various schemes in which to place the innovative Sheffield pro-ject. This latter led especially to schemes in Liverpool. None of them considered differences between the gender or race of parents.

In other countries, such as the US and Canada, the ways in which parents were involved in the democratic political processes were already fundamentally different, given the existence of specialist, 'single issue' school decision-making by elected school boards in the US (David 1975; 1976) and school board trustees in Canada (Levin 1987). In Australia, too, the system of decision-making was also rather different (Connell et al. 1982). There is an excellent study of the influence of gender in the running of Australian primary schools (Evans 1988). Given these differences, the evidence and arguments for more extensive parental participation in decision-making became the subject of ana-lysis in Britain by the end of the 1970s (David 1980; CCCS 1981). Beattie has, however, concluded that, for Britain, France, Germany and Italy at least, a broad theory is needed.

> In each of the four cases presented, it has been suggested that the 'reformist' theory . . . offers a less adequate account of the emergence of parent participation than the 'general crisis' theory. There appeared to be strong evidence in each

country that the new structures were set up more to meet the various short-term needs of the political apparatus than to implement long-term idealistic plans. In addition, it appeared that favourable circumstances for 'learning' participation (as in England and Wales) did not lead to spontaneous demands for formal parent involvement with schools. (1985: 233)

Typologies of parental involvement

We can see now, with the benefit of hindsight, that by the end of the 1970s, various different models of parental participation or involvement in education had been developed. In chapter 5 we discussed the initial development of parental involvement. Several authors have subsequently attempted typologies or classifications of these various schemes of parental involvement or participation. All focused on the assumption of the school's need for more parental involvement, whether of an individual or collective kind, rather than the corollary, the effects of school reforms on family life. This latter is a point to which we shall return in chapters 9 and 10.

From the vantage point of the late 1980s, Epstein (1990) for the US, Bastiani (1987), Macbeth (1989) and Tomlinson (1991) for Britain, and Beattie for England and Wales together with France, Germany and Italy (1985) developed typologies of parental involvement. Epstein and Tomlinson saw these as discrete and different types of parental involvement, whereas Macbeth saw the issues as a process of development and different stages in the debate about family–school relations, culminating in a partnership. Bastiani (1987) has also summarized the trends in home–school relations as a series of quasi-historical developments, but has also recognised the extent to which there are conflicts in the debates about different types of parental participation. Beattie was only concerned with parental participation as a form of citizen or community political involvement, although he reviewed the stages of development. Although Epstein and Tomlinson do not refer to the conflicts, their typologies acknowledge the divergent nature of different types of involvement. Moreover, given the policy changes in Britain and the US implemented by the New Right from the late 1970s which overlay and interacted with the developments in different schemes of parental participation, it would be difficult not to recognise divergent and conflicting notions.

What none of the typologies or schemes paid any attention to, however, are the definitions of and changing practices with respect to the notion of *parent*. In particular, the gendered and racialised notions of parent were not acknowledged, nor was the idea that family forms have changed to such an extent that the exercise of a parental role may now be fundamentally different. The term parent *qua* parent still lay at the heart of the typologies, despite the fact that it may be an inappropriate social category. It is certainly worthy of more detailed social investigation. Yet curiously, as we shall see, it has only slightly influenced the nature and development of these strands of social research. They all remain within a particular paradigm of social investigation, which Eichler (1986) has referred to as the 'business-as-usual' approach.

Eichler has developed her own typology of different types of social scientific research, based upon Kuhn's theoretical approach (1970), in order to consider the ways in which gender is made visible. She argues that the vast majority of social scientific investigations ignore, or at best only 'add-on', the question of gender. She then presents two of her own possible alternatives – the feminist and the non-sexist. These alternatives have been rendered relatively invisible in much of the work on parental participation, especially the development of typologies.

Epstein's typology, which will be fully elaborated in chapter 8, is a five-fold spectrum of parental involvement. It coves 1) the basic obligations of parents to create 'positive home conditions' for their children's learning; 2) the basic obligations of schools to communicate with families about children's progress and performance; 3) individual parental involvement at school as volunteers; 4) individual parental involvement at home in learning; and 5) parental involvement in governance and advocacy or decision-making for schools, such as in PTAs, school district boards, etc. It is this last issue of a *parental voice* that we will focus on in this chapter, returning to the others in chapter 8.

Tomlinson's four-fold distinction replicates this in the sense that she groups together Epstein's first two and second two into two different types. She then separates the formal and informal aspects of parental involvement in school matters such as formally on governing bodies as parent governors and informally through parent organisations. This difference partly reflects the development in both policy and allied research around parents' political and supportive roles in Britain in the 1980s. In the US, these developments have not been as marked as in Britain, given the American more democratic base beforehand. Moreover, the differences are also partly a reflection of the particular concerns of the two social analysts. Epstein, in the US, wanted to focus largely on issues to do with individual parental involvement and responsibilities. Tomlinson, a British researcher, was more concerned to focus on issues to do with the wider forms of parent–school partnerships and contracts. Curiously, this also underpins the kinds of social research developed in the two countries during the 1980s. In chapter 8, we shall return to a reconsideration of these various individual approaches to home–school relations in the research literature, and the further developments of the analysis.

Beattie (1985) has provided a developmental typology along the lines of Macbeth's which is only concerned with the *political* element in citizen or community involvement. He writes:

> . . . there is something similar in the four national experiences presented, and surely that similarity is somehow focused on the decade running from the late sixties to the late seventies. Over that period we see three factors:

(i) traditional elites striving to restrain control of
(ii) politics in the grip of unfavourable political and economic circumstances and producing
(iii) a series of attempts at modernization through administrative devolution and the redrawing of traditional boundaries.
. . . Parental participation in education is very far from a purely educational matter. (1985: 239)

Review of changing reformer–researcher partnership over participation in Britain

Given the lack of emphasis in the comparative research literature, I now wish to turn to the accumulated research around parental participation, especially school governance, formally and informally in the British literature. I shall, however, look at the ways in which some of the work of the New Right in the US as well as in Britain has become highly critical of particular forms of parental or political participation, arguing for a 'consumer' rather than a 'producer' or political model of participation. This is the particular shift that has influenced the policy and research debates in the 1980s.

Woods (1988) has provided a neat overview of the ways in which these complex debates have influenced strategies in the 1980s. He starts by pointing to a quoted assertion made by Mitchell about the extent of progress around consumerism, such that '"consumer" control has become as important as professional self-control and that of elected representatives or appointed officials' (Mitchell 1985: 4) Woods tries to classify the three different perspectives on participation in school education in Britain in the 1980s. He calls them '(a) market-orientated; (b) partnership; (c) instrumental' (1988: 325). The first is the strategy that has been used by he Conservative government to promote parental or consumer influence. Woods argues that

> . . . participation here should be understood in the context of the intention to move towards a market-like system. At the same time, by bringing consumers and producers together in the decision-making process, it contradicts the separation between the two that is characteristic of market systems . . . the success of participation is likely to be judged . . . [by] Conservative proponents in terms of how far its effects approximate those that would emerge from a free, private market in education . . . and close down schools that failed the 'market test.' (1988: 325)

The second perspective was that participation emerged from the presupposition of shared responsibility and is based, as in Tomlinson (1991), Macbeth (1989) or Sallis (1988: 115) on the notion of partnership. The third perspective, in Woods' terms,

> ... values participation principally for the benefits it offers or is believed to achieve (better examination results, more effective homework) ... This conceives participation as an instrument ... to bring about various ends, though unlike the first, market-orientated perspective it is not limited to the goals of a free market. (1988: 326)

However, although these three contrasting perspectives may have influenced policy in the 1980s – and we shall return to a fuller consideration of these in chapters 7 and 8 – their relative influences on research on parental participation have been less evident.

Most of the research has been rather more descriptive of the effects of policy implementation. It divides largely into research around the implementation of particular aspects of educational legislation. First, there is research on the 1980 Education Act which first set in place a system of parent governors, of schools giving information to parents and of a more judicial approach to parental 'choice' and appeals against particular decisions. Most of this latter is reported in Stillman (1986) and Stillman and Maychell (1986). Second is the research on changes to the system of school government and particularly the role of parent governors in the 1986 Education Act, as well as the role of parental influence over particular issues in the curriculum; and third is research on new political roles for parents through changes implemented by the Education Reform Act 1988. In this latter case, research has focused upon case studies of particular types of school, such as city technology colleges (Walford and Miller 1991) or the establishment of grant-maintained schools (Fitz and Halpin 1990, 1991). There is also ongoing research on the effects of a more market-oriented system (Ball 1991) and local management of schools.

Most of the research, however, has centred upon the developments in the system of parent governors, in the context of the changing role of governing bodies (Kogan 1984; Sallis 1988; Golby 1989; Golby and Brigley 1989; Golby and Lane 1989; Deem 1989; Brehony and Deem 1990; Hughes, Wikley and Nash 1990; Deem 1991). There are also case studies of particular forms of parental participation in schools and their relationship to parental power (Macleod 1989) and integrated schools in Northern Ireland (Morgan et al. 1991). Both the National Foundation for Educational Research and the National Consumer Council have conducted surveys of the new school governing bodies in relation to particular issues (Streatfield 1988; Jefferies and Streatfield 1989; Streatfield and Jefferies 1989; Community Development Foundation 1990; Keys and Fernandes 1990).

Interestingly, although the 1980 Education Act legislated for a new system of school governors, including, for the first time in British educational history, parent governors, this was not generally the subject of educational research or policy evaluation. In the early 1980s, most educational policy research was still focused upon a critical evaluation of the effects of policy on educational performance or on the general evaluation of social inequalities (David 1980;

CCCS 1981). In particular, the authors of CCCS's *Unpopular Education* saw educational policy changes, including the role of parents, as part of a process of restructuring the educational system to fit the needs of the economy more appropriately. For example, the authors argued:

> In that context, parental 'interests' were to be represented through the rational organisation, by the state of the school to work transition, and the matching of the appropriate skills and aptitudes to the needs of the labour market. Schooling and its social purposes were therefore to be politically subordinated to the perceived needs of a capitalist economy in the throes of a crisis. A restructuring was required because of the failure of schools to fulfil the older social democratic equation that investment in education would produce economic benefits. (CCCS 1981: 220)

This analysis drew on wider social research in both Britain and the US and was at that time the dominant form of approach (see especially Bowles and Gintis 1976).

However, some social researchers did focus upon the details of the 1980 educational legislation, and were concerned in particular with issues about both accountability and parental choice (Stillman (ed.) 1986; Woods 1988). Indeed, research into a parental role in school accountability began before the actual passing of the legislation (Elliott et al. 1981; McCormack (ed.) 1982). Elliott, for example, looked into how parents in one school chose their secondary schools as part of the process of making schools more accountable. Indeed, the major parts of the educational legislation of 1980 which became the subject of research investigation were those centred around the issues of 'parental choice'. This will be further discussed in the next chapter.

The balancing of parental preferences with LEA decision-making over the allocation of either primary – or secondary – school places was seen as part of the process of either making schools more accountable to parents or allowing for more parental influence and participation. Giving parents more information in the form of brochures or prospectuses as well as allowing for a system of quasi-legal appeals were all seen as part of the process (Bull 1980, a and b 1985). Indeed, Bull has carefully monitored the role of legal appeals against LEA decisions (1985). The main emphasis in Stillman and Maychell's study, however, was on the reasons for and process of parental choice of school (1986). We shall consider this kind of research in the next chapter.

A by-product of the research commissioned by the Inner London Education Authority (ILEA) in the early 1980s to consider how to 'improve' London's schools was the question of the role of parents not only in their individual child's learning either at school or at home but also in the wider political processes. Hargreaves, a major sociologist of education in Britain at the time, was appointed to chair the committee of inquiry: A traditional social-democratic educational researcher, he recommended not only wider home–school liaison, but the establishment of 'home–school councils which could act as a think-tank for home–school relations' (Hargreaves 1984: 50). These councils were to be part of a wider system of parental participation or involvement in schools and their decision-making. The model was to make schools more effective. Similar recommendations were made by the Thomas inquiry into primary schools published by ILEA (Thomas 1985).

Research on parent governors and governing bodies

Formal research results into school governing bodies did not begin to emerge until the late 1980s, although Kogan's edited collection published in 1984 was an important starting-point. There have been two major research projects on parent governors and governing bodies: one based in the Department of Education at the University of Exeter, which has disseminated a large number of different types of research findings – by Golby and others (1989, 1990), by Wragg (1989, 1990) and by Hughes (1990) – and one based at the Open University in the School of Education, directed by Deem. This latter project has also produced a variety of different findings.

Golby, together with Brigley, was interested in exploring the roles and experiences of parent governors. Their fascinating official research report was published in 1989. Golby, however, reports on the essence of the approach and findings in a paper in a collection debating the range of contemporary challenges about parents and schools (Golby 1989). He argues:

> Only systematic research can help us to clarify what is going on and little enough of that has been done. Can it be an accident that policy-oriented research is now so hard to get funded while research on technicalities such as assessment and testing is relatively easy to set up?
>
> Fortunately, some evidence about the parental frame of mind comes to hand from the Leverhulme Parents as Governors Project. A team of teacher-researchers interviewed eighty parent-governors in Devon secondary schools and then conducted intensive case studies of individual governors at work. (Golby 1989: 139)

Although this was in essence a fairly small-scale study, it is important, as Golby noted, because of the paucity of other such research. Despite the small sample and the relatively homogeneous social area of Devon, Golby found that 'parents were not all of a like mind'. He identified three different types of parents who held three types of educational values, ranging across those committed to *meritocratic*, but selective, education, to those committed to *egalitarian*, comprehensive education. He described them in the following way:

Parent governors were definitely not motivated by purely personal or selfish interests and they generally greatly respected the endeavours of professionals . . . There was no commando force of parents ready to leap into ideological battle with the school system.

Instead it was possible to identity three broad categories of parents subscribing to rather different educational values. There was a substantial number of parents who adhere to what may be called grammar school ideology. There was another set who saw schooling as a service industry, principally to employment. A smaller third group of egalitarians promoted comprehensive school ideals. Respectively, these groups stressed the values of the traditional grammar school curriculum and all associated forms of behaviour, dress, etc.; the skills required by the world of work, especially all the modern guises of computer technology together with associated attitudes towards earning a living, industriousness, etc,; and the broad curriculum and cooperative ethos of the supposed good comprehensive. Thus parents . . . exhibited . . . the deeper political and social assumptions current in the broader political debates. (1989: 140)

Golby, however, was not content just to describe these different perspectives. He located them in the contemporary debates around the legitimacy not only of a parental democratic or consumer's role but also that of local government. He was particularly concerned to demonstrate that parents as governors should not be seen as *the* critical decision-makers. He tried to show how that relationship was seen and evaluated by the parent governor:

The relationship of LEA nominees was central to parents' accounts . . . In this way parents recognized the legitimacy of the local authority but they did tend to regard [it] . . . as a distant bureaucracy rather than a supportive presence . . . Parents are indeed the 'parents of the day' and there will be a new set of parents with each new intake to school. Parents as such have a temporary interest in the work of their child's school but their children are certainly of permanent interest, so to speak, to all of us . . . Parents as governors should therefore not be accorded the status of ultimate consumers of education. (1989: 142)

Golby's own perspective is certainly not neutral. He sees school governing bodies as part of the extension of democratic and citizen participation in the work of public institutions, rather than as consumers. However, in order properly to achieve this, parent governors have to be representative in some way of the parent body. In his research Golby found that PTAs were beginning to provide that link between the parent body and the parent governor. Moreover, the co-option of community or industrial representatives added to the balancing out of differential forms of representation, along with teachers. Golby therefore concluded that 'parent power which has come into political play for one set of reasons may well serve broader, more liberal and democratic causes in the long run' (1989: 144).

The research report by Golby and Brigley (1989) provided more evidence in the form of both quotations and analysis of the different approaches of the three types of parent governor in secondary schools. It also gave more detail of the extent to which parent governors felt themselves to be effective. As the authors conclude:

> The next few years will surely see a clarification in the practice of the role of the school governor and of parent governors in particular. We have discovered parents working under the constraints and inhibitions of traditional practice as well as parents staking out fresh ground. The majority seem to muddle along, more or less helped by schools and the LEA. The 'honest endeavour' we noted among teacher governors in 1985 (Golby 1985) is equally apparent among parents. (Golby and Brigley 1989: 87)

However, given that their sample was in Devon, it is perhaps no surprise that 'it was exclusively white, predominantly middle class . . . and [that] parents with professional occupations made up the majority of parent governors' (p. 88). Golby and Lane (1989), in a study of primary–school governorships in both Exeter and Hounslow, confirmed this finding.

The finding that the majority of parent governors were white, professional and middle class is also confirmed rather than challenged by both the NFER surveys and the Community Development Foundation [CDF] survey of minority ethnic communities and school governing bodies. These two sets of surveys were both based on all governors, not just the elected parent governors *per se*. The NFER found that of all the 2,686 governors sent questionnaires in 1,134 maintained primary and secondary schools, 'the great majority (98 per cent) were English/Scottish/Welsh/Northern Irish' (Keys and Fernandes 1990: 3). Almost half of all the sample, even when teachers were excluded, held a professional qualification, and mainly in the broad area of education. This was higher in secondary than primary schools. Interestingly, 'the main occupation (sic) of the governors taking part in the survey were teachers/other education or training occupations (39 per cent)' (p. 3). The CDF survey was of 60 LEAs, 22 of whom filled in the questionnaire. As the authors state, 'we suspect that this low response rate is an indication that, as yet, most LEAs have not tackled the problem of the under-representation of minority ethnic communities' (CDF 1980: 2). The authors found that

> . . . evidence indicates that in areas where there is a concentration of minority ethnic groups [these] mechanisms have not yet produced representative governing bodies – that is, a mix of governors broadly mirroring the population served by the school. (p. 1)

They also mention that although most of their respondent LEAs 'encouraged local people to stand as parent governors, only eight LEAs particularly tried to involve people from minority ethnic communities' (p. 4). This led them to conclude that '. . . fewer than fifty per cent of LEAs were taking positive action to recruit minority ethnic community parents and cooptees' (p. 10). Yet they continued to argue for this to be encouraged especially by LEAs and central government. The majority of governors, even in working-class areas and areas with large proportions of minority ethnic communities, did not achieve representation of these groups. Rather, interest in governing bodies remained a middle-class phenomenon.

Golby and Lane (1989) also reported on their survey of primary schools in Exeter and Hounslow. They contacted 'all twenty-three Exeter primary schools' setting up new governing bodies, and had 23 replies from Hounslow primary head teachers (1989: 5). In particular, they were interested in 'levels of interest' in governing bodies and found it greater in Exeter than Hounslow. Their most interesting finding, however, was of the gender of the parent governors as opposed to coopted governors. They found that mothers tended to be parent governors, whereas men, not necessarily fathers *per se*, tended to be community representatives in these primary schools. They wrote:

> In both Exeter and Hounslow, female parent governors are in the majority, in Exeter by 57% to 43%; in Hounslow by 51% to 39%.
> Among the cooptions in both Exeter and Hounslow males (sic) are in the majority in Exeter by 66% to 34%; in Hounslow by 59% to 41%.
> These figures are remarkably consistent and indicate parent governorship is seen as a mother's role, community representation a male role. (p. 6)

The type of mothers who choose to be parent governors, however, seemed to vary between Exeter and Hounslow. In the former, the majority of mothers who were parent governors were educators or professionals, while in Hounslow they were housewives (p. 6). This finding, of the predominance of mothers among parent governors, was not confirmed for secondary schools, because Golby and Brigley did not consider it. It has also not been reported in other surveys.

However, the NFER survey had a similar and rather sexist form of reporting their findings on the gender of all governors: 'Just under half (47 per cent) were male. The proportion of male governors in secondary schools (57 per cent) was higher than in primary schools (38 per cent)' (Keys and Fernandes 1990: 3). The CDF, NCC survey of minority ethnic community governors also did not consider or raise the question of gender. Golby, however, in association with Brigley, Lane, Taylor and Viant (Golby et al. 1990) interviewed 39 parent governors, half of all parent governors in Exeter primary schools, to consider whether 'the balance of power [is] tilting from professionals to parents . . . in the new era for education' (n.p.). They were concerned to find out why people became governors, and considered the differences between the men and women, in terms of qualifications. They found that 60 per cent of parent governors were mothers; 40 per cent fathers. The researchers commented again that this was the reverse of ratios of coopted governors, where the majority were professional men. They therefore asked why the mothers considered it a role they wished to play, and presented as evidence the words of the mother governors themselves. A typical one, which resonated with other studies, was:

'I am an ordinary Mum. Parents are somewhat in awe of the school and its staff whereas they are quite happy to talk to me. I'm in a good position to help. It's helpful to have ordinary people as governors to create a balance.' (Housewife, Middle School) (Golby et al. 1990: 6)

By contrast, another mother said:

'I bring absolutely nothing in as a parent. I went in by default. Before this I was a political appointee. I bring experience of how things are done. My role is now limited and likely to decrease.' (Housewife, First School) (1990: 6)

Jane Ribbens (1990) found that mothers of primary-school children did indeed find it difficult to approach the school staff as opposed to other mothers. But those mothers who became governors did not see themselves as representatives of other mothers; rather as representing children. Golby et al. report that 'Of our thirty-nine respondents, 24 perceived themselves as representing children as an important part of their role . . . The majority did not see themselves as delegates' (1990: 8). What was crucial about this piece of research, however, was the extent which these new school governors, mainly mothers, saw their new roles as being about their parental role and not just a political one, which they felt was rather burdensome. Golby et al. conclude:

. . . the powers and responsibilities which have been stipulated on paper are not attractive additions to the armoury of the active and ambitious parent governor. Essentially the parents seek a moral right to exercise influence on schools in part-nership and negotiation with those who know and work most closely with pupils . . . unless and until they feel they have achieved some . . . empathy with the educational mission, parent governors will be reluctant to take up the political reins offered them in the latest reforms. (1990: 22)

Deem's evidence about both the social and sexual composition of governing bodies and the beliefs of governors is somewhat at variance with that of the Exeter research team led by Golby. This may be because Deem studied *all* members of governing bodies rather than just parent governors. However, it may be the case that both teacher and coopted governors may also be parents. Indeed, some of the evidence already collected would indicate that some of the teacher and coopted community governors are also parents. No study has looked at this issue of the role of parents in relation to different types of governorship. This raises a complex question of having dual roles in relation to families and schools – a professional and a parental role.

Deem and Brehony began a research study in 1988 of the power dynamics and coping strategies of 15 school governing bodies in two southern LEAs. Both primary and secondary schools were represented in the study, with a variety of catchment areas ranging from affluent white middle-class to working-class Asian inner-city areas (Deem 1989: 258). The results of the research have been widely and variously reported (see especially Deem in Flude and Hammer (eds) (1990) and Brehony and Deem (1990a) as well as papers given at conferences). Deem summarises the sexual and ethnic composition of her sample as being overwhelmingly male and middle class (Deem 1989). Only one-third of her sample were women and they tended to be concentrated in the primary school governorships, though not necessarily as parent governors. However, black and Asian women governors were likely to be parent governors. Whatever the position, there might be dual commitments as both professionals and as parents, a point to which we will return. Deem summarises the women governors as follows:

> Only one of the governing bodies in the study has more female than male governors. Women are most numerous in primary school governing boards. The secondary schools are much more male dominated. Women are most likely to become members of governing bodies as teacher or parent governors. Over half the teacher governors in the project are women ... and a large minority of the parent governors are women (there are most in primary schools). Black and Asian women and men are more likely to be LEA or parent governors than teacher or coopted governors, although some schools have used coopted places as a way of increasing or getting ethnic minority membership. There is very low representation across all the 15 bodies of black and Asian women, regardless of categories. Coopted governors are overwhelmingly white males, which has much to do with the emphasis being put on co-opting high-status business people. Where women are coopted, they are usually either accountants (accountancy has a high proportion of women compared to many professions) or else they have jobs in a community organisation or are primary head teachers of feeder schools. The great majority of all governors (250 in all 15 schools) in our study are male and middle class. One-third of the 250 are women and 7% are black or Asian. (Deem 1989: 252)

Deem also reports interestingly on the dynamics of school governing bodies (1989: 254–7). She argues first that

> ... there is a tendency in some governing bodies in our study to treat *parent governors* differently, appealing to them only on particular issues and apparently not expecting them to contribute on other matters: this is especially marked where there are female and black or Asian parent governors. (1989: 255)

She shows that this might vary with the educational expertise of parent governors and their ethnicity in particular social contexts. She argues therefore that ethnic minority governors 'have a hard struggle and are amongst the quietest in our study' (p. 255).

She also makes particular points about those she called intriguingly 'women parent governors'. She states that most of the silent governors were mothers, especially in primary school boards, and adds that they 'appear to feel that they should only voice opinions on things that are of legitimate concern to them, such as passing on parental views about classes who are constantly taught only by supply teachers' (p. 255). However, she notes that when they did contribute, they appeared to be able to stick to the point better than men. This point about gender differences in meetings has been made by others for example, Marshall (1987) and, in the US, Shakeshaft (1988). However, Deem's particular point about mother governors may also be of special significance in the context of such women feeling they only have limited knowledge and expertise.

Deem also alludes to the fact that some governors with difficulties other than parent governors may also be mothers for she pointed to the fact that the 'typical' governor is one with *no* domestic commitments. She also draws attention to the rate of resignations from amongst female governors 'because of the pressure of domestic commitments and the difficulty of arranging child care for meetings whose duration may vary from an hour to five or six hours (p. 257). She therefore concludes by drawing attention to their need for further support and help, especially with training, as the tasks of school governors increase and become more burdensome. What is also significant here might be the difference between those with professional commitments as business people or educationalists and as parents.

Together with Brehony, Deem also extends this consideration about the ways in which governors could pursue their new role, especially in the light of the debate about 'charging for aspects of free education' (Brehony and Deem 1990a: 333–45). Indeed, they show that the issue of consumer power is a weak one in the context of the new school governing bodies who need professional educators to administer schools effectively. They also show that so-called 'consumer governors' did not necessarily identify with the parent body any more than other governors. They state that 'the majority of parent governors took no or minimal part in the charging discussions ... despite the clear centrality of the issue to parents' (p. 344). This is an important point in relation to the role that parent governors might be expected to play, moving from a community-oriented or representative role to a more individualistic consumerist role.

This kind of detailed research study fleshes out the evidence about the conflicting perspectives underpinning the roles for governing bodies and for parents, especially as parent governors, in particular. Similar evidence is beginning to be accumulated by other researchers about the changing balance between parents on governing bodies as political representatives and as consumers (Ball 1991). This is beginning to substantiate the arguments made by Beattie (1985) about the differing political theories underpinning such roles and relationships. He argued that the original justification was for an extension of liberal democracy rather than a consumerist position. However, the implementation process has entailed a substantial shift of argument.

Hughes, Wikeley and Nash (1990) have also shown that parents do not see themselves as 'consumers' and, indeed, with respect to the national curriculum in primary schools are not expected to. The same is true of secondary schools. However, this adds to the evidence about the contradictory tendencies underpinning the ERA 1988 which, on the one hand, increased 'parent powers' through their roles and powers on governing bodies and, on the other, gave powers to central government to control the curriculum. There is a growing accumulation of evidence about that shifting balance, which seems to be pointing, albeit uneasily, towards greater parental power rather then central control. This has been presented by Flude and Hammer (1990) as well as by Ball (1990a & b). Recent studies of schools and teachers seem also to add to this (Mortimore and Mortimore 1991).

Morgan et al. (1991) provide evidence of the time-consuming nature of parent-created and parent-run schools. They demonstrate that such family schools do not necessarily allow for the amount of individual parental or family control suggested or implied by economic theories. Morgan et al. investigated the roles of parents and teachers in integrated schools in Northern Ireland. This was a very particular case-study of schools which crossed the religious or sectarian divide. Interviews were conducted in three integrated schools – one secondary and two primary – to get a picture of parental attitudes:

> Freedom to exercise choice is fundamental to integrationists, so founder parents were unlikely to deny others the right which they claimed for themselves . . . founder parents regarded integrated schools as an alternative to, not a replacement for, maintained and controlled schools. (Morgan et al. 1991: 2)

The researchers found that the types of parental involvement changed from the original intentions of the founder parents of such schools to their opening. The founder parents had set up the schools to develop a close relationship and religious harmony for their children but they realised that ongoing parental involvement would be more complex than the creation of such schools. However,

> . . . since it was seen as important that the spirit of co-operation should be maintained, many founder parents continued their association with 'their' school, as trustees, directors and parent governors. They also began to realise that their work in setting up schools was only a beginning, and that the real task now lay ahead. This realisation was to be crucial in their thinking about parental involvement. At the start they had chosen parental involvement as a major aim, but as time went on they began to appreciate that this was a more complex process than they had expected . . . when founder parents were asked why they chose integrated education most said they were initially attracted by the prospect of having a close relationship with their child's school. (pp. 32–3)

Morgan et al. considered the various forms of parental involvement in the schools and found that few parents wanted to become involved in being school governors or on school councils, saying that they did not have the skill. The researchers compared and confirmed these misgivings with those found among parent governors in Birmingham primary schools in the early 1980s (Pascal 1988). They also considered that poor communication between boards of governors and parents' councils possibly exacerbated the perceived image of the governing board as rather remote (p. 35). Parents' political participation was thus seen to be arduous and difficult and did not necessarily mean a better or close relationship with their own children's school.

The researchers concluded, however, that the 'immense time inputs' that teachers and parents had to put into the development of the schools had implications for the changed system of parental involvement and increased local management of schools in England and Wales as well as Northern Ireland. They felt that there

> ... must be uncertainty about whether large numbers of parents can be expected to input so much time and skill. Our evidence suggests that parents want to be involved in their children's education but that for most this does not imply a wish or even a willingness to be heavily committed to meetings on a regular basis. (p. 55)

The researchers also echoed Golby's point about the difference between parents' short-term perspectives and longer-term educational issues. The majority of parents in both research settings had the short-term goal of developing better education for their own children rather than political participation in order to develop schooling in general.

The creation of grant-maintained schools through ERA 1988, on the basis of parental ballots organised by school governing bodies, runs directly counter to this. The system set up by the Tories in ERA allows for one generation of parents unequivocally to influence the long-term status of a school. A parental ballot to opt in or out of LEA control will have very long-term implications for generations of school-children at that particular school. However, the decision may in fact not be exactly what the parents had bargained for if the evidence Morgan of et al. can be generalized. Fitz and Halpin's investigations of the creation and establishment of grant-maintained schools (1990; 1991) will be able to confirm whether parents feel their involvement in the running of these schools is burdensome and inefficient compared with traditional bureaucratic structures. Evidence will also be available about the effects of local management of schools on the roles of governing bodies, including parents (Ball 1991).

Westoby has also tried to speculate on the effectiveness of 'the ERA's strategy for improving schools that parents are dissatisfied with'. He argues that

> ... it is not the actions of parents who opt away from them that will produce changes but rather the behaviour of those – parents and others – who get and remain involved in them. And whether the second 'prong' of the ERA's strategy for parental power will be effective turns on how far parents prove able to wield

sustained and constructive influence in school decision-making and micro-politics. Some of the evidence suggests that their capacity to do this may be quite limited . . . Apathy, however, may only reflect past impotence . . . the autumn 1988 parent governor elections were contested in about half of primary schools and three-quarters of secondary school, with energetic contests and substantial polls in a significant minority of schools (Westoby 1990: 77).

He also considered how parents as a body express their views to the governing body and generally wield political influence. In other words, he considered the more informal ways in which parents have become involved in school political processes through PTAs and annual parent meetings, etc. The evidence for these latter parent business meetings as part of the process of extending parental power through governing bodies is not very sanguine. The majority of such meetings have been found so far to be inquorate, parents preferring involvement through their individual children rather than more general political meetings. HMI reported on aspects of parental involvement in 1989–90 (HMI 1991). They found that some of the least well-supported were the governors' annual meetings for parents. Of the primary schools visited, only three reached a quorum. None of the secondary schools reached a quorum, although some had large numbers of parents who attended (p. 5).

Nevertheless, Macbeth (1989), Bastiani (1991) and Tomlinson (1991) have argued for the extension of such informal developments in home–school relationships on the instrumental grounds that Woods referred to. Their argument is for a mix of a 'parental political voice' in decision-making and a more effective partnership between parents and schools to improve their children's education. We shall have occasion to return to these issues in chapter 8.

Arguments about consumer power and influence do not always rest on a parental voice or role in decision-making. Indeed, one contradictory strand in the contemporary British debates is the creation of city technology colleges, initially at the request of business as well as government. Although these schools were given additional government sponsorship through ERA 1988, as well as a steer from business, they were not to be parent-run bodies. The aim was to extend the range of consumer choice of types of school through the creation of a mixed system of schools, reliant on a variety of types of sponsorship. We shall return to this issue in the next chapter.

American research into parental political involvement

It is important to note both kinds of argument about parental power and consumer choice have also been used recently in the US as a basis for considering changes in the form and organisation of their systems of schooling. They have also underpinned a new educational research agenda in the US. As we saw in chapter 4, the National Commission on Excellence in Education spawned a whole new set of studies about the workings of the American educational system and particularly school democracy. A number of researchers have pointed both to the ways in which there has been a shift in power from professional educators and school boards to business and community interests (Mitchell and Goertz (eds) 1989). However, as noted earlier in this chapter, in the US the traditional systems of community control of schools tended to allow for more parental involvement than in Britain. It is this system that has recently been called into question by critics of liberal schooling who have been advocating a more consumerist approach to education, on the lines similar to British arguments.

A major study by the traditionally 'liberal' Brookings Institution has recently presented both research evidence and radical policy proposals to remove schools from traditional local democratic systems of control (Chubb and Moe 1990). In a large-scale re-analysis of 1,015 high schools and nearly 60,000 students, Chubb and Moe pointed to the persistence of educational inequities largely on the basis of family differences. They argue, however, that it is school bureaucracies that have inhibited the development of quality education and especially quality teachers. Teachers have been constrained by petty bureaucratic rules, especially in the large inner-city school systems. The argument is as much about empowering teachers as about empowering parents to be able to choose good and effective schools.

> The schools' most fundamental problems are rooted in the institutions of democratic control by which they are governed; and, despite all talk about 'restructuring', the current wave of grab bag reforms leaves those institutions intact and in charge. The basic causes of America's educational problems do not get addressed . . . The schools remain subordinates in the structure of public authority – and they remain bureaucratic . . .
> Our guiding principle in the design of a choice system is this: public authority must be put to use in creating a system that is almost entirely beyond the reach of public authority . . . the best way to achieve significant, enduring reform is for states to take the initiative in withdrawing authority from existing institutions and building a new system in which most authority is vested directly in the schools, parents and students. (Chubb and Moe 1990: 217–18)

The new system that they envisage consists of the individual states setting minimal criteria for accrediting schools as 'public', whether they were hitherto public or private. All schools which met the criteria would be chartered as a 'public', that is, a state school, and granted the right to accept students and receive public money. The money would never go to individual parents or students, but, via a Choice Agency, directly to the schools. The amount of parental 'add-ons' to funds would be limited so as not to produce 'too many disparities and inequalities in the public system' (p. 220). Despite these latter genuflections towards a system of equity, Chubb and Moe remain implacably opposed to the traditional systems of schooling, concluding that 'democratic control normally produces ineffective schools' (p. 227).

Conclusions

In this chapter, we have seen how the education reformer–researcher debate subtly shifted over a 30-year period. It changed from a consideration of the ways to make schooling more effective through more local or community forms of political participation to those concerned about individual parental involvement as consumers. The origins of the political debates lie in discussions about citizen participation in local democracy. These influenced studies and strategies about parental participation in education not only in Britain but also other advanced industrial societies. As a result, political strategies were revised to ensure more parental involvement. In the process, arguments changed from community to consumer involvement. Nevertheless, a considerable body of knowledge has been amassed about how effective these particular reforms have been, especially the local or community control of schools through governing bodies and the role of parent governors. Interestingly, here evidence has been collected to assess the effects of the gender and race of parents on the changes. During the course of this evaluative research, policy has further shifted in terms of a role for parents as consumers.

We turn now to the issue of parental choice itself, about which Chubb and Moe are so celebratory, to see the extent to which new systems in Britain or the US have so far been effective. However, these new approaches tend to be located within the context of traditional democratic systems and are part of what Chubb and Moe call 'grab bag' reforms. The 'grab bag' reforms were those which extended democratic citizenship or community roles to parents on the premise of making schooling more effective. As we have seen from the British research evidence, governors, and particularly parent governors, did not want to be *the* critical decision-makers in the running of schools. However, as the decade of the 1980s progressed, shifts in political rhetoric and policy implementation led to changes in the notions of parental involvement. Instead of parental involvement being about parental participation as a form of partnership in the running of schools, it has shifted towards a notion of parental power as consumers, as Woods (1988) has noted. This has also inexorably led to new ideas about parental choice. We turn now to look at these arguments and the associated research evidennce.

7

Parental or Family Choice of School, or of Education?

Introduction

In this chapter I shall review the research debates over the various notions of choice in education for parents or families in the context of changing educational reforms. Choice of education, whether of school or course/curriculum, has been enshrined in public or state systems of education in the majority of advanced capitalist societies. For example, as Beattie has noted:

> The Universal Declaration of Human Rights (1948) mentioned parents who, it stated, 'have a prior right to choose' the kind of education that shall be given to their children ... [but] the relationship between parents and the state as the provider of education was complex and controversial. (1985: 2)

The notions of parent and/or family and those of education are difficult to unravel, especially when it comes to choice, itself a complex notion. Choice is about trying to assess relatively unknown processes and relationships. As Midwinter has claimed, 'A major difficulty for parents is lack of information about how particular schools operate and, in the nature of things, a lack of prophetic instinct about how their children are going to develop' (1980: 10). As we saw in the previous chapter, in discussing various typologies of parental participation or involvement, Woods (1988: 325) has also pointed out how policy developments affected the notions of 'choice' from a concern with parental partnerships to a more market-oriented notion of 'consumerism' in education.

Most of the research in Britain has been developed in a specific policy context – that of changes in legislation developed largely by New Right governments in the decade of the 1980s, as we noted in chapter 4. However, some of this work is presaged, as Johnson points out in her excellent monograph on the topic entitled *Parental Choice in Education* (1990), on research on private education and parents' choice of such schools, largely either by advocates of this system or their detractors. There is also little by way of serious full review, and most of the British evidence on choice prior to the 1980s is incidental to other research. By contrast, the US literature is replete with earlier evidence, such as the volume of essays by Coleman and others, entitled *Parents, Teachers and Children: Prospects for Choice in American Education* (1977), and Coons and Sugarman's 1978 study.

In Britain, as we shall see, the vast majority of the research is focused upon the question of choice of school rather than issues such as choice of courses or subjects within school. It is about choice at key stages, either primary or secondary, but usually the latter. It is also largely about the event rather than the social process. This is by contrast with some of the research in the US, which looks at a range of such choice questions (Raywid 1985). However, we shall also have occasion to refer to the review of 'choice of school' conducted for the US Department of Education and published in 1989. This study, by Glenn (1989), contrasted the US with six other nations, namely Great Britain (looking separately at England and Wales, Scotland and Northern Ireland), France, the Netherlands, Belgium, Germany and Canada, having looked carefully at the educational systems in 25 nations. However, this study was one which focused very much on policy-oriented research, and was not, in Glenn's own words, 'an academic exercise' (1989: 213).

Indeed, the starting-point of most of the research on choice in education is the policy shift from a liberal or social-democratic approach to educational systems, providing some measure of equity or equality in education whether by individual or community-based political involvement, to one in which individual choices by families or parents as 'consumers' are paramount. We noted in the previous chapter the various shifts in the definition of parental roles. It is worth drawing attention at this point to Glenn's somewhat surprising conclusion to his seven-nation study:

> As the U.S. Department of Education prepares to publish these papers for the use of American educators and policy makers, I have asked for the opportunity to step out of my temporary role of amateur researcher, describing the experience of other nations with an attempt at objectivity, and to make some concluding remarks in my own voice, as a practitioner deeply engaged in issues that face American schools, on what we can learn from this experience about parent choice of schools. . . .
>
> For nearly 20 years I have been responsible for equity and urban education programs in the Massachusetts Department of Education. In this capacity, I have been deeply involved both in limiting parent choice, when it works against educational equity, and in promoting choice, when it is harnessed to improving schools . . . Massachusetts has ample experience to set alongside that in other states and nations, but it is different experience, under different conditions and

intentions, and it has been valuable for me to lift my eyes from my own tasks to see what is working and not working elsewhere . . . I am, of course, not representing the Massachusetts Board . . . though support parent choice among public schools subject to appropriate constraints required by equity and by the interests of all pupils. (1989: 213–14)

Glenn's personal remarks sound more like those of a 'liberal educationalist' than of the education reformers who have initiated the policy changes either in Britain, to which most of the British research refers, or in the US. His remarks resonate with those of Midwinter in his pamphlet produced for the British Advisory Centre for Education in 1980. Midwinter is also a 'liberal' educationalist, and became known for his action-research in community education and parental involvement in the running of schools. In *Education Choice Thoughts*, which is a discussion of the pros and cons of parental choice of school, he concludes:

> Properly defined, it has sound justifications, professional as well as democratic, but it is as well to realise that it would only make sense and lead to educational improvement if it were part and parcel of a broader educational policy. In the development of our public services there is even what has been called 'a necessary tension' between liberty – with individuals having as many freedoms to choose and act as possible – and equality – with the community accepting that some rights and resources should be fairly and universally distributed. With educational choice . . . one should perhaps approach the discussion in the mood of the third feature of the celebrated social democratic trinity. If 'fraternity' were adopted as the moving force . . . of teachers . . . and parents . . . then children could be, as is right and proper, the chief beneficiaries of such brotherhood. (1980: 18)

Despite the unthinking patriarchal or sexist conclusion about the kind of educational community he wishes to create, Midwinter also draws attention to the tension between different political values underpinning policy developments.

In Britain the motivating force behind the policy developments was what was considered an inappropriate balance between liberty and equality, with the emphasis having been pressed too far in the direction of equality, rather than 'individual' freedom of choice. Thus, there were a number of legislative attempts – as outlined in chapter 4 – to redress the balance, shifting from a rather bureaucratic 'producer' dominated system, which emphasised equal opportunities, towards one which put more emphasis on individual choice, largely as 'consumers'. As we have seen in the previous chapter, this changed policy relied more on an 'economic' model than one devoted to a social analysis. Indeed, a number of writers have pointed to the economic theories underpinning these developments. They have been most clearly articulated by the Hillgate Group (1986) and by the Institute of Economic Affairs (Ashworth et al. 1988). There has been a slow but concerted attempt to allow for more 'consumer' choice over a range of public services and at the same time to try to develop markets for traditional public social and educational services. However, the extent to which either or both of these has been achieved with respect to education is dubious. It is this that has been the subject of much research analysis and debate.

However, the other factor that has not been clearly articulated in the policy debates is not only the notion of choice itself but also the concepts of the 'individual' to whom the choice refers. As Walford (1991: 68) has pointed out, in Britain, this has been very clearly articulated as being the 'parent' of the school-child rather than the entire family. In other countries and other places and at other times, the notion may refer to the family as a whole. Indeed, Glenn's concept seemed to imply some balance between parent and child in the choice of school. In other studies in the US and in most of the prescriptive work around educational choice, the concept has usually been of the undifferentiated family. For example, an early text in the field that gave both the historical background to the ideas and an argument for the exercise of educational choice, including the application of education vouchers, was that of Coons and Sugarman (1978) which referred chiefly to family choice. In that case, however, Coons and Sugarman were concerned to develop a broad argument which focused upon an array of methods and techniques of implementation, and over the boundaries between public and private services.

Similarly, Hirshman (1970) developed a set of arguments about the interrelationships between individuals in organisations as consumers and as participants. Indeed, his theories had general applicability to a range of public and private organisations. As we noted in chapter 6, his argument was essentially that competition between or within organisations did not necessarily have the results expected by traditional economic theory. This led Hirshman to revive his views and develop them (1981).

As Westoby has recently commented:

> One reason why exit can be ineffective is that voice to exit may pull in opposite directions ... Making exit easier may well atrophy voice; voice may be loudest, and perhaps of greatest effect, when monopoly conditions prevail and customers are securely 'locked-in.'
> Hirshman takes state education in the United States, with private schools competing with the state schools, as one of his main examples to develop this point, and to establish the sorts of cases where easier exit may most weaken the recuperative effects of voice. These cases are most likely to be found, he argues, where suppliers compete for customers most of all on quality and relatively little on price ... Hirshman's concept of 'exit' need not be limited to those who are already consumers ... Many ... points apply to consumers' decisions on which suppliers choose on first entering the market. (1990: 71–2)

Westoby tried to apply these ideas to a consideration of the implications particularly of the Education Reform Act (ERA) 1988, using the evidence developed by other British researchers on parental choice of school. The notion of choice here refers to that also of 'exit'. What is critical in this analysis is the consideration of how parents exercise 'choice' and balance it with expressions of a view of how the organisation – in this case the school – is operating. We have already had occasion to review the evidence about 'voice'. We shall review Westoby's consideration of the notion of 'exit' later, in the context of looking at ways in which parental choice has been enhanced by the ERA.

British researcher–reformer debates over parental choice

What is particularly interesting about the British research on parental choice of school in the state system is not only its narrow and particular focus but also the fact that a great deal of it is concerned with reviewing the effects of the implementation of particular pieces of legislation. This is similar to the more recent work on consumer involvement and on parent governors as reviewed in the last chapter. This is in marked contrast to the parallel developments in social research on parental involvement in education, which have gone beyond the rather particularistic concerns with policy analysis, review or evaluation. Nevertheless, there is a certain parallelism with the original social research that was spawned after the 1944 Education Act, as we noted in chapter 5. However, as it developed it distanced itself from the specificity of the legislation and developed a rather more strategic view of the application of research findings to policy developments. As we have seen in the previous chapter, the research on parental involvement is now so complex that it covers a multitude of issues that can only be condensed into four or five different approaches. Research on parental choice in some senses could be seen as a by-product of one of those approaches, as is much of the work on 'parental voice' and partnership. These two areas are also born of particular policy concerns.

Although most of the research, especially that about parental choice of state education, has been about the implementation of particular policies, the researchers are neither advocates nor necessarily detractors of the system. They all view, relatively dispassionately, the effects of policies on parental choice. However, they are also more concerned with cataloguing and classifying the reasons for particular choice than with detailed elaboration of particular economic or social theories. Indeed, the majority of the research methodologies stand in the old tradition of social surveys and quantitative social analysis. There is very little sense of the underlying social processes behind the 'choices'. Perhaps this is where the contrast with the research on parental involvement is at its greatest. Most of the researchers, in any event, are educationalists or social policy analysts, rather than psychologists or sociologists, who might be concerned to develop deeper theoretical insights on social processes. Moreover, the perspective tends to be related more, as noted above, to economic and political theories rather than social or psychological ones. By contrast, most of the work on parental involvement in early education has, as already mentioned, been carried out by sociologists and/or psychologists, while that on parental participation has been carried out by policy analysts.

The studies that we shall therefore review are first, a study of the implementation of the 1980 Education Act by Stillman and Maychell (1986); second a study of a particular aspect of the 1980 Education Act – the assisted places scheme – by Edwards, Fitz and Whitty (1989); third, two studies about the implementation of the 1981 Education Act in Scotland, one referred to as the Glasgow study, by Macbeth, Strachan and Macaulay (1986), the other as the Edinburgh study, finally published in book form in 1989 by Adler, Petch and Tweedie and an article by Echols et al. (1990); fourth, studies of parental choice in the Inner London Education Authority by Hunter (1991) and West and Varlaam (1991); fifth, studies of parental choice in relation to ERA by Hughes, Wikeley and Nash (1990), Westoby (1990), and Coldron and Boulton (1991) as well as studies of particular types of school, such as the grant-maintained schools (Fitz and Halpin 1990, 1991) and city technology colleges (Gerwitz et al. 1991; Walford and Miller 1991). In addition, we shall look at wider issues in relation to parental choice by looking at choices of private education (Fox 1986) or the balance between state and private education (Johnson 1987) or related issues about secondary-school choice (Elliott et al. 1981, Elliott 1982). There is also work in progress by Ball and Walford as well as David and West which cannot yet be reviewed. We shall not, however, have occasion to look at issues in relation to parents and particular types of special education (Barton and Tomlinson 1983) since these can bear only tangentially on the question of 'choice'.

The balancing act of 1980

The study by Stillman and Maychell (1986) conducted under the auspices of the National Foundation for Educational Research (NFER) was the first attempt in Britain to survey the ways in which parents made decisions about the secondary schools to which to send their children. However, the researchers were not concerned with the issue of choice entirely from the individual parent's point of view. What they wished to elucidate was the *balance* between the LEA and the parents, following the implementation of revised clauses about the balance between 'parental wishes' and reasonable public expenditure, in the 1980 Education Act. As we noticed in chapter 4, the legislation did not use the term parental 'choice', but the rather milder notion of 'preference'. It also changed the notion of 'unreasonable expenditure' to that of 'efficient use of resources' (see, David 1980, for a discussion of these issues in the draft legislation). Indeed, Stillman edited a series of papers from a conference which he entitled *The Balancing Act of 1980: Parents, Politics and Education* (1986). The papers in this volume mainly focused on issues to do with changing legal processes, their implementation and the processes of decision-making and appeal. What was particularly significant about the legislation, as Bull (in Stillman 1986) pointed out, is the extent to which choice was subject to a more justicial process, including appeals at quasi-legal tribunals and the ultimate authority of the ombudsman. Thus parental choice was far from unconstrained; on the contrary, it was, in fact, hedged around with an array of constrains of both a legal and resource nature.

Indeed, Stillman and Maychell's survey of parents in four authorities found this. They sent questionnaires to over 3,000 families whose children were transferring to secondary schools from primary schools. This, in fact, is a feature of the narrow but detailed nature of their research. The schools were all located in one of four LEAs which varied in the extent of selective or comprehensive secondary education. The questions over the decisions about transfers to secondary schools were to some extent based upon Elliott's study of secondary-school choice (1981, 1982).

However, Elliott's study was part of a much wider analysis of accountability in education, although based on one LEA. He grouped the reasons for choice into two sets of factors – those he called 'process' and those called 'product'. By 'process' he meant the extent to which the management of the school appeared to contribute to overall pupils' happiness. By 'product' he referred to the general academic achievements of the pupils in terms of examination results. He also discussed factors to do with the accessibility of the school, which could for these purposes be considered the third 'p' factor, namely proximity. Elliott had found that, on balance, 'process' and 'proximity' factors predominated over 'product'. However, the study was very small-scale and did not take into account the extent to which these factors might overlap with each other. He also did not take into account the extent to which these ideas were based upon reputation and rumour rather than more 'objective' indicators. And of course, this applies to all the research in this area; as Midwinter (1980: 10) pointed out, parents cannot reasonably predict their children's development.

While it is always going to be the case that parents cannot guess how their children will develop in relation to the particular characteristics of the school, there was in fact more information on which parents could base their choices in the Stillman and Maychell survey than there had been before the 1980 Education Act. Schools had been required, under the legislation, to produce general information booklets both about admissions criteria and the appeals system.

From the point of view of the criteria by which parents made their decisions about schools, Stillman and Maychell used the three groupings that Elliott had found, using the same terms as his for the fist two, namely 'process' and 'product', and adding a third which they called 'geography' rather than 'proximity'.

They were able to group the vast majority of their 97 'reasons' under these three categories, although they found that there were a few that could not be thus grouped. They found the most frequently recorded reason to be that of 'product' rather than 'process' or 'proximity'. Over half the sample saw the educational outcomes, such as examination results, as important in their decisions, whereas nearly 40 per cent gave 'process' reasons such as the school's 'ethos', as contributing to the child's happiness. Many families, however, gave a combination of reasons for their choices, and in that respect 'process' reasons turned out to be far more important than 'product', cited by almost all in the sample (1986: 90). Despite its narrow remit, Stillman and Maychell's survey is important in that it was the first of its kind. However, given its originality, it is a very 'board brush' approach to the issues, concerned as much with setting out the detailed administrative and legal context in which the reasons were expressed as focusing upon the issues in relation to choice. Indeed, perhaps as much was left uncovered as was covered by this large survey. For example, there was no consideration of the social, sexual or racial characteristics of the parents or the children and whether or not these factors contributed in any way to the process of decision-making. Moreover, the reasons themselves were not linked in any particular or theoretically informed fashion.

The study of the implementation of the assisted places scheme (Edwards, Fitz and Whitty 1989) is of a rather different order from the NFER survey. The authors looked at the history of the political process of developing the scheme as well as carrying out detailed investigations, through interviews rather than questionnaires, of many of the participants in the implementation of the scheme, including parents of pupils at a number of independent schools. In other words, Edwards, Fitz and Whitty were concerned with rather more than just how a particular type of group of parents came to 'choose' private or independent education. In fact, parental choice was not a key factor in their study. Rather they were concerned, again, to look at the balance between different types of educational provision and the ways in which resources were being redistributed between types of selective and/or private education as against comprehensive and/or state education. Indeed, the assisted places scheme started off, as we noted in chapter 4, as a modest way of reintroducing state financial support to low-income parents of academically able children to enable them to participate in elite, private academic secondary education. To this broad end, Edwards, Fitz and Whitty conducted studies of schools, parents and pupils in three different areas of the country and tried to look at the balance between private and state education. However, because of the politically sensitive nature of the issues, the researchers experienced great difficulties in obtaining access to schools – private or state – and to parents. In the event, they managed to interview over 300 families, including both parents and pupils, from both state and private schools.

In the course of the interviews they asked both the parents and pupils a range of questions about the reasons for their choice of school. Although they did not use Elliott's terminology, the nine main factors in relation to school choice cover both 'product' and 'process' as well as 'proximity': however, these were slightly differently named and valued. Two main factors cited by parents with children either in private or state education, and whether fee-paying or assisted-place holders, were examination results and school ethos. Prospects for higher education came a very close third, except for the parents of children going to comprehensive schools. Thus 'academic' factors were by far the most important for these parents. The authors considered that 'ethos' was about more than the 'civilising characteristics' of schools, but was about providing a challenging and competitive setting to 'stretch' academically able pupils. Interestingly, 'ethos' did not figure highly for comprehensive school parents, whereas, comparatively speaking, 'child's friends' was more significant. This had to have been a factor of great importance to Stillman and Maychell's parents. On the other hand, given that the assisted places scheme was more about academic merit as the chief criterion than simply parental choice, except within the criterion of being a low-income family wishing to avail itself of academic and private education, it is little wonder that children's friendships did not play a major part in the reasoning.

What is important from this study, which we shall have occasion to return to, is the kinds of families, within the socio-economic category, that were chosen for assisted places. It transpired from this study, plus some further evidence from the Assisted Places Unit in the DES, that low income is not entirely correlated with traditional measures of social class. Indeed a large minority of families in receipt of assisted places were lone-mother households. Many of these mothers were found to have substantial amounts of education, including higher education. They have been referred to as the 'artificially poor' (Douse 1985) or as the 'sunken middle class' by reason of divorce, marital separation, widowhood or unemployment (Edwards, Fitz and Whitty 1989: 166).

Both these studies showed the constraints on both family decision-making and administrative decision-making, in the context of balancing resources. More important, however, are the issues surrounding balancing values between liberty or freedom of choice on the one hand and equality or collective consumption on the other. Given the so-called incremental approach to policy changes in Britain, it is not surprising that the evidence shows how hedged-in parental choice is by other considerations. The two Scottish studies add further weight to this, in particular the Edinburgh study since it was concerned with how the balance between individualism and collectivism could be accomplished in the state system. Adler, Petch and Tweedie (1989) were concerned to show the difficulties in implementing a wide system of individual parental choice in the context of a social welfare or social policy approach which valued collectivist goals.

Scottish 'choice' research

The study by Adler, Petch and Tweedie was concerned not only with issues to do with what in Scotland are called 'placing requests' of parents at both the primary and secondary stages of schooling but also their implications. The study was a detailed survey of how the process of making 'placing requests' occurred in a number of Scottish authorities at both stages, interlaced with an analysis of administrative factors. The researchers interviewed 1,000 parents, 400 of whom were sending children to primary schools and 600 to secondary schools, so that they had a large sample on which to base their analysis.

The considerations which parents gave to the questions of school choice were again similar to the findings of Stillman and Maychell, rather than those of Edwards, Fitz and Whitty. Parents were more influenced by the geography or location of school (proximity) and by issues about discipline in the school – what might be considered general reputation – than by wider educational considerations, such as curriculum, teaching methods and examination results. Nevertheless, these 'geographical' reasons led only to a small proportion of 'placing requests' – namely 10 per cent in the key period of the research (1984– 6), rising later to 14 per cent (Adler, personal communication, March 1991). Of these requests the vast majority were granted either initially or on appeal. However, if the issues were considered by LEA Appeal Committees they tended to uphold the LEA's decision, whereas the courts tended to uphold the individual parents' request. Although placing requests appeared to come from right across the social class spectrum, and were linked to specific areas rather than class groupings, LEA decisions on appeals were more linked to social class, especially the affluent working class.

Adler, Petch and Tweedie found it quite hard to draw clear conclusions from their very detailed and complex analysis. They noted a shift from both an LEA-wide and collective-welfare approach to a more child-centred and individual client-oriented approach to school admissions. But this represented only a modest shift for, on the whole, parents seemed satisfied with the schools available for them. Where changes were requested they might have the effect increasing social segregation. In addition, it appeared that the schools which gained the most were those with high reputations and those that lost the most were those which were on the periphery of traditional housing estates with poor educational attainments. This is in an area, Scotland, where few schools are overcrowded and thus the effect is to create a few chronically under-subscribed schools. The overall conclusion that can be drawn is that this leads both to a more inefficient use of resources, and to widening inequalities between schools and between pupils, in terms of opportunities. As Adler et al. pointed out, it might be quite rational for one parent to choose but it is irrational for all parents. The threat to equality of opportunity that these parental choices give rise to has serious implications in a democratic society. Indeed, the optimum balance between individual rights and collective welfare did not seem to have been achieved by these measures. However, Adler and his co-authors were clearly committed to a more collectivist approach and their research confirmed them in their disapproval of a rather costly and inefficient administrative new system, which the vast majority of parents eschewed.

The University of Glasgow study conducted by Macbeth, Strachan the Macaulay was altogether a more modest affair than the Edinburgh one. Although there were some overlapping issues – the investigation of the parental choice clauses of the 1981 Education (Scotland) Act – the Glasgow researchers chose to concentrate entirely on attitudes to parental choice. As the authors state:

> The main purpose of the study was to examine the parental responses to the provisions and their impact upon schools. Since parental responses are related to parental understanding, assessment of the extent and modes of information made available to parents were integral, as were indications of parents' knowledge of and views about the new system, the reasons why parents had or had not taken action relating to school placement, who influenced choices and the extent to which parents found the system easy or difficult to operate. We were also concerned to know what kinds of families made placing requests. We considered it important to obtain both breadth of coverage and detailed knowledge of parental perspective. (1986: 2)

They carried out a massive survey of 1,500 parents, supplemented by around 200 home interviews, and some interviews with headteachers. The report of this study was not published in book form but as a University of Glasgow mimeograph (1986). It was, however, a full and detailed account both of their methods and of the reasons parents gave for their choices of school. It is also similar to the Edinburgh study in that the authors were concerned to locate issues about parental choice in the debates about, on the one hand, comprehensive secondary education and on the other, diversity, freedom and social justice. More important from these authors' perspective is the wider issue about choice as part of a broader concept of parental involvement. Given Macbeth's earlier work (Macbeth et al. 1984) and subsequent work on school effectiveness through home–school contacts (1989) to which we have referred in chapter 6 and will return to in chapter 8, this is not surprising. The authors of the Glasgow study state:

> The view that education, including schooling, should be a partnership between home and school, has gained momentum. The reasons . . . lie . . . in accumulated research evidence that there is a relationship between a child's home background and his/her attainment in the school . . . the broad correlation is generally accepted.
> The problem facing those responsible for the schooling system is what, in practice, to do to enhance a sense of education partnership between home and school

without escalating costs. Parental choice of school seems to be one step which the government has felt able to take rapidly, either because it is deemed appropriate on non-educational grounds or it may contribute towards an awareness of the parental dimension in education. (1986: 7–8)

Given this overall perspective it may be of interest that the authors found the detailed analysis of their material difficult to classify, not being certain how to balance family as against other reasons for choice. They found, in the event, that across six different types of area surveyed, each family gave on average two reasons. But for the urban areas 'choice of school is more real . . . than in the rural areas' (1986: 334). As with the Edinburgh study, although the parents knew their rights few parents made placing requests. Where they did so, the grate majority (over 90 per cent) were successful either initially or on appeal. The requests were made, again confirming the finding of Adler et al., from across the whole social range. The vast majority of parents, then, chose the local school. The reasons they gave were 'divided fairly equally between those based on assessments of schools and those which were non-school reasons'. The 'school-based' reasons could be divided between families making placing requests and those not. The former tended to give detailed consideration, whereas the latter were concerned with 'generalized reputation' reasons; curricular reasons were only one-tenth of the reasons given. 'Of non-school reasons most concerned convenience', but 'there was a progression from rural to urban areas in which convenience became less significant and school-based reasons more so' (1986: 336). Among some of the factors cited were those that Edwards, Fitz and Whitty had called 'ethos'; namely, schools having 'traditional values' (such as a structured learning environment, good discipline, academic emphasis) (Macbeth, Strachan and Macaulay 1986: 336). Similarly, 'public examination results' influenced half of those families making secondary placing requests and one-third of the others. In sum, the Glasgow study chimed in very well with the Edinburgh one and the English studies referred to. Although the emphasis in the Glasgow study was on parental preferences, the authors did also acknowledge the constraints under which both parents and education authorities have to operate.

Public versus private choice of school

That parental choice is based on other than educational standards is also confirmed by the various studies conducted by the Inner London Education Authority's Research and Statistics branch and subsequently as the Centre for Educational Research at the London School of Economics. Indeed, some evidence has been collected of the detailed application of social factors. Hunter (1989, 1991) and West and Varlaam (1991) found in examining choice of secondary school that the parents of girls were more likely to choose single-sex schools than the parents of boys. Another study, carried out in an outer

London LEA, however, failed to find this difference (West, Varlaam and Scott 1991). Two studies (West et al. 1984; West et al. in preparation) have found that parents from Asian backgrounds are more likely to choose single-sex schools for both their girls and boys than families from other backgrounds; black African/Afro-Caribbean pupils are more likely than pupils from other ethnic groups to express a preference for a religious (Church of England or Roman Catholic) school. What is significant about these studies is the balance between parent and child reasons, which had not been fully addressed by the other studies reviewed so far.

Both Fox (1986) and Johnson (1987) looked only at parental choice of school; in the context, however, of *private* education. Fox's study was a relatively unique analysis of the reasons given by parents who sent their sons to elite public or independent schools. She interviewed 190 sets of parents and found to her surprise that they were not all of an elite social background. Indeed almost half of the schoolboys' fathers had been educated in the maintained grammar schools, and had created rather than acquired their wealth. So her sample turned out not to be socially homogeneous but instead rather mixed, with a minority having inherited social privileges. For the 10 per cent of her sample where private education was simply part of the general culture of the home, parents had given little thought to any alternative to the private system. And another 20 per cent had such a commitment to the private sector that she did not find further analysis possible.

Fox did find three clear overlapping reasons given by two-thirds of her sample: these were that pupils would 'get on better in life'; that schools would provide academic advantage and that schools would 'develop character and foster discipline'. As Walford, in discussing Fox's research, notes:

> ... the most frequently mentioned reasons were the ability to produce better academic results and to develop the character by instilling discipline. Both these aspects were also seen to be of major importance by the boys questioned in my own study of a major boarding school (Walford 1990: 43).

Johnson's study of 25 families, self-selected through a newspaper advertisement, did not yield quite such clear-cut reasons for moving from state to private education. Given her sample, the study is rather more problematic. As Walford mentions, 'Those with an axe to grind are bound to predominate' (1990: 43). Indeed, a large number of Johnson's families were teachers, or had been or were 'refugees' from the state system. The majority again saw academic reasons as important to their choices, while some had an unquestioned faith in the private sector. Johnson also identified what she called a 'domino effect': once parents had decided on private education for one child they would consider it for others. This was mainly in the context of comprehensive secondary school reorganisation and many did not like the abolition of 'grammar' schools in favour of comprehensives. Fox had also found this a factor with some of her sample, but not those choosing boarding education, who did so for other reasons.

Morgan et al. (1991) studied the roles of parents and teachers in integrated schools in Northern Ireland, as we saw in the previous chapter. As part of the analysis, they looked at why the parents had chosen these schools. In fact, they assumed that 'the distinctive feature was their cross-community dimension and parents would have chosen to send their children these because they were religiously mixed' (1991: 24). In fact, they found a much more complex set of reasons ranging-from the ideological, to the educational, to dissatisfaction with current schools, to convenience and mixed marriages. Moreover, given these diverse reasons, choice did not necessarily deal with all the issues raised.

Parental choice in the new ERA

All of the above studies were begun prior to the passing of the Education Reform Act (ERA) 1988. However, since its passage, there have been a number of different types of study, from general issues about parental choice to specific issues about schools. Coldron and Boulton (1991) followed on the tradition established by the NFER and the two Scottish studies, and looked into 'the criteria used by parents when selecting secondary schools'. What is most important about this albeit brief study is the emphasis they place on it being a process, rather than a snapshot:

> Regardless of the amount of time and thought given to the issue, parents' choice of secondary school is addressed over time until a deadline is reached, when a decision has to be taken. It involves a developing relationship between parents and their children and demands important judgements that will affect these people's lives and their future. (1991: 170)

Coldron and Boulton interviewed 16 families and analysed 222 questionnaires returned from parents. In response to an open question about their reasons for choosing a particular secondary school, they got 30 categories of stated reasons. So they had to find some way of summarising their data which would also do it justice. The majority of the parents wanted to use the nearest school if possible, a criterion they also called 'proximity'. However, they also felt that there was a range of factors, including happiness and discipline, which interacted to make a nexus. They characterise it:

> More than anything else, parents wish their child to be happy and secure at the new school.
> They want their child to want to go to the school that is chosen.
> They want this for the sake of their child and to avoid for both their sakes the difficulties of a confrontation caused by rejecting the wishes of their son or daughter.

Many children determine their preferences on the basis of where their friends will be going or where their sister or brother attends. This in turn is determined by a strong and understandable desire for some continuity to give a sense of security in the new school. (1991: 176)

They have tried to theorize a social process, but are also concerned to be of relevance in a policy debate, seeing parents' concerns with happiness and security as essentially short-term. But parents, from their analysis, are *not* preoccupied with academic standards. So they conclude that schools and LEAs should, in their marketing and concepts of school image, not pay this too much attention.

Another study in Exeter, as we briefly noted in the previous chapter (Hughes, Wikeley and Nash 1990) has looked at parental choice of *primary* school in the context of the implementation of the ERA and specifically the national curriculum. This is probably the only study of 'choice' which focused directly on primary rather than secondary schooling. In their interim report, the authors drew attention to a range of factors; but most specifically, almost 80 per cent cited *locality* and two-thirds *reputation*. Within these two reasons, however, there is some diversity and, given the area of the sample, some constraints on choice. Those who did not choose a local school tended to favour one with a good reputation, chosen, significantly, from the mothers' friendship networks (1990: 9). As Ribbens (1990) has carefully pointed out, few studies pay any attention to these more 'social' questions and/or the differential role of mothers and fathers in the various processes of decision-making. However, given these two major factors, Hughes et al. concluded that 'the majority of parents are not exercising a wide range of choice' (1990: 11). In any event, at least at primary-school level, parents tended to choose the local neighbourhood school, unless they had definite reasons for rejecting it. But three-quarters of the parents (over 100) felt satisfied with the choice. The majority, in any event, did not see themselves as 'consumers' in the classic economic sense. However, given the lack of substantial choice, this probably would be difficult.

Westoby, in a rather more speculative analysis of the choice components of ERA, considers this issue of consumerism. He writes:

Many of my observations so far can be drawn together in the simple prediction that, if ERA's strategy for improving schools that parents are dissatisfied with is to work, it is not the actions of the parents who opt away from them that will produce changes (except very indirectly) but rather the behaviour of those – parents and others – who remain to get involved in them. And whether the second 'prong' of the ERA's strategy for parental power will be effective turns on how far parents prove able to wield sustained and constructive influence in school decision-making and micro-politics. (1990: 76)

This question of parental power, through the exercise of a parental voice, is not the subject of concern here, given that we have already discussed it in chapter 6.

There have been two studies of particular forms of parental choice as understood through the ERA as 'opting out': one is the creation of city technology colleges and the other the development of grant-maintained schools. Walford and Miller (1991) have studied the setting up of the first college in the context of the development of the policy, changing from entirely industrial sponsorship to that of part public funding. But the chief criterion of the CTC was not parental choice *per se* but a type of academic selectivity. The Principal and staff would be free to choose from among the applicants for places. The authors (1991: 112) presumed, as had others, that the majority of parents would be middle class. In fact they did not find this to be the case at Kingshurst: they noted in fact the low percentage of parents in professional or similar occupations. They stated that the vast majority seemed to have skilled manual or non-manual occupations, although they were not able to be sure since their information was based upon pupil reporting of parents' occupational backgrounds. However, the researchers also considered whether the parents were exercising choice in the sense that they would not automatically have accepted an LEA allocation. They found that these was 'a fairly high level of choice being exercised' (p. 118) but that it was in the specific context of the creation of a CTC. In the absence of that school, similar results might not have occurred. In other words, given that a new school had been created in the area, with better funds than state schools, both parents and children wanted to choose it.

In the same respect, Fitz and Halpin's work is about the ways in which the processes of creating new grant-maintained schools occurred (1990, 1991). In the first instance, they have looked at the development and implementation of the policy. A second stage of the research (in process) is the detailed investigation of how parents have voted in the parental ballots organised by school governing bodies to create such schools. This is part of a new process of rather more collective parental choice of school. A majority of parents have to vote for the school to 'opt out' of the LEA system of control. Even then, once the choice is made, the school has to be approved by the Secretary of State for Education. However, as Fitz (personal communication, March 1991) pointed out, 212 schools had considered the matter in the two and a half years since the legislation: of these 63 had been approved and 50 were operating. The assumption of the government had been that Conservative-dominated schools would choose to 'opt out' of Labour-held LEAs. Interestingly they were not all in Labour-controlled LEAs and indeed some of the schools were themselves Labour-controlled rather than Conservative. However, this evidence needs to the fleshed out by a more detailed study of the parents in a selection of the schools which Fitz and Halpin have embarked upon.

It is, however, clear that ERA 1988 has spawned a diversity of approaches to parental choice which are less constrained by bureaucratic factors than hitherto. It is not yet clear what the implications of this are for the exercise of parental choice. What is obvious is that the choices parents have made hitherto have not been dominated by consideration of academic or educational standards as the policy-makers presumed they would be. Rather, consideration has been given to a variety of issues, including social factors. In any event, it may be that the factors across the range are not as distinct as policy-makers would have us believe. Certainly the policy of examination league-tables would seem to suggest that parents, choosing within the state or private systems, would opt for those schools with the 'best' results. However, their choices would necessarily be constrained not only by 'proximity' but probably also by 'process' as well as 'product'.

Patterns of parental choice abroad

The ways in which parents choose has also been the subject of research in other countries as well as Britain (Westoby 1990). The issues of choice affect what kinds of parents or families choose and what kinds of choices they make. Raywid (1985) has reviewed the American literature over family choice, focusing not only on choice of school but also options and curricula, etc., within schools. Given the proliferation of such schemes in the US and the array of diverse options, it is difficult to be precise about how parents choose and what they choose. She covers the development of the notion from the education voucher schemes of the late 1960s through to alternative schools, magnet schools, etc., and discusses the advantages and disadvantages of each type of scheme. She draws some important conclusions:

> Although the evidence is mixed, there has been concern that alternatives might increase racial isolation; and family choice patterns clearly can increase socio-economic segregation in schools of choice. Accordingly, there is concern that individual alternatives may become programs for minorities and the poor, on the one hand and programs for the elite on the other. (1985: 461)

This effect may in fact be an *aim* for some policy-makers and may be based upon evidence about how schools in fact can and should operate. For example, Chubb and Moe (1990), as we saw in the previous chapter, argue that choice has not gone far enough in ensuring effective student achievement. They are perhaps the clearest exponents of the view that individual family choice rather than bureaucratic or collective decision-making should be paramount. They are less concerned with equity, more with individual freedom. They argue that school choice should be implemented without 'grab bag' reforms of a democratic or political form:

> If choice is to work to greatest advantage, it must be adopted without these other reforms, since the latter are predicated on democratic control and are implemented by bureaucratic means. The whole point of a thoroughgoing system of choice is

to free the school from these disabling constraints by sweeping away the old institutions and replacing them with new ones. (1990: 217)

Raywid is not of the same political persuasion as Chubb and Moe. She went on:

> Without doubt, parents of all socio-economic levels and of children of all ability levels can be encouraged to exercise their options. But if the system is to be equitable in this regard, careful plans and extensive efforts are necessary. . . . (1985: 462)

She does consider the debate about diversified public schools for family choice and sees it as unresolved, but recognises it as a trend under right-wing administrations that is likely to continue. Indeed, Chubb and Moe, writing five years later, confirm the fact that it has become a dominant theme in American educational research as well as policy. They provide substantial evidence from a reanalysis of high-school data covering 1,015 high schools and nearly 60,000 students (1990: 260) as well as a parent survey. They try to demonstrate what effective schools are and how they influence student performance and achievement. Their argument is rather traditional: that the main 'causes' of student achievement are family background, together with ability and school organisation. Hence their plea for radical reform to provide unconstrained schools, which can supply what particular parents choose on the basis of their children's abilities. Similar arguments have been deployed at a more local level in the US. For example, Domanico and Genn from the Manhattan Institute of New York (1992) have argued about using choice to improve New York's public schools. They have shown concern about the stifling yoke of a massive public bureaucracy in New York. They, too, have looked at choice for teacher empowerment as well as consumer use.

This 'radical' argument is, however, not taken up by Glenn (1989) in his survey of six other nations for the US government. Glenn covers the political debates and associated evidence in each of the six countries surveyed. He also concentrates on some aspects of certain countries, Belgian Flanders and Northern Ireland, as well as giving a detailed review of the Scottish studies I have discussed. The reason for looking at Flanders and Ireland is to consider issues of religion in relation to family choice. The motivation for the study is perhaps best expressed by the US Secretary of Education: 'The growing demand for parental choice in the United States derives not simply from a desire for improved test scores but changing perspectives on liberty and equity' (Glenn 1990: iii). These seem more balanced than the view presented by Chubb and Moe or Domanico and Genn (1992). Glenn (1989: 5) expands these objectives to consider, first, choice based upon a desire for education informed by a particular religious or 'world view' perspective, second, choice based upon vocational goals in the broadest sense, often including some measure of social class maintenance or aspiration, third, choice based upon a desire for a particular type of teaching, fourth, choice based upon a desire to maintain a particular minority language or culture.

Against this backdrop, Glenn draws some of the following conclusions:

> If choice based upon denominational loyalty is a somewhat diminished phenom-enon (though asserted with renewed vigour by religious minorities in recent years) the same may be said of opposition to confessional schooling based upon a militant secularism, a foi laique. Apart from the United States there seems not to be among national elites the horror towards religious 'indoctrination' in school that so embittered debates during the century and a half before World War I. (1989: 208)

He then looks at other factors that have dominated choice debates about religion and draws the conclusion that 'public funding of non-governmental schooling is neither destructive of national loyalties nor a guarantee of religious loyalties' (p. 210). A more disheartening conclusion is over social factors associated with the choice debates and evidence. In drawing the conclusion, however, Glenn dissociates himself from the kinds of arguments put by Chubb and Moe, and sees the US as still more concerned with equity and integration than the six other nations. He argues:

> For those who fear that public support for parent choice will result in race and class segregation and unequal opportunities, the survey provides confirming evidence. Whether it be non-Catholic German parents using Catholic schools in the Ruhr to avoid Turkish children, or English parents demanding one Church of England school rather than another to avoid Asian children, individual parent choices clearly can result in injustices for the children of other parents. (1989: 211)

He then presents his personal reflections, in which he is more sanguine, ending on this note:

> The experience of other nations yields no conclusive evidence that parent choice has a decisive effect, either positive or negative, on the quality of schooling. Evidence is extensive that choice may have an . . . effect upon equity.
>
> What parent choice of schools *does* affect powerfully, is the satisfaction of parents, their sense of being empowered to make decisions about their own chil-dren, the accommodation of their deeply held convictions about education. (1989: 220)

Conclusions

Glenn's conclusion from his qualitative survey located the evidence about parental choice in a wider context, looking at philosophical issues of equity versus debates about types of parental participation or involvement in children's education. As Macbeth et al. (1986) note, in discussing the complexity of the notion of choice, it can be part of the wider strategy of home–school partnerships so that it may contribute to school effectiveness.

Most of the research that has been conducted on family or parental choice, however, as we have seen, has not had such a broad canvass. Most of it has been particularistic, concerned with the detailed evaluation of legislation's effects and administrative or bureaucratic implementation. Indeed, the political concern with 'choice' as one aspect of developing new administrative systems of education is of relatively recent origin. Given different political systems it is hard to compare particular effects. Glenn's assessment is that although 'choice' may not affect quality of schooling, it probably does affect parental attitudes of satisfaction, since it makes parents feel empowered to control their children's education.

However, this assessment, as we have shown, has not been and probably could not be satisfactorily tested. As Midwinter (1980) commented in a remark to which we referred at the beginning of this chapter, it is impossible for parents – or educationalists or researchers, for that matter – to be able to predict social relationships and educational achievement, especially not on the basis of past aggregate factors. In any event, some of the crucial evidence for some groups or categories of parents is and has been lacking. Although there is some research on religious or denominational schools, and on social class factors, such as forms of private schooling, there is no evidence for minority ethnic group parents. Moreover, no consideration has been given to whether or not 'choices' vary depending on the gender and/or family status of the parents. There is also no evidence about the processes and effects on boys versus girls.

Nevertheless, key political changes have been mooted on the basis of negative factors related to race. For example, a group of white working-class parents in Kirklees in Yorkshire refused to allow their children to attend a middle school whose composition was predominantly Asian. Instead, they chose to have their children taught by a retired headmaster in a 'pub' for almost a year (Naylor 1989). Similarly a mother of a mixed-race child in Cleveland, N. Yorkshire sought to remove her child from a predominantly Asian primary school to a school in a more predominantly 'white' neighbourhood, fearing the ill-effects of such inter-racial mixing. Both sets of parents were eventually 'allowed' their choices of schools, despite the lack of evidence of ill-effects and the considerable evidence of inequitable distribution of resources. Decisions about 'choice' here were made on 'moral' rather than 'social' grounds, in terms of particularistic rights rather than community developments. In other words, parental choice of education in Britain, in the late 1980s and early 1990s, was seen to take precedence over promoting racial or religious harmony and preventing racial discrimination.

Part of the reason for this kind of legal decision has been the shifting political balance in family–school relations from issues of equity and community participation to notions of consumerism in education, as Woods has clearly pointed out. Yet the research evidence for these shifts has not kept pace with the changes themselves. What the evidence has demonstrated is the effects of particular pieces of legislation or policy. It has also shown that parental or family choice has operated within narrow parameters and contexts. Concern about choice, especially for academic attainment, may be more appropriate for those parents who can properly exercise a choice than for those living in constrained circumstances. Yet the policies on choice have tended to assume that all parents can exercise their choices equally. It has also shown that choice for one type of parent may have deleterious consequences for other families. Given the previous social research, referred to in chapter 5, families clearly do not start on an equal footing. Indeed, the evidence about family–school relations remains far more complex than that about 'choice' alone, despite the fact that here, too, race and gender perspectives remain curiously absent. It is to this kind of research that we now return.

8

Parental Involvement for School Effectiveness or Home Improvement?

Introduction

In previous chapters we have looked at how the researcher and reformer part-nership about the relation of parents to education gradually became more complex. As we noted, the origins of the post-war 'liberal' policy reforms and allied social research centred on the goal and implementation of equality of educational opportunity. Eventually, in the late 1950s and early 1960s, social researchers changed their approach from policy evaluation to ways of influencing strategies. This entailed a role for parents in order to iron out differences between families on the basis of their socio-economic circumstances of either privilege or poverty. We have reviewed these reformer–researcher developments around parental participation in chapter 5. In particular, the idea of individual parental involvement was developed gradually, first from American social scientific evidence, particularly for pre-school and early child-hood education, and secondly from work in Britain on primary schools, as well as pre-school provision. In the 1970s, as we have seen in chapter 6, the notion of parental involvement was extended to the wider idea of citizen or community participation as a political process, especially in educational decision-making processes; sometimes referred to as the idea of a parental voice. This again drew on American experience and debates as well as those of Europe (Beattie 1985). At the same time, ideas about parents as consumers were beginning to be devel-oped, as we have seen in chapter 7.

Woods (1988: 325) has shown how, in the 1980s in Britain, the notion of parental participation was used to justify three different approaches. As we noted in chapters 6 and 7, he has argued that there was a shift from professional and/or political control of educational processes to the idea of 'consumer' or parental control under the Conservative government in the 1980s. However, he has tried to show that there were three rationales for these kinds of individual parental participation in education, viz (1) market-orientated, (2) partnership and (3) instrumental. The first was to try to establish a free, private market in which schools which were unpopular in market terms would close; the second was to develop a sense of shared family–school responsibilities; and the third was to use new systems to achieve the goals of better educational standards. But in the process Woods remarked that parental roles became more complex. He has commented:

> Parents, because of their social and legal responsibilities, can be seen as consumers by proxy, acting on behalf of their children. Their position, however, is not a simple one. Parents have a complex mix of roles in relation to schooling: for example, they can make consumer choices . . . though these, like all consumer decisions, will be constrained by resources and circumstances; they can act 'politically' within the school as an integral part of school government; they can take part in the larger political process at local and national level concerning education matters. This complex of roles is a creature of the state's involvement in education . . . (1988: 323)

In the 1980s, this complex of roles which developed through the reformer–researcher partnership became more difficult to disentangle. However we have already reviewed the research evidence and strategic developments concerning both 'consumer choice' and a 'political voice'. What remains to be considered is how notions about parental involvement continued to be applied and developed strategically, by social researchers.

It should be noted, however, that despite the complexity neither gender nor race perspectives have predominated in the strategic developments; nor has family change been the subject of detailed consideration. Most of the research evidence has, in fact, been oriented to trying to improve 'home–school relations' to achieve educational effectiveness. This has taken a variety of forms of parental involvement in schooling. Little, however, has been written about the indirect or reverse effects of such developments in schooling on family life. Ulich (1989) is rare in attempting to assess the effects of such strategic developments on family life. We shall have occasion to refer to such effects in this chapter and in the next, where we will consider in more depth the implications of new strategies for parental participation for mothers' involvements in education.

In this chapter, I will look at the range of research that was developed in this country and in Australia, the US and Europe, to make notions of parental involvement both more sophisticated and applicable to strategic developments. Indeed, it would be fair to say that the objectives of the researchers and reformers underwent major changes during this period. There was a shift from attempts to ensure children's educational achievements to ideas about school effectiveness and to more legalistic notions of parental partnerships with schools, through ideas about home–school contracts, or compacts.

Reviewing and summarising the research on 'home influence on education' for the Commission of European Communities in the early 1980s, Macbeth was led to conclude:

> What we *can* say is that a very large number of studies in different cultures has indicated that parental attitudes have an influence on children's attainment, even if we cannot put an exact value to that influence: there is relative dearth of contrary evidence, in-school factors seem to be related to these home factors. At the very least, home seems to influence school performance and it would appear that a strengthening of partnership between home and school could improve the quality of children's learning. (1984: 185)

Indeed, it was around the idea of improving 'the quality of children's learning', rather than attempting to reduce socio-economic disparities or to provide equal opportunities on the basis of academic ability and educational achievement, that the research was developed, spurred by the changing policy context, both nationally and internationally.

Typologies of parental involvement revisited

In chapter 6, we reviewed the development of a variety of different typologies of parental involvement or participation in education. Essentially it is possible to group these into two kinds: those which attempt to show the underlying historical and political processes in the creation of forms of parental involvement and those which classify and categorise different schemes of home–school relations. In chapter 6 we were more concerned to look at the former: the ways in which forms of 'political' or citizen participation had developed out of 'liberal' strategies around a parental role. Beattie (1985) reviewed the specific political developments by comparing and contrasting two different theories, both in the 'liberal' tradition. Macbeth (1989) and Bastiani (1987) have also viewed developments in parental participation as part of an historical political process, within a liberal democratic tradition. Woods (1988) has looked at the underlying philosophical or theoretical arguments within changing and competing political ideologies, as we have just seen. Glenn's review of parental choice in seven different nations including the US also attempted to classify the notions in terms of underlying political or philosophical arguments. His conclusion that 'choice' may not have special substantive effects but rather affects parental attitudes or feelings of satisfaction is important.

Here we want to look in greater depth not only at the other typologies as classifications in themselves but at the evidence that has been collected which fleshes out the complexities in the ideas of parental involvement. We will therefore consider both Tomlinson's (1991) and Epstein's (1990) typologies again and review the evidence that has been collected under each category. However, since we have given detailed consideration to the notion of parental involvement as political in chapter 6, we will only briefly refer to this. Interestingly, neither typology gives consideration to the notion of parental choice in this context, despite Woods' justification of it as part of the process of 'consumer' or 'parental' control in education. Rather they are more concerned with specifying different types of ongoing parental activities in education. As mentioned in the previous chapter, parental choice is not generally viewed as a process, although it may be, but as more of an one-off event.

Tomlinson has noted for Britain that by the 1980s,

> the extent of home–school contacts could perhaps be summarised as follows:
> - Contact via shared communication: visits (parents to schools, teachers to homes), letters, circulars, pupil reports, pupil records of achievement and compacts, Government reports, schools prospectuses.
> - *Parental involvement*: (a) in learning, via home-school reading and maths schemes, homework agreements, etc. (b) in day-to-day activities as classroom helpers, technicians, translators, materials-makers, assistants on outings, etc.
> - *Parental informal involvement* in school matters via Parent Teachers Associations and other parent organisations. Parental fund-raising.
> - *Parental formal (and legal) involvement* in school decision-making as parent-governors, and the annual parents' meeting. (1991: 5)

An official British survey conducted in 1990 by Her Majesty's Inspectorate, entitled *Parents and Schools: Aspects of Parental Involvement in Primary and Secondary Schools*, also develops a typology of four types of home–school contact. They group their evidence, drawn from '32 primary and 38 secondary schools during the academic years 1989–90', and visited in the course of their work, in a similar way to Tomlinson, while using rather different terminology. They categorize the first type as 'what the schools do for parents'; the second and third as all aspects of 'what parents do for schools'; finally they cover 'parents as governors', Tomlinson's fourth type, as a separate issue. We have already referred to this latter in chapter 6.

Bastiani (1987), in a thought-provoking discussion of changing attitudes in the study of 'home–school' relations, points to the difficulties of interpretation, based on a typology of changes, from studies of compensation to participation. His typology of home and school ideologies ranges from compensation, to communication, to accountability and finally to participation, and locates the characteristic methods and forms of research within each. He draws the conclusion that:

> Nevertheless there has been what amounts to a steady shift in attitudes in the home–school field which is also reflected in the area of application of findings, in policy-making and in practice . . . Above all, however, a contemporary perspective

on home–school relations is obliged to recognize its paradoxical nature. On the one hand there is some evidence of more constructive communication taking place between families and schools, involving parents and teachers . . .

Set against this argument . . . is a growing recognition that families and schools are very different kinds of institutions between which tensions are inevitable. (1987: 104)

This may, however, merely mean that developing a typology of types of parental involvement either over time, as he had done, or in terms of Tomlinson's and the HMI types, in the contemporary context, is rather more complex than anticipated and needs to take account of competing ideologies.

Curiously neither Tomlinson's typology nor HMI's differ significantly from that developed by Epstein (1990) based upon her own American research studies and those of others in the US, as we noted in chapter 6. Epstein does not refer to any British studies and yet the types of perspectives on parental involvement on home–school relations are remarkably similar. At a more theoretical level, rather than one grounded in educational experiences, the typology could be fitted into Bastiani's developmental process, especially covering communication and accountability as well as the complex notion known as participation. Epstein's notions are, like those of Tomlinson, HMI and others, somewhat prescriptive. She sees them as a necessary part of a 'comprehensive program for family and school connections, in every school' (1990: 133). She looks at each type basically from the point of view of the school and classifies them:

Type 1 *The basic obligations of parents* refers to responsibilities of families for children's health and safety; parenting and childrearing skills to prepare children for school . . . and *positive home conditions* that support school learning . . .

Type 2 *The basic obligations of schools* refers to the *communication from school-to-home* about school programs and children's progress, including . . . communications . . . and conferences to inform all parents . . .

Type 3 *Parent involvement at school* refers to parent volunteers who assist teachers, administrators and children in classrooms . . . and parents who come to school to support and watch events . . .

Type 4 *Parent involvement in learning activities* at home refers to parent-initiated, child-initiated requests for help and . . . ideas from teachers for parents to *monitor and assist their own children* at home on learning activities that are coordinated with the children's classwork.

Type 5 *Parent involvement in governance and advocacy* refers to parents in *decision-making* roles in . . . PTA/PTO, Advisory Councils . . . at school, district, or state levels. . . . (1990: 113)

These five clearly cross-cut with Tomlinson's and therefore could be regrouped. Both type 5 and Tomlinson's third and fourth types are obviously very similar, in language about decision-making which is most appropriate for a national context. We have already dealt with these in some depth in chapter 6. Epstein's types 3 and 4 are quite similar to Tomlinson's types 2 (a) and (b), although some of Epstein's type 3 might be covered in Tomlinson's type 3, namely parental support of school, which could cover fund-raising. Finally Epstein's type 2 clearly fits in part Tomlinson's type 1, whereas Epstein's type 1 goes beyond issues of parental communication with schools. It deals more with the issues that Bastiani was attempting to address and ones that Tomlinson later addresses in her report: about developing more justicial forms of contact between home and school, essentially legal contracts. This is also what HMI referred to as the school's statutory obligations.

In looking at the research evidence around different types of parental involvement, across the nations as well as across the country, I shall rely on Epstein's typology but discuss it in inverse order, ending with a review of the new developments around parent–school partnerships and contracts, which are implied in Epstein's first two types. I shall only briefly refer to Epstein's type 5 since this has been covered in chapter 6.

Parental involvement in decision-making

As regards the schools' work for parents, HMI were chiefly concerned, albeit from a brief one-day 'bird's eye view', to see whether schools were in accordance with their statutory obligations. They found that, for the most part, the ways in which schools informed and contacted parents was 'satisfactory'. They provided nice anecdotes and descriptions of the particular practices of certain schools, especially over the style of their documentation.

On the more formal aspects of parental involvement in decision-making, HMI's rather fair picture becomes more bleak. The main finding was:

> As is the case nationally, the schools succeeded in attracting parents in greater numbers to parent evenings and meetings to discuss children's progress than to the Annual Governors' Meetings for parents. The latter were invariably poorly attended; no secondary schools and only three primary schools achieved a quorum. (HMI 1991: 1)

Changes in home–school relations may have been developed in the 1980s, but at least from this slender official report do not seem to have achieved anything beyond parents' consideration that schools are doing 'a reasonably good job' (HMI 1991: 1). But this report does not delve very deeply into the aspects of parental involvement, merely classifying a range of responses on a one-day visit. Nevertheless this report, being official, may have a more significant impact on policy changes than any independent research report.

We have already noted, through this discussion of the HMI report, some aspects of parental involvement in decision-making in England and Wales. Clearly, this is not seen as a major issue at the level of general meetings.

However, there is considerably more evidence about the roles of parent governors that has already been presented in chapter 6. In addition, however, parents are involved in other kinds of decision-making activities, such as through parent associations or parent–teacher committees, that build up towards what Mortimore et al. (1988), Bastiani (1989) and Macbeth (1989) consider to be 'effective schooling'. Such schooling develops what Bastiani calls a 'whole school approach', incorporating different kinds of home–school liaison, not only around parents' individual relationships with the school, concerning their own children, but also focused on wider processes, and possibly issues related to the community. Macbeth's stages of development in home–school relations saw this kind of involvement as perhaps most crucial (1989); indeed, the prescriptive subtitle of Macbeth's book is *Effective Parent–Teacher Relations*. I shall have occasion to return to this when discussing the question of partnership contracts, notions which have been developed recently in this country and others of the European community.

Parental involvement in education: at home or at school

There is perhaps most evidence collected around the twin questions of parental involvement in learning activities at home and at school, here looking at parental involvement much more in relation to individual children, most usually the parent's own. However, some aspects of parental involvement at school, while based upon the notion of developing the quality of children's learning and educational progress, may do so in an indirect way rather than focusing only on their own child. Moreover, aspects of Epstein's type 1 – *positive home conditions*, as a prelude to or supplement to school's work – may need to be discussed in the review of research about supporting children's learning at home. Inevitably, as Bastiani (1987) was suggesting, most social research is complex and it can be difficult to disentangle contradictory notions and ideas.

The notion of parental involvement in learning at home is of relatively recent pedigree, both in Britain and other European countries. Although the idea of 'homework' has a very long pedigree in relation to schools in Britain, as elsewhere, this has not necessarily meant to include parental involvement on a systematic basis. In Britain, at least, the notion of homework was reserved for secondary-school children until the last decade or so. It is only with developments in the idea of closer family–school connections, making families deliberately part of the educational process as educators, that the idea of 'homework' and parental involvement in learning at home has grown. In its early origins schooling was seen as an entirely 'professional' process and the preserve of professional educators rather than the amateur parent, as we have noted in chapter 6.

There is more research on the complex relations between home and school from Germany (Enders-Dragasser 1982; Ulich 1989) and from Smith in Canada.

We have referred to some of this latter in chapters 2 and 5 in discussing the development of a feminist perspective. Most of Smith's work is a critique of previous non-feminist work, pointing up its lacunae. But she has also pinpointed the preconditions for successful schooling through the work in the family for pre-school children. We shall return to the detail of this in the next chapter on mothers' involvement in education. The research in Germany has also pinpointed the impact of the school and school processes on the family, and especially the kinds of conflicts evoked (Ulich 1989).

The changed picture has largely developed as a result of relatively sophisticated research which has attempted to show that families and schools are not separate institutions with no reciprocal influence on each other. One of the most complex and intricate pieces of social analysis in this respect was a study by Connell and colleagues, published initially in Australia and reliant on Australian evidence (1982). It was a complex analysis of the interactions between families and schools and how social divisions were sustained and reproduced. One of the more important findings that concerns us here, however, was that

> ... family and school are [not] separate spheres containing separate processes. 'The family' does not form a child's character and then deliver it ready-packaged to the doorstep of 'the school.' The family is what its members do, a constantly continuing and changing practice, and, as children go to and through school, that practice is reorganised around their schooling. . . . (1982: 78)

Connell et al.'s research, however, could only be conducted in a social climate that was conducive to this kind of sophisticated and systematic analysis of data. Connell's study drew on previous kinds of research, albeit much less intricately woven, about family–school interactions, developed in Britain and the US.

Another strand of influence on this developing research agenda was work on early childhood education and how best to prepare families to prepare their children for formal education or schooling. Much of this work was influenced more by developmental and social psychologist than sociologists. In England, for example, a particularly critical study was that conducted by Tizard and Hughes at the Thomas Coram Research Unit in the early 1980s. It was eventually published, to enormous media acclaim, in 1984, entitled *Young Children Learning*. This study compared and contrasted children's early language development at home and in a pre-school nursery setting. Interestingly, the sample consisted entirely of daughters and, when at home, their mothers. The key feature of the research findings was the idea that girls' language development was much more rapid and effective at home in one-to-one settings with their mothers than in nursery-school environments. This argument was on occasion twisted to imply that nursery education was therefore unnecessary: that children's educational development prior to schooling was most effectively conducted at home. However, little extensive comparison was conducted of the two

settings and the various kinds of development that make up educational progress. Tizard and Hughes' study certainly gave credence to the importance of
home as a learning environment for young children, even emphasising the
particular pedagogical role of mothers. It built upon studies largely conducted
in the US, especially the work of William Labov, the socio-linguist.

Subsequently Walkerdine and Lucey (1989) have reanalysed and recon-
textualised this study, from a feminist and 'working-class' set of perspectives,
considering the range of factors that contribute to children's development,
especially that of girls. In particular, they are concerned to pinpoint the ways in
which class intervenes and revises the forms of educational development among
children learning at home with their mothers. They entitled their study most
evocatively *Democracy in the Kitchen: Regulating Mothers and Socializing Daughters*
and illustrate the complexity of home-based learning from a variety of social
and economic, familial settings:

> The whole discourse of parental involvement assumes that teachers must teach
> parents (almost always mothers) how to prepare and help their children in the
> right ways. The target is, almost always, black and white working class parents.
> There is no sense of listening to and learning from the parents – for they are
> already defined as wrong and reactionary. But the working-class mother who
> 'lacks' also knows a lot ... She ... implies that the world is frightening ... She
> prepares her for the world as she sees it, but this is a frightening lesson and not a
> cosy reassurance. Often, then, the working-class girls acquire at school knowledge
> which their mothers do not have ... The middle-class mothers 'know' ... [But]
> our evidence suggests that the transition for middle class girls may be only partly
> bridged by the mothers' knowledge of the school pedagogy as well as (not
> unproblematically) her own experience of education. Often, in stark contrast to an
> easy familiarity with educational discourse, we witness working class parents' fear
> of school ... Going to school then is not simply a place where autonomous girls
> can skip happily towards independent and fully fledged entry into social democ-
> racy. (1989: 181–8)

There have been few other studies in Britain, at least, that take as their focus
learning at home, and highlight the issues from a feminist perspective. We shall
return to this in the next chapter.

Most of the work on this is a by-product of work on either parental socio-
economic backgrounds or parental participation in school. Toomey (1989) notes
that

> ... there is a large body of evidence, produced mostly by psychologists and
> educationalists, that the home exerts a substantial influence on children's know-
> ledge and skills 'independently' of socio-economic factors; this evidence refers to
> the pre-school, primary and early secondary levels of schooling ... The body
> of US evidence is considerably larger than the British ... [and confirms] the
> substantially greater predictiveness of family environment than socio-economic
> variables. The rate of natural-setting experiments leading to a similar overall
> conclusion is considerable, from long-term evaluations of Headstart and the

Parent Education Follow-Through Program, to a variety of intervention studies using parents as teachers of school knowledge to their own children in disadvantaged and non-disadvantaged localities. . . . There is a substantial body of case studies depicting the influence of the family environment on children who learn to read without formal instruction . . . The success of programmes involving 'disadvantaged' parents as teachers of their own children is particularly telling evidence of the independent influence of the family environment . . . (1989: 394–5)

Many studies in Britain of parental participation also pinpoint the critical influence of family or parent rather than social class on children's learning.

In particular, the work of Wolfendale on parental participation, first in children's early childhood development and education (1983); later with Topping (1985) investigating the specific issue of reading, has shown the crucial importance of family to child development. Wolfendale's work concentrates on early childhood and primary education, with a particular emphasis on reading as a form of educational development. Apart from language development, through an analysis of children learning to talk, psychologists have tended to focus on children's educational development through reading, comparing and contrasting the effects of parents and school. Wolfendale's work in particular pinpoints the part played by parents in improving early reading performance. She looks at both the contribution of parents at home and at school, reaching the conclusion of the importance of the family. She does not, however, consider the differential effects of the gender of the parent, although this may be inferred. Bloom (1987) also focuses attention on the contribution that parents can make to children's reading development, showing that they have relatively more influence than the school itself. Again, no consideration is given to the differential effects of the gender of the parents; nor is the issue of race of parents made problematic.

An early study by Cyster et al. (1979) began to set an agenda for parental involvement in early childhood or primary education. They did not pursue the question of family influence at or from home but focused entirely on issues to do with school. They were more interested in general types of 'volunteer involvement' through a national survey. At the early stage they were unsure of the extent of potential benefit of amateurs instead of professional educators. They concluded that

The 'syllogism of parental participation' proposed by Young and McGeeney (1968):

A rise the level of parental encouragement augments their children's performance at school.
Teachers, by involving parents in the school bring about a rise in the level of parental encouragement.
Teachers, by involving parents in the school augment the children's performance.

remains largely unproven. (1979: 150)

In other words, Cyster and his co-authors were unable to demonstrate that parental participation in the actual educational process at home or at school had decisive effects on children's educational performance.

However, this has been followed up in Britain by a range of studies, from pre-school parental involvement at home or in nursery schools to more detailed case studies of particular forms of involvement or participation in primary schools. For example, a series of studies published under the auspices of the Oxford Pre-School Project, edited by Bruner (1980), considered a range of issues about parental involvement. Smith looked at parents' roles in pre-schools (1980), while Tizard, Mortimore and Burchell (1981) considered the question of involving parents in nursery and infant schools. All these studies pointed out the greater efficacy of education for young children with the help of parents whether in classroom or play activities, or generally in support activities during the school-day, or in preparation for school. But these studies did not demonstrate the differential effects of particular kinds of parenting on child development and educational success. No consideration was given to the gender or race of parents. Yet we have seen the significance of this from subsequent studies especially of parent governors, etc.

These early studies of pre-school and school involvement of parents led to more detailed case studies of particular aspects of the curriculum. Nevertheless, although the concern was with the effects of different types of parental involvement, there tended to be a clear dichotomy between work on pre-school or early childhood education and that on junior schools, at least for Britain. Indeed, perhaps this separation draws on the different social scientific approaches, in that early childhood education and pre-school provision tend to be dominated by social psychologists, while studies of home–school relations in primary education tend to be influenced most by the work of educationalists and, to some extent, sociologists. However, by the end of the 1980s there had been a series of summaries of the state of the art in parental involvement covering both pre-school and school-based relationships.

The HMI report (1991) referred to earlier in this chapter briefly reviews a range of formal and informal aspects of parental involvement, from the perspective of 'what parents do for schools': 'In all but two primary schools some parents helped regularly with some aspects of the work either in classrooms or elsewhere in the school. By contrast, only four [out of 38] of the secondary schools made use of parent help in such ways' (p. 7). Moreover, HMI cite interesting examples of parental help, which include mainly maternal involvement, but with some particular instances of a 'multilingual parent' and the example of 'a father helping four girls to make a wooden boat' (1991: 8–9).

Second, there has been a series of case studies of aspects of parental involvement, especially in primary education, in the 1980s. These studies have a more contemporary perspective and at least consider issues of both race and gender although they do not make them central. What is most significant is the fact that parental involvement in school or in education is taken as a given. For example, Edwards and Redfern (1988), in a case study of one multi-racial primary school in Reading, argue that the official policy of the school is to involve *all* parents in the activities. Their study, *At Home in School*, considers a range of issues, but largely with the focus on parents *in* school, rather than at home. At the beginning of the book, in an authors' note, they state:

> We would like to make it clear that our understanding of 'parents' is much broader than the traditional concept of the two-parent nuclear family: we use the term as a convenient short-hand for the very wide range of family patterns which make up any school community. (1988: 1)

Indeed, they point out that the school they studied might be considered very unusual by some, and was indeed dismissed by the headmaster of another school, 'because Redlands is an inner city school with a high proportion of ethnic minority children' (1988: 2). Edwards and Redfern are concerned to demonstrate the current complex ways in which teachers and parents relate to each other and their relevance for children's educational development. They consider in detail parental involvement in classroom activities and point out that nearly all the children talked of how such involvements improved their relationships with their *mothers*. However, this was not a crucial issue for the authors. We shall return to this issue of mothers, rather than parents per se, in the next chapter.

Tizard et al. (1988) have looked at issues to do with young children's schooling and development in the inner city, and considered again the role of parents. They, too, concentrated on schools with large proportions of ethnic minority children. While Edwards and Redfern looked at junior schools, Tizard et al. focused on infant schools. Tizard et al. also spent a lot of time considering the role of parents in terms of their effectiveness in aiding children's learning, on the assumption of its validity. Both these studies concentrate on issues to do with multi-racial schools, and see as crucial the question of how to elicit effective parental involvement to improve the quality of children's learning. But neither study raises the issue of the gender of parents as being of much significance.

A major study of junior schools in the Inner London Education Authority by Mortimore et al. (1988) also raises the question of the complexity of parental involvement in the context of a multi-racial society. It is concerned to build upon the new tradition of how to make schools more effective in the contest of changing social and familial trends. It draws upon a tradition developed in this country by Rutter and his colleagues (1979) in a book called *Fifteen Thousand Hours* looking at secondary school effectiveness. Rutter had attempted to contrast this with the plethora of school research in the US, as we saw in chapter 5.

Parallel to the Mortimore study is a study by Smith and Tomlinson (1989) which is a major survey of multi-racial secondary comprehensive schools. Entitled *The School Effect*, the study shows that it was possible to achieve successful learning for children at school despite the fact that the children came from a variety of multiracial and multicultural home backgrounds. In all of these studies there had been a subtle shift of emphasis from the notion of reducing disparities between children on the basis of differential home backgrounds in order to achieve equal educational opportunities, to that of effective school-based learning.

This has more recently been considered as ways of evaluating school effectiveness in terms of 'value added'. The shift has been towards seeing that the school can achieve successful educational performance despite poor socio-economic home circumstances or family backgrounds. At its best it can do so by involving such families in the processes of learning and in the life of the school. Successful educational performance has been shown to be particularly true at the level of primary schooling. Mortimore et al. (1988) and Smith and Tomlinson (1989) also indicate differences in school effectiveness on the basis of the ethos and school management, particularly with respect to parents and families. In other words, the locus of concern has shifted from a consideration of policies to attract families and to teach better educational practices, to policies, again, of school management.

Jowett has recently produced surveys of the research evidence about both primary schools and early childhood education (with Baginsky 1988) and in terms of early childcare (1990). She has reviewed the various different methods of working with parents and their relative effectiveness over different kinds of issues, such as social and linguistic development. Jowett (1990) has argued:

> It is frequently assumed that parental involvement is 'a good thing' without any real understanding of what the phrase means, and there is a lack of agreement about what work should be developed . . .
>
> The NFER research found much evidence of contact between parents and staff that was well-regarded and valued by the participants . . . It was also clear that there was great potential for enhancing work with parents and a widespread desire to do so. Indeed, some staff said that developing work with parents was essential to good practice . . .
>
> Although much valuable work with parents is being developed, the limitations of existing structures and approaches are clear. There are differences between and within schools that cause confusion and provide a 'hit and miss' element to the contact with parents . . .
>
> Parental involvement should not be concerned simply with getting parents into school. It demands an approach to learning that recognises and draws on the contribution of the home and sees contact with parents on a variety of matters as fundamental. (1990: 46)

Hannon and James (1990) pay particular attention to literacy development among pre-school children, showing different perspectives among parents and subsequently the children's school-teachers.

Scott (1990) conducted a survey of parental involvement in pre-school provision in Scotland from a critical and feminist perspective. She demonstrates the continuing pervasiveness of traditional approaches to gendered parent involvement: in other words, the implicit if not explicit assumption of maternal rather than paternal involvement. She claims:

> Modern educational politics has not as yet addressed the problems here – the impact of different family experience on demands, and the conflicting attitudes towards provision on offer. Instead, the usual response has been merely to acknowledge that not everybody wishes to, or can be, involved, whilst at the same time, predicating provision on the assumption that all good mothers should really want such involvement and be able to participate. (1990: 6)

A most interesting development, however, in the area of parental involvement, especially at the stage of primary schooling, has been the attempt to apply new methods in the area of mathematics, as well as reading and literacy or linguistic development. A major project in England has been the action-research entitled IMPACT: Mathematics, Parents, Children and Teachers. It has been a project to get teachers to involve parents in teaching and learning about mathematics both at school and at home. The innovative aim has been to get teachers to share their educational processes with parents, in order that they can continue the children's learning processes and experiences at school in the home. In other words, learning 'maths culture' begins at school but is transferred by both children and parents into the home. The project director, Ruth Merttens, has argued that:

> It is an initiative which mirrors the PACT schemes in reading, seeking to involve parents in their children's mathematics in the same sorts of ways that parents have, in many schools, become involved in their children's learning to read. IMPACT is of necessity a materials based project, since once it is decided that children are to take mathematics home, the next question is of what precisely the mathematics that is done at home should consist? . . . IMPACT has developed new ways of working, in which the mathematics that is to be done at home becomes, in some way, the focal point for the classroom work in the subject . . . It is this sense of the unity of the child's mathematical experiences, whether at home or at school, which creates the particular environment within which changes and improvements in children's learning can be brought about. (Merttens and Vass 1987a: 263, 265)

The project has been very proactive in developing materials for school teachers that can be shared with parents and families and can be used in home-based learning as well as schools. It has also provided a range of evidence about the effectiveness of this particular strategy of involving parents in learning mathematics (see Merttens and Vass 1990). Indeed, the authors also argue:

> Parental participation involves setting up and maintaining the dialogue between parents and professionals. On the one hand, the parents, with their intuitions and

intimate knowledge . . . of their child and how they learn . . . On the other the teacher, with her professional expertise, ideas and knowledge . . . It is the dialogue between these two that should create and construct the environment of the child . . . The implications of sustained parental participation are far-reaching . . . It is schemes such as PACT and IMPACT which may prove to have more power to initiate change in education than moves to strengthen the parent's position on governing bodies. (1987a: 270–1)

This strategy is not confined to Britain. Indeed there have been similar developments in Europe and the US as well as in Australia. Evans (1988) has looked at a range of issues in a case study of one Australian school, including parental involvement in mathematics. Epstein (1990) has also developed an action-research project called TIPS – Teachers Involve Parents in Schoolwork. She writes:

The TIPS process is designed to assist teachers to increase parent involvement in math and science homework and discussions, encouragement, and enjoyment of these subjects at home . . . We hypothesize that parent involvement in specific subjects – such as math and science – will increase student skills and positive attitudes in those subjects, just as our early data suggests about reading. In addition, some specific results concerning math or science may occur. For example, mothers' involvement in TIPS math and science activities over many years of schooling may increase daughters' interest and attention in math and science, the number of courses students take in these subjects and, perhaps in the long term, occupational orientations. (Epstein 1990: 111–12)

By the end of the 1980s the notion of parental involvement in education, whether at home or at school, had become the accepted practice of most state school systems, especially at the primary or early childhood education level. Most teachers and educationalists had devoted considerable time and attention to developing particular schemes to ensure the involvement of parents. As we noted in chapter 5, referring to Lady Plowden's own assessment of the impact of her report, the key issue has been the development of a professional–parent relationship over schooling. However, as she notes, there have been some adverse effects, to which we will draw attention.

Parental involvement for ethnic minority communities

Further indications of the centrality of the idea of parental involvement in education are to be found in official as well as independent research reports. For example, the Swann committee in Britain, reporting in 1985 on the education of ethnic minority children, accepted the necessity of parental involvement in education and schooling. However, the methods that were proposed did not necessarily draw on the evidence that had been accumulated in the previous decade in either Britain or other countries. They did not accept the argument that in early childhood education children should be taught in 'mother-tongue' languages. Lord Swann, in his personal summary of the report, argued:

> The Committee lays great stress on the fact that a good command of English is essential to equality of opportunity, to academic success and, more broadly, to participation on equal terms as a full member of society. First priority must therefore be given to the learning of English. The Committee regards pre-school provision as particularly important, and much prefers that the teaching of English as a second language should take place in mainstream schools as part of a comprehensive programme of language education . . .
>
> While believing that the linguistic and cultural identities of ethnic minority communities should be fostered, the Committee does not support the arguments put forward for teaching school subjects using mother-tongue languages as a medium of instruction (bilingual education). Nor does it think that mainstream schools should take on responsibility for the teaching and maintenance of ethnic minority languages. It does recommend, however, that LEAs and schools should offer help and advice for community based provision. (1985: 11)

In other words, the committee accepted the now conventional wisdom that the school had an important role to play not only in fostering equality of opportunity but in reducing educational disadvantages that accrued from socio-economic circumstances and family backgrounds. Indeed, the committee paid considerable attention to re-reviewing the research literature, with especial attention to the work on ethnic diversity of family backgrounds. They accepted the evidence that, on balance, educational under-achievement of ethnic minorities was more to do with schools than family circumstances or family forms.

Lord Swann himself was 'struck . . . by the importance the minorities attach to education . . . This perception of education as central to success in adult life is held, contrary to a commonly held view, if anything *more* deeply by ethnic minority parents than by those of the majority culture' (1985: 2). Nevertheless, although the central conclusion was that 'society must not, through prejudice and discrimination, increase the social and economic deprivation of ethnic minority families' (1985: 9), the recommendations were only for 'a change of attitude' and 'a greater sensitivity in the education of the ethnic minorities'. They were not for a shift towards responding more directly to the needs of such families or altering education in that direction, or involving parents in 'teaching' their own cultural patterns.

Tomlinson (1990) has reviewed the extent to which education has changed for an ethnically diverse society, focusing especially on 'multicultural policies and practices in white areas' (1990: 9). She suggests that:

> . . . an overview of evidence of white parental views since the 1960s suggests that the overt antagonisms some white parents felt about the education of their children alongside minority children still persists in some areas in the 1980s . . . However, there is also some evidence of greater acceptance of multiracial schools by white parents in multiracial areas.

The views of white parents in white areas are not well-researched, but evidence indicates that antagonism towards those regarded as racially or culturally different is still the norm, and white parents continue to influence their children to hold negative views of minorities and to condone or ignore racist behaviour.

On the positive side, these is some encouraging evidence from the Swann data, and the north-east schools, that some pupils are thinking in terms of acceptance, sympathy and respect for minorities, and are beginning to concede the unfairness of discriminatory treatment. There is also evidence that there are committed practitioners who are attempting to capitalize on pupils' positive views, and are attempting to develop curriculum and classroom practices that will begin to educate pupils towards a belief in equal citizenship and equal respect for ethnic minorities. (1990: 68)

Nevertheless, the development of closer home–school relations, especially through parental participation, had not brought about a marked shift in attitudes but had perhaps made schools and teachers more 'sensitive' to diverse, ethnic cultures. Parental involvement, in other words, remained very much an individualistic notion both for white and non-white or ethnic minority families.

Effects of parental involvement at home and at school

Although teachers have been engaged in developing better home–school relations and particularly parental involvement within school, not all are entirely sanguine about either the process or the results. There is some evidence to suggest that this may lead to some school-based difficulties and exacerbations of the tensions to which Bastiani earlier referred. For example, Lareau, writing of these developments in the US from the point of view of the classroom, mentions:

It is not surprising to learn that teachers feel parental participation in schooling improves children's educational performance. Other studies have demonstrated this. As a result, it is predictable that teachers believe that failure of parents to participate in schooling reduces children's potential for school success.

It *is* surprising, however, to learn that parental involvement influences *teachers'* job satisfaction. Indeed, when asked what was the least rewarding aspect of their job, 1/4 of the sample of 85 (22 teachers) replied that family–school relationships were the least rewarding part of their work . . . The problems children bring to the classroom impede teachers' effectiveness . . . Thus family–school relationships appear to shape not only children's school experiences but also those of their teachers. Many teachers seek a broad range of activities from parents and are severely disappointed by the lack of response. (1989a: 252–3)

Curiously, however, there have been few studies in Britain that point to the effects of changing family life for parent–teacher relations from teachers' point of view. There is evidence, such as that of Bastiani, that the changing context makes the situation more problematic. It is certainly within that context that there have been deliberate attempts to change home–school relations from the point of view of particular kinds of pupil. Macbeath, Mearns and Smith (1986) in a study entitled *Home From School* attempted to address this issue by developing strategies for pupils with particular types of disabilities.

Ulich (1989) has, however, looked at the effects of changed home–school relations in Germany, not on teachers but on parents and their relationships with their children. In other words, he has looked at the impact of changed expectations about the educational process on family life. This is indeed unusual. He has identified two key practices – that of homework and that of examination marks. He argues essentially that these changed practices produce considerable stress in family life. He interviewed 12 older pupils (15 to 19 years old) and eight parents, and so had only a small sample on which to base the indicative conclusions. Nevertheless, the findings may be important to the broader consideration of changes in the educational process and home–school relations. He argues:

> Through school all families experience an important extension of the world around them, through which new stresses and problems (may) arise. Two short empirical pointers may serve to show that school does, in fact, frequently bring about stress in children:
>
> – primary school pupils feel least happy at school (compared with family and playgroups); a quarter of the children do not like going to school and 407 suffer from school phobia (Lang, 1985)
> – many parents of school beginners notice the strain on their children due to having to adapt . . . working class parents express such problems more frequently than white collar workers (Sass/Holzmuller 1982: 34 ff.)
>
> . . . Parents too have constantly to take school into account: help with homework, providing support and motivation; coming to terms with disappointments (including their own); contacts with teachers, adapting the allocation of time within the family to school requirements, etc. (Ulich 1989: 2)

He goes on to flesh out the difficulties felt in particular around homework and around the marks given by teachers. He states:

> If the very act of formally checking homework (has it actually been done) implies a moment of parental authority induced by the school, then the demand of parents for redoing the homework (or the threat thereof) puts them in a position of censorship or giving orders, comparable to that of the teachers . . . [It] leads to the parent–child relationship resembling that of school. My thesis is that it is this very emphasis on success at school which becomes an area of conflict for the family . . . (1990: 7)

The development of parental involvement either at school or at home has not been without major consequences. Although the idea is now accepted in most educational systems of advanced capitalist societies, the consequences are not all felicitous. The aim of such development was not necessarily educational equity or equality but greater school effectiveness and enhancing the role of the school in the process. The role of parents has shifted not only into the school but into becoming 'informal educators' and thereby affecting family relationships. We shall return to these issues in the next two chapters.

Home and school responsibilities or partnerships elaborated

More recently there have been attempts to develop a more didactic approach to parental involvement from the informal ways in which school and home impinge upon one another. This means developing appropriate notions of parental and school responsibilities. Both Macbeth (1989) and Atkin and Bastiani (1989) have written about ways in which this could be achieved. Macbeth has been concerned to develop more effective home–school relationships, but in the context of some measure of teacher resistance. He has suggested that there are four stages in the growth of home–school partnerships:

> *Stage One – The Self-Contained School* is characterised by teacher autonomy, limited to formalised contacts with parents, little parental choice or consultation, a denial of access to school records, and with a curriculum and teaching methods regarded as the teacher's domain.
> *Stage Two – Professional Uncertainty* is characterised by tentative experiment with home–school liaison and participation but teachers still restricting consultation and blaming homes for low pupil attainment.
> *Stage Three – Growing Commitment* is the stage at which the school leadership encourages liaison and consultation with parents, recognises the value of home teaching, encourages parents on to governing bodies and generally begins to adapt the school system to include parents.
> *Stage Four – The School–Family Concordat* represents the ultimate stage in the attempt to involve all families in formal schooling, recognising that home learning is part of education and the role of parents is crucial in this, and emphasizing the obligation of parents to be involved and to cooperate with schools. (quoted in Tomlinson 1991: 6)

This kind of 'progression' or stages of development which is at the root of Macbeth's idea is based on a notion of what might be considered 'reciprocal inequality'. In other words, as Lareau (1989a and b) has pointed out for the US, teachers and parents do not have equal responsibilities. Parents have to submit their children to particular school routines. Woods (1990) also made this point in his analysis of parental participation and the shifting emphasis, as we noted at the beginning of this chapter.

Nevertheless the notion of a 'home–school contract of partnership' has gained considerable currency in recent years as a way of specifying and clarifying different parent–teacher responsibilities. Indeed, in Britain there is now a major organisation committed to its development. Bastiani, the editor of the newsletter of this organisation, has tried to define the idea of 'partnership' more succinctly. Drawing on the work of Pugh (1990) and her studies of pre-school parental involvement and that of Wolfendale (1989) and her work specifically on reading, he draws up a tentative definition:

> *Sharing of powers, responsibility and ownership* though not necessarily equally or in obvious ways.
> *A degree of mutuality* which begins with the process of listening to each other and incorporates responsive dialogue and 'give and take' on both sides.
> *Shared aims and goals*, based on common ground, but which also acknowledge important differences.
> *Rootedness in joint action* in which parents, pupils and professionals work together to get things done. (Bastiani 1991: 2)

There is in this idea an entirely changed emphasis: the shift to a limited notion of educational effectiveness rather than any view of equal opportunities. This, too, seems to be the implication of Macbeth's more scholarly but prescriptive approach (1989). Similarly Tomlinson (1991) in her report on *Home–School Partnerships* has abandoned such a commitment and is more concerned to clarify obligations and roles, on the basis of legal developments in Europe and England. She is concerned to ensure that relationships between home and school are more structured and not based on voluntary cooperation which may not be effective. She therefore provides some models of what 'educational agreements' might look like, the aim being that 'to optimise the effects of schooling and raise standards for all pupils, partnership is the key' (Tomlinson 1991: 4). She based her evidence on a survey of four European countries – France, Italy, Germany and Denmark – which seemed to indicate such effectiveness. She also produces examples of the more formal legal agreements.

Conclusions

By the end of the 1980s, home–school relations had been transformed from simple research models to more complex ones in which issues about clarity of purposes and policy aims had become paramount. They have taken as given that there is no clear and unique association between type of home background and school attainment. In other words, the complex social research findings, based on notions of reducing inequalities in economic and educational opportunities, are taken as given. Particular features of family backgrounds may be more or, at least, as important as social class in determining children's educational progress and success. But a positive association between home and school is now commonly accepted as necessary for educational progress. The shift had taken place not only through developing research but also through changes in the legal and policy contexts and their aims. Tomlinson's recommendations for home–school partnerships fit in with the changing policy context in recommending ways to achieve new policy objectives on the basis of more careful research or scholarship.

However, as we have seen, there are at least four or five types of home-school relationships, most of which centre on parental involvements in education either at home or at school. All of these types of involvement have been elaborated both in Britain and in Europe and North America over the last 20 to 30 years. They have meant, therefore, far more complex relationships between families and schools. They have entailed, in particular, far more 'educational' activities for parents both in school – as helpers, volunteers, workers, fund-raisers, or in decision-making – and at home. This has transformed the nature of the school, from the point of view of both teachers and pupils, and the nature of family life. It has implied both greater school effectiveness and the possibility of educational success through home or home improvement. The idea of home–school concordats or partnerships is one attempt to address these transformations and put them on a more formalistic footing. It enables a more clear-cut legalistic picture to emerge. However, it does not deal with the effects on family life and the different roles for parents at home. It is to this that we now turn to elaborate the changed effects, particularly on gendered parenthood; or rather, motherhood.

9

Mothers in Education, or Mum's the Word?

Introduction

In this chapter, I shall review the evidence about parental involvement in education from the point of view of *mothers*, rather than simply from that of parents as an ungendered category. In particular, I will focus on the ways in which there has been implicit rather than explicit gender differentiation in the strategic developments around parental participation. Despite the fact that there has been an enormous amount of research evidence about different aspects of parents' roles in education – from individual parental involvements in early childhood education, as reviewed in chapter 5, to a parental voice in decision-making, as commented upon in chapter 6, to parental choice of types of education, as noted in chapter 7, to complex types of parent–school partnerships, as reviewed in the previous chapter – little of it has differentiated explicitly between mothers and fathers. Those reformer–researcher developments, framed within a liberal social-democratic mould, have taken as given a traditional family form. The shift to a more right-wing 'consumerist' orientation by both researchers and reformers also has accepted the assumption of the traditional family, with a clear differentiation between fathers and mothers in their roles in relation to child-rearing and occupational responsibilities. I shall try to highlight the implications of these strategic developments in parental involvement for women's roles as mothers both at home and at school, looking at both the positive and negative effects.

These developments in parental involvement have also taken place against a backdrop of expanding educational and occupational opportunities as part of the policies of social-democratic reformers and their developments of the welfare state. This has meant increased opportunities for women in the labour market and in education, especially further and higher education, as a prelude to paid employment. It has also entailed changed family patterns as mothers have either remained in, or returned to, work and education while their children are themselves at school. More recently, with changed economic and political circumstances, and more right-wing social policies, women have also been encouraged or enticed back into the labour market or the educational system. The 'demographic time bomb' or the notion that the labour force will be insufficiently large to care for a growing 'dependency population' of children and elderly people has provided the occasion for these developments in work and education. I shall therefore consider the implications of these complex developments for mothers' involvements in education; not only as mothers of children in pre-schools or schools, but as mothers in education themselves, either also as 'consumers', that is as students, or as 'workers', that is as teachers. Indeed, I shall also look at the implications of expanding educational opportunities on the basis of gender and race, especially for women's lives with respect to their families, their jobs and their education, as well as at the impact of reforms which deal directly with parents *per se*. I am concerned to make explicit, insofar as the evidence permits, the extent to which changes in education affect women's lives not only as parents of school-children but also as members of families, the labour market and the continuing-education system.

It is, however, a matter of some curiosity that despite the vast amount of scholarship on motherhood, both in the feminist and social scientific literature, internationally as well as nationally, there has been very little which has concentrated on motherhood in relation to schools or to education. (David, Edwards, Hughes and Ribbens 1993). Most of the work on motherhood and childcare in Britain and the US as well as internationally has concentrated on caring in relation to very young children rather than in relation to school-children. There has, however, been some recent statistical work in Britain which has looked at mothers' opportunity-costs in relation to childcare, again rather than in relation to children's education (Joshi 1987). Similarly, there has been little systematic work specifically on mothers' involvement in either the labour force or education, rather than on the involvement of women without regard to their responsibilities for children. The vast majority of the studies in Britain have focused upon motherhood as an experience and an activity in relation to men and children (David, forthcoming). Mothers' educational experiences and involvements are dealt with only tangentially, so to speak. However, there is a growing literature in Europe on the implications of educational developments for mothers and family formation.

Maternal involvement at home and at school

As we have already seen, one of the early objectives of social-democratic policy-makers was to reduce disparities between families on the basis of parental privilege or family poverty, in order to provide educational opportunities on the basis of academic merit. This objective became translated into strategy through the research evidence of a number of social scientists, including both psychologists and sociologists. The gradual consensus of social scientific opinion was that the best way to help children's educational progress and development was through a lack of dissonance between home and school. The objective was to ensure a lack of social or economic differentiation between children in educational outcomes.

Perhaps more important, however, was the notion of parental participation in children's schooling on a regular and daily basis, particularly in early childhood and primary education, as the starting point to ensure either educational success on the basis of merit or academic merely sound schooling. These ideas were complicated and led to a variety of different strategies. However, two key ones were eventually, as Bastiani (1987) notes, that families should become educators in partnership with schools and that parents should become involved in school work on a regular and daily basis, if necessary to learn how to become an 'effective parent'. These were two key types of parental involvement to which we referred in the previous chapter, and which were types 2 and 3 of Epstein's typology of parental involvement.

As a result of this attempt to reduce differences between home and school, schools began to alter their expectations about the roles of parents in relation to school, as well as in the period before the start of compulsory schooling. Hitherto, as we have already argued, education had been seen as a prerogative of professional educators, the teachers themselves, sometimes referred to somewhat pejoratively as 'producers'. Inevitably, these changing expectations about how children should be educated in the family and in partnership with the school had implications for roles within the family. The new post-war educational consensus built upon a general social welfare consensus about a sexual division of labour between adults in families. This latter assumed what is now considered to be the traditional family in which the father was the breadwinner and the mother was the housewife and the one responsible for daily childcare and child-rearing. The presumption was, therefore, that it was mothers' role in family life an early child-rearing that would be transformed, rather than there being any particular effect upon fathers' activities with respect to daily child-rearing and schooling. Nevertheless, the presumptions built upon rather middle-class notions of 'educated parenthood'.

Bernstein (1974,1990) was able therefore to note this gender differentiation in parenting in his careful theoretical analysis of primary schooling; in particular, he pointed to new forms of maternal activities as 'visible and invisible pedagogy'. However, Bernstein's analysis remained highly theoretical. It has only been more recently that social analysts, particularly feminists, have begun to pinpoint the special effects of these changed presumptions. Eisenstadt (1986) has looked at the issues with respect to early childhood education, from a feminist perspective.

As I have noted before (David 1985: 35), schools expect mothers to have done a lot of 'educational' work with their children before they come to school. For example, teachers receiving new infants expect them to be able to count and to know their letters. Those children who have not already been taught a lot by their parents need special attention to compensate. Videotapes for mothers of pre-school children have been developed to help them with early learning. Teachers set clear standards for what work mothers have to do to prepare their children to go outside the home and into school. Dorothy Smith provides a beautiful example:

> A little pamphlet addressed to parents published by the Ontario government makes recommendations for how children's reading and writing skills can be improved ... the list of suggestions includes many items which are like the kinds of activities children might be engaged in in kindergarten or primary grades ... all presuppose and make invisible expenditures of time, effort, skill and materials. Paint, crayons, scissors, paper, photographs, works of art are supposed to be available. Many of the activities suggested presuppose also some if not consider-able preparatory work on the part of the parent in preparing photographs and reproductions of works of art, in making puppets and certainly considerable further work in cleaning up after these events have taken place. Space is presupposed in which these messes can be made without damage to household furnishings, etc. Presupposed also are skills involved in knowing how to discuss works of art with your children, how to extend their vocabulary, etc. . . . It is the investment of mothers' work and thought in activities of these kinds which prepares children for school. (Smith 1987: 16–17)

What Smith is pointing to, however, is the changed generalised assumption, on the basis of Canadian evidence and example. These changing presumptions are rather more complex than the general one of maternal, rather than parental, involvement.

Walkerdine and Lucey (1989) have considered the effects of social-democratic reforms on mothers' roles in bringing up children, daughters specifically, as we saw in the previous chapter. What they are particularly concerned to highlight is that, despite the rhetoric of social democracy and expanding opportunities, mothers' roles are still themselves regulated. These roles have crucial implica-tions for the ways in which the mothers 'socialise' their daughters, or educate them to be women and/or mothers themselves, in the family:

> There grew up within feminism a new myth ... of the perfect mother ... The mother became the guarantor not only of the liberal order, but of the new libera-tion. It is this account which we want to challenge, by showing not only that women's labour of natural love is profoundly oppressive but also that natural mothering is a historically constructed phenomenon. While the production of the normal family has been seen as vital to the maintenance of democracy, this has meant the different regulation of proletarian and bourgeois women, often pitting one against the other. (1989: 15–16)

They set out to reanalyse and recontextualise the study by Tizard and Hughes (1984) which developed a 'liberal' account of how working-class and middle-class mothers dealt with their tasks of bringing up young children. Tizard and Hughes' argument was one which sought to 'rehabilitate' working-class mothers and family life, seeing their pedagogical practices as 'equal but different' to those of the middle class. Tizard and Hughes pointed to the educational principles in working-class households, which they commended above those of nursery schools. Walkerdine and Lucey provide a critique of this approach, pointing to both methodological and substantive flaws in the arguments. They point to the ways in which different practices in the home around women's domestic labour and childcare, such as play, learning and housework, became celebrated and advocated in the development of post-war welfare policies:

> The facilitation by mothers of young children's play thus became loaded with ... investments ... Throughout the 1960s and 1970s such notions were popularized and special 'educational' toys and kinds of play were favoured, usually those which were supposed to aid language and cognitive development. Parents could aid their children's educational success by provision of the 'right kind' or play materials and by playing with them. The 'wrong' kind of (non-educational) toys were frowned upon, as was overt teaching. More than anything, however, play was the opposite of work ... because it was pleasurable ... just as mothering was not seen as work either, but as 'love' ... The learning environment becomes the entire home ... a(n) ... opportunity for a valuable lesson ... It must be directed carefully and sensitively taught, directed, by the mother, to ensure that the right lesson is learned. The good mother must always be there ... Given this, it is not so difficult to see why middle class mothers especially allow their time and space to be invaded much more than the working class mothers. And how, also, mothers who readily give up their own work to talk, play and rationalise with their daughters are 'read' by researchers as *sensitive* mothers, constantly attuned to their daughter's needs. (1989: 82–3)

Walkerdine and Lucey provide a very stringent critique not only of Tizard and Hughes' report but of all those social and developmental psychology studies which try to provide a basis for strategic developments in improving home–school relations.

The changing presumptions have had different implications and effects for different classes of parents, or rather mothers, as well as for different ethnic minorities or races, and are highly dependent upon the age and stage of education of their children. However, there is little systematic evidence of this in the literature, especially not for Britain, except for that of Walkerdine and Lucey. A case study of one Australian primary school has provided a careful and systematic analysis of the effects of such expectations on mothers and teachers, as well as pupils (Evans, 1988). Entitled *A Gender Agenda*, it looks at the ways in which expectations about men and women's roles in school impact on one group of people's lives. However, perhaps inevitably, this study is essentially a snapshot rather than a review of the wider processes at work.

A similar study conducted in England in 1988, *At Home in School* by Edwards and Redfern, does not explicitly address the question of gender, as we saw in chapter 8. By implication, they are concerned to tease out the various ways in which parents, often through teachers, have become involved in educational processes and what the implications are for their lives and those of their children. Most interestingly, in their review of parental involvement in the primary classroom, they consulted the children, who nearly all talked of their relationship with their 'mum'. For example:

> Why do I like parents' mornings? Mmmmm . . . it's just nice to see my mum in school, you know. I like her to be here because she helps me and I think it's really good. She gets to know all the children because she didn't know them before. (Edwards and Redfern 1988: 155)

Although there is some evidence, both here and elsewhere, to suggest that children both like and benefit from their mothers' involvement in classroom activities, there is also contrary evidence. It also suggests that children find mothers' involvement an obstacle to their own developing relationships with peer-group friends and with teachers.

For example, Best (1983) conducted a cohort analysis of boys and girls in one elementary school in the US. She was interested initially in why boys learn to read more slowly than girls. She found that the reasons lay in a complex mix of issues from teachers to peer relationships. She also expanded her study to investigate a range of home–school factors. She found that older children did not always appreciate, or even benefit from, their mothers' involvement in school activities. Many of the children felt that it inhibited their own personal and social development.

Moreover, not all mothers can or are invited to be involved to the same extent. This may, then, have differential effects on children's educational progress. Given that the original desired effect was to reduce disparities on the basis of socio-economic circumstances, differential involvement may have the opposite effect. It may, moreover, accentuate disparities between mothers within class groups rather than between them (David 1985). Edwards and Redlfern imply that parental involvement in classroom activities is variable and somewhat dependent upon parental circumstances, whether of a broad socio-economic or material kind, or more specifically to do with involvement in paid employment. The surveys conducted by the ILEA into primary and secondary education in the early 1980s (Hargreaves 1984 ; Thomas 1985) found that parental involvement was a function not only of paid employment and socio-economic circumstances, but also time. Furthermore, as Edwards and Redfern have implied, the precise nature of the family situation may have a bearing upon opportunities for daily and regular involvement. Scott (1990) has also demonstrated this at the level of pre-school services in Scotland. I shall also return to discuss the implications of these issues for children's educational performance and success in the next chaptter.

Particular groups or categories of mothers may also find it difficult or choose not to become involved in schoolwork. For instance, many children do not have positive experiences of education and school, and may be resistant therefore to overtures for them, as mothers or fathers, to become closely involved in their own children's schooling. Lareau shows, in her study of elementary schools in the US, that there are differences between parents, from the point of view of teachers, in how they get involved in schools:

> Children's social class played an important role here. Teachers working in districts of high socioeconomic status were most likely to face the problem of *over-involved* parents . . . In one relatively small elementary school, for example, parents racked up over 1000 volunteer hours . . . In general, teachers in urban communities with working-class and lower-class families faced the task of building up levels of parental involvement in schooling . . . Teachers repeatedly said that children were bringing more problems into the classroom, that they did not have the attentiveness of earlier cohorts . . . Teachers attributed these problems to changes in family life, particularly the lack of parent involvement in children's lives because of the rise of women's labour force participation and single-parent families. (Lareau 1989a: 251–2)

Lareau also argues that changes in family life have led to unrealistic expectations about parents' increased involvement in education and might have differential social effects. She also argues that it might have negative consequences on families.

Ulich has also argued about these in the German context, stating:

> The role of the parents is also changed and extended with the advent of school: parents, especially mothers, now have school-oriented tasks in caring for their children (including getting them up, meals, clothing and homework) and this involves in part new activities and skills. In any case, everyday life at home and the parent–child relationship are influenced by school, as regards time, activities and the psycho-social aspect . . . in this, the emotional resources and psychological skills of the parents are of crucial importance in order to help their children to overcome the stress caused by school (Furtner-Kall-Munzer, 1983: 87). However, these abilities are rather unevenly distributed and depend on the social status of the parents in our society and their own work-stress. (Ulich 1989: 2)

Ulich argues that changes in schools and educational practices have all had the implication of involving parents, especially mothers, more. But they have not found it easy and have seen the developments, especially in homework and examinations, as well as in their involvements in school, as difficult.

School practices in any event vary. In some cases, school may try to engage *all* parents, regardless of their circumstances or previous experiences. Edwards and Redfern claimed that this was the official policy of the school that they studied. Other schools vary in their approach, borrowing from the examples of early childhood schemes. In some it is the practice to try to involve only the more distant and possibly disadvantaged in order to 'teach' them informally at least through their experiences at school how to 'parent'. This policy was one advocated by Pugh and De'Ath (1984). Indeed, this form of 'parent education' draws on a social welfare model developed for pre-school provision and nurseries, and elevated to the practice in family centres. Here the general idea of parental involvement is entirely 'educational' – to teach mothers, in the same setting as their children, how best to parent at home (David 1985). This has also been developed in other countries as a policy, based upon similar presumptions.

This approach is one now used not only by official agencies but one which has also been developed by voluntary groups, organisations and societies, mainly at the pre-school stage. 'Parent education', as it is known, although it is almost invariably targeted at mothers rather than fathers, is a form of informal education (David 1985). It has a range of theoretical underpinnings, from that of community development (Flett 1991) to developmental or social psychology (Poulton 1980). Particular schemes therefore use different theoretical models, yet they all target mothers for help and education about how best to parent. Very often the volunteer schemes use middle-class mother volunteers to visit poor, usually working-class (and possibly from a minority ethnic group) mothers and teach them informally how to rear their children.

This experience of 'parent education' may have unintended consequences, as Finch (1984) found in her study of pre-school playgroups. Instead of eroding class differences it exacerbated them. In that respect, mothers may then choose not to become involved in school-based activities, finding too much dissonance between their lives and those of school. Certainly such voluntary schemes do not always have the intended effects of providing positive images of motherhood in respect of education. In any event, such schemes are rather limited in their scope and may only have the effect of preventing mothers from not being able to cope at all adequately with motherhood (New and David 1985). So despite their best intentions, they may achieve only a limited effect in ensuring 'good standards' of motherhood. Scott (1990) found 'considerable ambivalence' towards parental participation in her sample of 150 Scottish mothers in Strathclyde:

A total of 27% of working mothers and 34.5% of non-working mothers felt that they *were* involved in the activities of the establishment that their children attended. When asked a more general question about whether they *wanted* to be involved, parents showed that there is no universal acceptance of this role. A fairly high number of working parents (31.7%) wanted to be more involved (as against 23% of non-working parents). On the other hand, a significant number said they would prefer *not* to be involved – 26.8% of working parents and 35.6% of non-working. (1990: 5)

Scott's study of these mothers of pre-schoolers showed that the way they felt about the issue of parental involvement was not entirely dependent on work status but rather was related to class and a complex set of attitudes. As she goes on, 'the lower interest of those not in work could reflect a *realistic* appraisal of the limited nature of what is on offer' (p. 6). It may also relate to their class position and feelings in general about education. Her study also illustrates the fact that significant numbers of mothers are involved in paid employment.

Mothers' involvement in school and at work

Many mothers are now placed in material and socio-economic circumstances, whatever their type of family circumstances – two-parent, lone-parent, young-parent households – that require their involvement in forms of paid employment. As we noted in chapter 2, there have been, internationally, major shifts in the rates of maternal employment even with the presence of very young pre-school as well as school-age children. The patterns differ, dependent upon national context:

> Employment rates among women with young children still vary considerably between countries. They are highest in Scandinavia, North America and France and lowest in the United Kingdom, Ireland and the Netherlands; moreover in the last two countries, most employed mothers work less than 20 hours per week, whereas in other countries most work over 30 hours a week (Moss, 1988). Even in these countries, however, employment rates are increasing and will continue to do so. The UK has recently entered a period during which employment rates among women with young children are likely to rise quickly . . . while in the Netherlands, the labour force participation rate among women aged 25–54 is expected to increase from 46 per cent in 1987 to 59 per cent by 2000, and much of this increase will include women with young children (OECD, 1988) . . . While the *issue* of non-parental care has come to the fore because of increased employment among women with young children, the *need* for such care is not the result of such employment. (Moss and Melhuish 1991: 1–2)

The need for care or education of young children is not related to mothers' employment, although the reverse, mothers' new rates of employment, may be related to educational ambitions for their children.

Expectations of a more educational style in motherhood, including involvement in childcare or school-based activities, may perforce conflict with involvement in forms of paid employment and lead to confusion on the part of mothers. Lareau, writing about the US, has argued that:

> . . . 'teachers' requests for parent participation in schooling are based on many assumptions. Teachers assume, for example, that parents have time to come to school during the day and in the evening, the transportation to get to school, the necessary child-care arrangements to attend parent–teacher conferences, and the

energy to work with the teacher and the child to improve their child's school performance. In addition, it is assumed that parents have the language skills to speak to the teacher, the education to understand what the teacher wants them to do and to help their children as well as to intervene in schooling by initiating contact with the teacher or principal. Successful family–school relationships require not just *some* of these resources, they require *all* of them. Yet these resources are unequally available. Middle-class families are more likely to have them than families at the poverty level. (1989a: 254)

Epstein (1990), in a careful review of the evidence for the United States, states:

In our research, only 4% of the elementary school parents were active at the school building 25 days or more each year. Over 70% never volunteered in official ways and over 60% worked full- or part-time during the school-day (Epstein 1986) . . . Parents respond in different ways to requests for involvement. For example, single mothers and mothers who work outside the home were less likely to come to the school building than other parents . . . (Epstein 1990: 108–9)

Similar evidence at the pre-school level has been assembled by Scott in Scotland, as we have just seen, although she found that more of the working than non-working mothers wanted to be involved in the school (1990:7). Epstein also stated that many parents in her studies did not know exactly what was expected of them either at home or at school. However, the studies reviewed in chapter 8 show that there are nowadays, at least for young children, clear expectations in some schools about mothers' involvement in what might be considered the traditional 3Rs – reading, writing and arithmetic, or what is known now as mathematics.

Merttens and Vass (1987, 1990) in the IMPACT action-research have developed materials which prescribe clearly what is expected of parents. However, as Brown (1991) points out, this might be suffused with class expectations, too:

One possible way of addressing this question is obviously to look at what it is that is being asked of parents, and how they are being asked, and to attempt to analyze the underlying class assumptions. A rich source of data on which to base such an analysis are the booklets, outlining how IMPACT will work and what the parent's involvement will be, that are produced for parents by all schools participating in IMPACT. (Brown 1991: 11)

Having reviewed these materials, Brown reaches a conclusion that confirms that of other researchers, particularly that of Lareau (1987), who had investigated two elementary schools in the US. Lareau had argued that there was a clear class bias in forms of home–school relations and the expectations of parents by teachers. Brown's exploratory analysis appears to confirm this. He writes:

There are two sets of acquirers to consider in the case of parent participation projects: the parents and their children. In the case of parents as acquirers, with teachers as transmitters, it can be seen that with the rhetoric of the IMPACT project the hierarchy is implicit. Parents are presented as being partners, peers with teachers. Sequencing rules and criteria are also implicit in that they are not made visible to the parent. Control of what counts as appropriate activities lies in the hands of the teacher, the criteria by which the parent is to evaluate their own and their children's behaviour is implicit and has to be imputed by the parent from communications with the teacher . . . the parent is encouraged by the school to establish a form of invisible pedagogy within the home . . . Bernstein also suggests that the basis of invisible pedagogy lies in the culture and material conditions of the new middle classes and thus (such) initiatives . . . in all homes are likely to favour these groups, particularly in the early years of schooling . . . (1991: 13–14)

Brown's essay, interestingly, is an attempt to indicate both the class and sexist biases underpinning of most of the research, albeit not 'a destructive critique' (p.15) but it also ends by referring to parents in an ungendered way, rather than to mothers. Yet he had also used Bernstein's theories which pinpoint maternal, rather than parental or paternal, pedagogies. Nevertheless his key point is that parental participation projects may not have their desired effects:

. . . there may be elements within the practice of teachers that, no matter how worthy our intentions might be, can act to maintain parents in a position of powerlessness in relation to schooling. What's more, some of the attempts we make, again with the best of intentions, to develop a way of giving parents a greater voice in education might act to even more effectively reproduce the very social divisions that we would claim we are trying to counter. (Brown 1991: 14)

Some schemes and schools, however, do not target all parents for involvement in classroom activities but choose those mothers who have been professionally trained – teachers, social workers, etc. – and who are not currently involved in paid employment (David 1985). The aims in this case are to reduce the social dissonance between children on the basis of school rather than home through the use of unpaid teacher substitutes. Ulich has also mentioned that parents, in their work at home, become substitutes for teachers, and that home learning or parent–child relationships become more like teacher–child relationships at school, rather than the other way around. However, these effects are contradictory because many parents are also teachers, and so the process is two-way. Merttens and Vass have written:

Parental participation in mathematics makes explicit some of these issues in a way in which participation in reading does not. This is partly due to the fact that most parents, or a sufficiently large number to be significant, had helped their children with reading at home, whether or not the school had encouraged them to do so, and in many cases, even against the specific advice of teachers . . . A good proportion of teachers are also parents and despite widespread and official disapproval of parents who 'taught their child to read' at home, most teachers recognised clearly the value and importance of parental involvement in this area. (1987: 267)

Thus at least in some areas, family life has become more 'educational', with mothers teaching reading at home. Hamilton and Griffith point out that 'all parents are teachers and very effective' (1984: 25). At school, it is either teachers who are 'mother substitutes' or volunteer mothers who act as teacher substitutes. Parental involvement at school may be maternal, and it is certainly almost invariably mothers who engage in it, yet it may not be for the sake of their own children but to improve many children's educational development. In any event, many teachers in early childhood education are mothers or potential mothers. In early childhood and primary education, the teacher is often considered, as Lightfoot (1978) put it so succinctly, 'the other woman' in young children's lives. Teachers, as many studies have shown, are often seen as 'mother substitutes'.

However, these schemes of 'parent involvement' too may have the counter-effect of increasing social differentiation, especially between mothers. Certainly some studies of young mothers (Sharpe 1989; Phoenix 1991) have found that they are not, on the whole, well-educated and indeed may have 'chosen' teenage parenthood while still involved in education. Nearly a quarter of Phoenix's mothers were still in education or training when they became mothers (1990: 14). Rockhill (1987b), in studies in both the United States and Canada, has found that mothers are often 'blamed' not only for their own inadequate education and 'illiteracy' but also for that of their children. Rockhill has argued that for poor and immigrant women education is a particularly contradictory experience. They see it as both 'threat and desire'; it would make their family situations extremely fraught and violent and yet they desire it as a way to better themselves and their children, usually their daughters. She states:

> Contextualizing literacy, breaking it down into literacy and languages practices, looking for differences between the experiences of men and women . . . has led me to see three ideas as important to explicating immigrant women's educational experiences. The first is that literacy is women's work but not women's right; the second idea is that the acquiring of English is regulated by material, cultural and sexist practices that limit women's access to the 'public', confining them to the private sphere of the home; the third idea is that literacy is both threat and desire. (1987a: 320)

In the event, many such women forego formal educational participation while they have young children or until the 'threat' of violence leads to family break-up. They 'voluntarily' confine themselves to the private sphere of the home. Such an approach inevitably prevents such 'disadvantaged' women from more close involvement in the educational system, confirming their feelings of educational inadequacy.

Moreover, official reports and recommendations have tended to build on rather than erode these kinds of differences. For example, in Britain, the official Swann report (1985) on education for racial and ethnic minorities considered questions of parental involvement as we noted in chapter 8. For children starting school whose mother-tongue was not English, it did not recommend maternal involvement to aid the transition from home to school, despite all the other literature we have just reviewed which has advocated closer family–school relations. It suggested, instead, the use of 'mother substitutes', particularly girls from secondary schools involved in childcare and parent education courses. Rather than such children starting school with bilingual education, they would be afforded 'bilingual resources' in the form of teenage girls. The implication of this kind of proposition was the inadequacy of minority ethnic group mothers in the support of their children's English education. Indeed, similar kinds of implication may be drawn from other official recommendations and reports. The effects of changing policies for mothers' roles in education are, in other words, clearly differentiated by social and material circumstances.

Indeed, there is substantial evidence to suggest that the effects of changing policies to increase educational opportunities have enabled some mothers – usually middle class and professional – to become more involved in aspects of their children's education, helping their children to take full advantage of educational opportunities offered. More middle-class than working-class parents or mothers have gained from policies to involve them in their children's education either at home or at school. If they have been involved in paid employment, especially professional and educational work such as being teachers, they may also further benefit from changes. For example, both Johnson (1987) and Fox (1986) have showed how particular types of families, including professional families where mothers might be involved in paid employment, sought private education for their sons, in the case of Fox, and for both sons and daughters, in Johnson's case. Johnson points to the fact that, in her albeit self-selected sample, mother-teachers sometimes chose private education deliberately because of their negative experiences of state education both as parents and as teachers. There is also some evidence to suggest that parents make educational choices for their children on the basis of their own experiences. As Elliott et al. (1981) have shown in a small-scale study, mothers tend to prefer schools emphasising 'process', that is 'happiness', whereas fathers opt for educational outcomes, or 'product' as a chief criterion.

As we have also seen, Edwards, Fitz and Whitty (1989) found that a large minority of the parents who opted for assisted places at private schools were lone mothers. These lone mothers, who comprised 40 per cent of their sample, were often extremely well-educated, including not only school-based achievements but university degrees and other higher-education qualifications. This led the authors to conclude that some of the individual recipients of state-funded private education were the 'sunken middle class'.

Other mothers have tried to create new contexts in which to bring up their children, also as a result of their own educational experiences. Gordon (1990), in a fascinating study which compared English and Swedish mothers, explored their attempts to create new forms of child-rearing. She investigated particularly the extent to which such mothers feel they are able to be feminist in their styles of child-rearing. The majority of her sample, too, were highly educated and largely middle-class mothers.

Other mothers who may be living in middle-income households for their child-rearing but may originate from more working-class backgrounds also emphasise child-rearing and involvement with their children's schooling. Ribbens (1990) in a fascinating, qualitative study of mothers' child-rearing practices, comparing and contrasting with their own mothers and husbands, found that the kinds of involvements they wanted were related to their prior educational experience. They were all middle-income mothers, and she found that such mothers were deeply involved in considerations about their children's education, and put a major emphasis on it. This was often in contrast to their husbands, but followed on from their own family upbringing (David, Edwards, Hughes and Ribbens 1993).

O'Donnell (1985) studied a group of mothers of similar income in the United States. However, the majority had, before child-bearing, been involved in forms of paid employment, professional and/or feminist activities, and were in the main highly educated, including college degrees. Nevertheless she found that the vast majority of her sample group of women in a town near Boston decided that they preferred involvement in child-rearing to full involvement in paid employment. They saw their involvement in their children's upbringing as both more stimulating and challenging than continuous involvement in the labour market. Calling her book *The Unheralded Majority*, she bears witness to the ways in which mothers find satisfaction in family rather than work life.

Mothers' involvement in family, work and education

The effects of increased educational opportunities on women's family lives have, however, clearly not been uniform. Not only have the differences been manifest in mothers' involvement in their children's education either at home or at school, they have also manifested themselves in women's family and work circumstances, as well as their own involvement in education. Although there were originally arguments to increase women's education among the middle classes in order to provide middle-class men with suitably educated partners, this argument has been somewhat reversed. Bourdieu (1977) and Bernstein (1974) both made allusions to the ways in which this process was at work. However, there is now some evidence to suggest that education, educational qualifications or involvement in education may lead to marital disharmony and breakdown. This may cross class boundaries. Lawson found in her study of couples involved in adultery, taking examples of such relationships from both the US and Britain, that educational involvement was on occasion the cause of marital difficulties or separation (1990: 187). The families in Lawson's study were virtually all middle class because of her methods of collecting her research data.

Similar effects have however been found for other groups or classes of women. It has been suggested by Rockhill, as we noted earlier, based upon her study of Mexican migrant women in Los Angeles, that their wish to become involved in classes to learn English led to marital conflicts and family breakdown:

> Marriage, rather than education, is the rite of passage for the Latino. Marriage is the only way out of her parents' home; it is the only legitimate option for her to get out from under her father's control . . .
>
> In general, unless they are more highly educated, husbands are opposed to their wives taking classes or learning more than the rudiments of literacy in English. Once the acquisition of literacy moves beyond a question of basic survival skills, it carries with it the symbolic power of education. As such it poses a threat to the power (im) balance in the family. Men want to feel in control, not only does this mean having more power than their wives, but controlling what they think and do . . .
>
> Many of the women live with a great deal of violence in their daily lives . . . It is the fact that I did not explicitly look for this information . . . that makes me aware of reconceptualizing how we think about literacy and educational participation where it involves women . . . not only is there the continuing threat of violence at home with which to contend, but lack of economic and social options for leaving. A husband does not have to oppose directly his wife's taking classes for the wife to censor herself. . . . (1987a: 325–7)

However, Rockhill goes on to note how many more of her women were involved in education once they had separated or divorced.

There are no equivalent studies of such issues and processes in England. Nor are there studies of the effects of increased educational opportunities on women's family patterns in Britain. However, two exploratory studies by feminist researchers in Holland and France indicate that the effects of higher education may modify women's family formation rather than that women's involvement in education leads to family dissolution. For example, Keuzenkamp has investigated the demographic effects of Dutch emancipation policy. She looked at two groups of women: 'lower' and 'higher' educated, and the implications of policies to encourage women's participation in paid employment on their 'life courses'. She argues that

> . . . most lower educated girls and women have a traditional view of marital roles . . . (and) of motherhood . . . Girls and young women who attend higher education aim at permanent relationships at a higher age . . . When these girls think of the combination of work and family they opt more often than lower educated girls for shared parenting . . . They do not consider motherhood as the only fulfilment in life. (1991: 10)

She then goes on to look at what might happen to these two groups of women as a result of Dutch emancipation policy:

> I envision two possible scenarios which will probably both occur. One is that the number of children that higher educated women will give birth to slightly increases and that fewer . . . decide to remain childless, thanks to improved opportunities to combine work and family.
>
> The opposite scenario is nevertheless possible as well . . . More highly educated women will give in to the pressure to work, the attraction of a career and financial independence, and renounce having children. (1991: 14)

Castelain-Meunier and Fagnini (1991) have also looked at similar issues in France. They have investigated the family and professional strategies of highly educated women in France. They show how dramatic both the increases in educational and economic successes and opportunities have been in the last two decades, particularly for those who have gone into higher education. They therefore looked at the 'coping strategies' and decisions of a group of highly educated women. They reached the conclusion that the decision to have a third child or not was based on two different values or 'esprits de famille'. Those who decide not to value autonomy and independence think that a third child may 'upset the family balance'. They have 'strongly internalised' the feeling of 'precariousness in the couple', whereas those who opt for a third have both strong organisational capacity and a more traditional view of mothers' roles within the family. These two researchers also saw changes in educational and economic opportunities having contradictory effects on women's lives in the family and in work.

In Britain, there is similar contradictory evidence. There also seems to be a similar pattern for mature women students. First, there is some evidence to suggest that mothers involved only in distance learning, such as through the Open University, become involved in forms of marital disharmony and family breakdown (McIntosh 1980). However, the evidence is not unequivocal, for it does not give clear enough indication as to whether such women chose courses because of family difficulties or became embroiled in marital disharmony as a result of engagement in educational courses. Both types of effect seem indicated. These processes would be clearly very difficult to disentangle and provide proof about.

A study by Edwards (unpublished Ph.D. dissertation 1991) has looked carefully at a group of mature mother students in higher education, reading full-time for degrees in the social sciences. Choosing a sample of women with partners and young children, she focused upon the ways these women made separations or connections between their family lives and their educational lives, and with what consequences. There were clear differences between women whom she considered to be the 'separators' and the 'connectors'. The former kept their studies entirely separate from their home lives, whereas the latter tried to involve their partners and children in their educational lives and work. They had different implications for family and for education. The implications were also different for their relationships with their partners and their children. In some instances, involvement in education as a 'connector' led to family, or rather 'marital' breakdown, in the sense of separation from a partner. Separators tended to use that strategy as a shield against such familial or marital adversity. However, perhaps more important in this case, none of the mothers considered the question of family breakdown as one involving the children. Rather it was an issue between themselves and their adult partners.

In point of fact, the mothers' involvement in higher education was often justified in terms of their children. They felt that such an education would be of benefit not only to themselves and their involvement in better forms of paid employment but also to their children. Their children would benefit from both a more stimulating educational environment and the longer-term financial benefits that might accrue. However difficult the short-term college involvement might be in terms of family-life organisation, there were longer-term more significant benefits to be had from such a 'sacrifice' (David, Edwards, Hughes and Ribbens 1993).

Indeed, involvement in various levels of education for mature mother students has often been justified in these terms. Flett, a researcher at the University of Aberdeen, found similar justifications for mothers' involvement in a range of schemes which could variously be considered adult or community education (Flett, unpublished Ph.D. dissertation 1991). In some cases these schemes were forms of 'parent education' but in others they provided other more instrumental or vocationally-based educational opportunities. They also created a context for a more community-oriented view of both childcare and children's education, providing a cooperative and collaborative environment for mothers.

Neither Flett's nor Watt's studies (1989) touch on the question of marital disharmony as opposed to family care. Educational involvement cannot be the sole or even main cause of family or rather marital separation and breakdown, despite some of the evidence presented above. Increased educational opportunities for girls and women have, however, led to different aspirations and expectations among women. They have certainly led some groups of women to expect more of either their marital or partnership arrangements in terms of social and economic independence and participation in paid employment. In a study of a small group of black girls in the south of England, Fuller (1983) found that such girls expected to have to be the main breadwinners and rearers of children and therefore saw schooling as critical to their gaining the necessary qualifications to be economically independent. Other studies, such as Sharpe (1986) and Riley (1985) have found similar expectations that they will be economically self-sufficient among Afro-Caribbean and Asian women. Edwards (1990) also found different expectations about economic and child-rearing responsibilities among the black and white mother-students, this time in higher rather than secondary education. Phoenix also replicated similar aspirations among her young mothers:

> A minority of women in the Thomas Coram study were married or cohabiting when they conceived . . . Over the two years . . . some women moved into and out of a state which can best be described as 'semi-cohabitation' . . . It seems likely that the reduction in rates of marriage to mothers who are under 20 years of age partly results from the negative attitudes towards men and marriage that many women (more than a quarter of the sample) held. But this is not a complete answer, since some married women felt that men benefit from marriage more than women do . . . Women did not mention economic reasons for marrying, but there was some evidence that women who married before they were pregnant were more likely to have male partners who were relatively affluent . . . Although relatively few women were married it seems possible that part of the reason for the decline in marriage rates in this age group may be a consequence of young men's poor economic circumstances. (Phoenix 1991: 119–20)

The kinds of mature mother students that Edwards studied are rather more typical of mothers in education at all levels in Britain than one might intuitively have expected. Despite the changes in educational opportunities for girls and women over the last two to three decades, the vast majority of girls still leave school at the conventional school-leaving age of 16 and do not go on to further or higher education. Of course, the same is also true for boys. However, more boys than girls enter vocational training schemes, as shown by the relatively new schemes such as TVEI (Gleeson 1990). However, given the changes in income support and training opportunities, both boys and girls in Britain have to enter a training scheme if they do not find paid employment. These schemes, however, tend to distinguish between types of skill and courses for boys and girls. And indeed there is some evidence to suggest that girls are not as heavily censured as boys if they do not attend by reason of domestic or family responsibilities. Indeed one study found that Asian girls, in particular, were excused because of their requirement to 'help at home'.

The majority of girls or young women, then, enter forms of paid employment as a prelude to family life and child-rearing. However, given the changes in household formation, families, family size, and maternal employment referred to in chapter 2 and earlier in this chapter, there is now a different balance between what is referred to as the 'dependency' population – chiefly the elderly or those over the age of retirement and children, including dependent adult children, with physical or mental disabilities – and the paid labour force. Part of the explanation for the changing balance is the ageing population and the lower rate of social reproduction, through a lower birth rate and general family size. Another part of the explanation is the expanded educational system, with the effect that the majority of people – male or female – expect to spend longer in education and commensurately less time in the labour force.

These changes in the balance between the dependency population and the labour force are occurring in all industrialised societies and with similar implications and effects. Indeed, as we have already mentioned, the term 'the demographic time bomb' has been coined in the US and used in Britain (Moss 1991: 133) to refer to the potentially hazardous implications of the shifts, in that there are fewer people, especially women, available to care for the 'dependency' population.

It is clearly the case in Britain that there are trends towards more single households, especially though not exclusively of elderly people. As noted in *Social Trends 21* (1991: 36) this trend to a quarter of all households containing only one person has been caused by an increase in the numbers of elderly people and young people who live alone. Moreover, the trends are also of more childless women, more small families and, where families are formed, over a quarter are families with illegitimate children.

> Most women have children, though families are on average becoming smaller . . . Corresponding to the upward trend in the proportion of women remaining childless, the proportion of women projected to have two or more children now looks likely to fall. It is assumed that the proportion of women remaining childless will level off, so that just over 80 percent of women born in 1975 and later years are projected to have at least one child. (*Social Trends 21* 1991: 42)

The percentage of births outside marriage has risen steeply, so that by 1989 it had reached 27 per cent of all births (p. 43). However, the vast majority of these births are registered in the name of both not only one parent. It is predicted that the dependency population, by the year 2,025, of those children under 15 years old and the elderly over 65 will be the same, at 30 per cent each (*Social Trends 19* 1989: 23). In 1985 dependent children were 30 per cent of the population, while the dependent elderly were only 23 per cent. However, a large proportion of the elderly are themselves women. Expectations are that women will have to be involved in paid employment to help care for the growing dependency populations.

The solution to these shifts in the balance of the population is also similar in most advanced industrial societies – to draw on new groups in the population to be involved in the labour force. In some nations, there has remained a reliance on migrant or immigrant workers: in others there has been a greater attempt to draw women into the labour force directly or through education and training schemes. In Britain, the gloomy prognostications have led to special education and training schemes.

Mothers' involvement in employment and 'adult' education

Special forms of educational and training opportunities have been created to draw women into the paid labour market. It is already the case that increasing numbers of mothers of young children are involved in paid employment. Moss, reviewing developments in day care in the United Kingdom, has written:

> ... in the late 1980s and early 1990s, day care for children under three is likely to alter more than in the previous forty years. The main reason is an increasing demand for labour, especially in the service sector ... This has coincided with a fall in the number of young people leaving school, the result of the decrease in birth rate which began in the mid-1960s; between 1985 and 1995, the number of 15–19 year olds will decrease by 26 per cent. As a consequence, women are taking most of the new jobs. Of the 1.6 million jobs created between June 1983 and March 1988, 1.3 million (740,000 part-time and 550,000 full-time) went to women, and women are projected to take up to 80 per cent of the 900,000 new jobs expected to be on offer between 1988 and 1995. Many of these women will come from the group who currently have the lowest employment rate, those with pre-school children, with a consequent rapid increase in their employment rate. (1991: 137)

He has also commented, however, on the lack of sustained policies to facilitate these developments for mothers, and the fact that most schemes available are local and private. These have, however, not been accompanied by schemes to help women with their childcare and child-rearing responsibilities. Of particular note, however, are the schemes through the Training Agency, in further education, including courses which are forms of access to higher education. As Sperling (1991) notes, many of these schemes of access were deliberately created for mature women students as alternatives to the traditional GCE 'A' level route into higher education. This latter was seen to be more appropriate for the conventional 18-year-old school-leaver, especially boys. However, there is now evidence to suggest that girls do at least as well as boys, at GCE 'A' level and potential entry into higher education albeit over a different spread of subjects.

It is, however, clear that increasing proportions of women are choosing to enter further and higher education as a route to increased work opportunities. They are, indeed, encouraged to do so by a range of governmental public policies over the last decade. Many of these women are mature students, and given the known evidence about the average age of childbirth, are likely already to be mothers. However, there is little substantial evidence to indicate the exact proportion of mothers. The number of students who enrolled on further education courses in the United Kingdom began to increase between 1980–1 and 1988–9. Female students accounted for the vast majority – over four-fifths of this increase (*Social Trends 21* 1991: 51). They were mainly part-time, since the proportion of full-time students remained the same.

Between 1980–1 and 1988–9 there was an increase in students in full-time higher education of 20 per cent (*Social Trends 21* 1991: 57). This increase took place almost entirely in polytechnics and colleges, rather than the universities. A large proportion of that increase was accounted for by female students: in 1980–1, they were 41 per cent of the total; by 1987–8, they were 46 per cent.

The women students were, too, disproportionately involved in particular subjects, as they represented 80 per cent of all full-time students on education degrees (and only 13 per cent on engineering and technology courses) and therefore were directly preparing to be teachers.

The changes in part-time higher education have, perhaps, been even more dramatic than in full-time higher education. Between 1970–1 and 1988–9, the numbers of places in part-time higher education more than doubled. By 1988–9, women accounted for 40 per cent of the places, compared to 14 per cent in 1970–1. Of these women, 75 per cent were over 25 years old. As noted in *Social Trends 21*:

> The increase in the number of mature women students was greater than for men regardless of the institution or academic level of study, or whether the course was full or part-time. In 1988 men accounted for 56 per cent of mature students compared to 66 per cent in 1981. (1991: 58)

Thus, by the end of the 1980s, women's lives as parents were becoming increasingly complex, juggling family obligations and responsibilities for child-care and education with the demands of not only parental involvement, but also forms of paid employment or further and higher education.

Although the balance between men and women in further and higher education has altered dramatically in the last decade, the educational facilities provided have not altered commensurately. The majority of mother students, as noted above, are involved in part-time study, fitting these activities in the interstices of childcare and domestic responsibilities, possibly as well as work responsibilities. Forms of part-time courses differ: some are in the day to accommodate those with school-age children, whereas others may be in the evening to provide for those who share private childcare responsibilities. Sperling also brings into focus the continuing barriers to participation in higher education that mature women students face. She comments in particular on the lack of change in admissions and assessment criteria and also in teaching methods. She argues that women students have actually been encouraged into 'traditional' courses, with traditional and formal methods of assessment such as examinations. Although mature students may do as well as conventional students the methods may be limited in scope, and in appropriateness for different students. She notes that:

> Indeed, in my own research into Open Colleges as routes into higher education for mature women, 72% of respondents to a questionnaire about their educational experiences, both in compulsory education and as adult returners, cited less formal, 'friendly' assessment and teaching methods as a reason for choosing Open Colleges as their reintroduction to study. Apart from the examination context itself, revision may be marred for mature women students by the intrusion of outside responsibilities and commitments, and examination timetables may not

fit into their schedule. The task of taking children to school and travelling to college before an examination, arranging after-school child care for afternoon
examinations and the worry that this entails about the reliability and suitability of
the care chosen, all serve to deflect concentration from the subject at stake.
(Sperling 1991: 204)

She is, however, even more critical of the general ways in which higher
education opportunities do not provide equal opportunities for mother
students, but continue to keep them separate and different, maintaining sexual
differentiation. She draws her critique from that provided by other feminists
which is not only about the provision of special and important family or
childcare facilities but also about the nature and the knowledge being produced.
Sperling's conclusion is indeed strong and forthright:

> ... the changes that are necessary to accommodate mature women students
> within higher education are considerable and challenge the fundamental building
> block of the sector – that of its patriarchal structures and hierarchies. Not only is
> it necessary to provide adequate and affordable child-care, suitable timetables,
> student-friendly teaching and assessment methods and educational guidance and
> counselling, it is also necessary to change the context of higher education to
> include the experiences of women as relevant bases of knowledge. The seemingly
> mundane experiences of many mature women have an important role to play in
> the learning experience. By their incorporation not only will higher education
> become more directly apposite to women but, as *bona fide* members of academia,
> mature women's needs will necessarily be acknowledged and accommodated as
> have the needs of men historically. (1991: 212)

To some extent, some aspects of women's needs have already been incorporated
into the academy, to wit the development of women's studies and/or gender
relations courses. However, for the most part they too have tended to ignore
the needs of mothers, focusing largely on questions and issues to do with
women in general. Although new courses and curricula have been developed in
higher education in Britain and even more so in North America and Europe,
where feminist studies are now the norm, these have not yet begun to challenge
the traditional, patriarchal structures of the academy or society at large.

Conclusions

In this chapter, I have reviewed a range of evidence about mothers' changing
involvement in education and the implications these have for their children. I
have surveyed both their involvements at home and at school on behalf of their
children and their own educational involvement. It is the case that on the whole
women's involvement and incorporation into education at all levels has been
different from that of men. Despite the opening up of educational opportunities
for women there has been no real recognition of the implications that there may

be for women's roles *especially as mothers within the family and in forms of paid employment*. Indeed, in order to try to expand educational opportunities for children, mothers have been relied on to contribute both at home and at school. In the first instance, this has meant foregoing their own opportunities for advancement in education or paid employment 'for the children's sake'. Secondly, women as mothers have recently been enticed back into education on the basis of needing to train to contribute to the labour force to care now not only for children but also for elderly people. In this case the evidence would suggest, again, that education is not provided for them in their own right. Indeed, it has often meant that they have had a 'double burden' much like the now classic one of work and family. In some respects, as Edwards and Sperling have shown, this may be even more difficult than work, since 'education' is also, like women's work, 'never done'.

Interestingly, there has been virtually no analysis of the differential effects of these educational involvements of mothers, whether at home, at school or in further and higher education, on their sons and daughters. All the accumulated evidence has tended to focus on children in general, much like most of the evidence here has been about parents rather than mothers and fathers. The one exception to this is the reanalysis of the Tizard and Hughes (1984) study conducted by Walkerdine and Lucey (1989). Their rather polemical account demonstrates the reproduction of class-based forms of womanhood and motherhood through mothers' relationships with their daughters at the stage of early childhood education. This would suggest that these patterns are then the building blocks for the forms of maternal involvment at all levels which we have investigated in this chapter. The patriarchal structures in higher education, to which Sperling has referred, are far more pervasive than just that part of the educational system. They pervade the whole of the educational system, often rendering women invisible and mothers clearly as 'other' in their various formal and informal structures. This is despite the fact that mothers are in most respects the mainstay of both formal and informal, home-based education. Indeed, given current demographic and family trends they are becoming increasing indispensable, and important for children's educational success or performance, as we shall see in the next chapter.

10

Debating the Effects of Family Changes and Circumstances on Children's Education

Introduction

In this chapter, I review the effects on children's education and subsequent life-chances of the changes in family life that have occurred over the last few decades. As we have already seen, it has become accepted in public policy, across the political spectrum of left and right perspectives, that a close and clear relationship between parents and schools necessarily will lead to more effective education of children. Given this set of assumptions, a whole range of strategies around parental involvement in education has been set up, from individual and collective involvements in pre-school and early childhood education, at home and at school, to political participation in running schools, to parental choice as 'consumers' as well as 'producers'. Recent right-wing public policy pronouncements in Britain have endorsed the idea of greater individual parental responsibility for children's education, through the Parent's Charter and the notions of 'choice'. The aims have variously been to improve children's educational achievements, to enhance their educational performance or to empower parents to feel more secure in the exercise of their parental duties over education.

It is not yet evident that these strategies have had the desired effects for all children from different social classes, racial or ethnic minority groups or of different sexes. Precisely what have been the effects of changes in parental roles for mothers and fathers on children's gendered educational developments? Although there is a paucity of evidence, I shall try to tease out the implications of changing and differential parental roles for boys' and girls' education. Changes in family life from the traditional two-parent family and developments in maternal employment may have influenced children's gendered educational developments. The evidence about the impacts of maternal employment, parental divorce and separation as well as remarriages will be reviewed, insofar as it exists.

As noted earlier in chapter 2, the assumptions about family life were of two natural, gendered parents, rearing their children in the privacy of the family. During the social-democratic period dominated by the idea of 'meritocracy', the aims were to ensure that children were not unnecessarily advantaged by privileged home circumstances, and that children from materially or economically limited home circumstances were not disadvantaged in educational opportunities on the basis of their academic abilities. Evidence was collected, as we have seen, to demonstrate that poor families or parents living in poverty were educationally disadvantaged. Strategies were therefore devised to ensure that children's disadvantages were restricted, often by means of involving their parent in their education at home or at school. However, the form of such families was rarely investigated to consider their characteristics and consequent effects on the particular form of disadvantage (Mortimore and Blackstone 1980).

Similarly, evidence was collected, particularly in the US, of educational disadvantage accruing from particular kinds of racial or ethnic origins. But again, although assumptions were made about differential family structures in the arena of public policy, this was not linked to issues abut educational performance. For example, Moynihan's now classic study *The Negro Family* (1966), often cited as the example of 'blaming the victim', claimed that it was black families themselves, given their approaches to family life, that resulted in their poverty. He did not link his argument to educational disadvantages for black or racial minorities.

The shift in the political arguments and strategies to the idea of 'parentocracy' has led to more of a concern with the private family taking responsibility for the children's education. The claim is that parents are best placed to decide on their children's appropriate schooling. But the characteristics of the private family have remained an enigma.

During this 40- to 50-year period of a shifting relationship between education reformers and researchers and their political arguments, there have also been changes in family circumstances. As noted in the previous chapter, some of the changes in family life, such as the extent of family or marital break-ups, have been attributed to changes in educational opportunities and aspirations. Similarly, some aspects of family break-down have to do with lack educational opportunities and/or the threats imposed by differential family or marital circumstances. Yet another aspect of major familial change over this period of time – the rate of maternal employment while there are dependent school-children, or pre-school children, to care for – has to do with changes in educational opportunities linked to arguments about economic growth.

There is also contradictory evidence about the extent to which increased educational opportunities have the same impacts on women's aspirations or desires for more involvement in education. Indeed, as noted in the previous chapter, there has also been a trend, both in the US and in Britain (less so in other European countries), towards young motherhood, especially among those still eligible to remain in school. This trend has been linked to broader trends towards young, out of wedlock, motherhood.

Against this backdrop, there has been a range of commentaries on the effects of these changes in family life on children's care and education. But there has been very little social scientific evidence that demonstrates a particular pattern. Epstein (1990), in her far-reaching review of these trends in the US at least, has called for more research on the issue. To quote her:

> Families are changing. The 'traditional' family of two natural parents with mum working at home is now 'untraditional' (Bureau of the Census, 1984). Most children live in other types of families – one-parent homes, reconstituted or blended families, joint-custody families, foster homes, extended families, relatives as guardians, and other variations. These arrangements cross economic lines and are not indicative of uncaring families. And, all schools and families must understand how they can influence each other to benefit the children they share. A continuing research agenda needs to focus on questions of the effects on students of family and school programs that provide developmental and differentiated experiences for families of children at all grade levels and for the special needs of different families. . . . (1990: 116–17)

Lareau has argued similarly that changes in family structure and family life have been occurring at the same time as the schools have been demanding greater involvement of parents. She has written:

> Indeed, the last few decades have been substantial changes in the family, notably changes in women's labor force participation, family size and family structure. For example, with the increase in divorce, a majority of school-aged children now spend some time in a single-parent family . . . We believe there must be a restructuring of family–school relationships to reflect the changes occurring both within schools and the larger society. Schools and families are in a synergistic combination. Teachers' expectations for parental participation in schooling have escalated in the last few decades, precisely at the same time that changes in family structure have reduced familial resources for participating in schooling. (1989a: 254)

She wants schools to give greater consideration and respect to these family-life changes.

The various political arguments about changes in family life

Many of the commentaries about changes in families, especially those from the US, have imputed reasons and a pattern to the effects. New Right or conservative commentators in the US, even those who are social scientists, have assumed that the changes in family life are 'morally wrong' and have deleterious effects on the affected families. Although educational consequences have not been chief among their targets, they have nevertheless been alluded to.

First, Gilder has pointed to the serious consequences of changes in family life for the traditional structure of society. His concern, however, was in particular for male motivation over economic activities, arguing that 'man has been cuckolded by the compassionate State' (1982). He was especially concerned that family or marital breakdown would reduce men's motivation to work hard. He also felt that state social support provided to 'errant' wives and mothers for their child-rearing responsibilities would reduce male economic responsibilities. His strategy was, therefore, to try to change the state's economic and social relationship with women in families, in order to stem the tide of marital break-down and ensure that women remained within marriages. Although Gilder wanted to try to reinvoke traditional family life, his focus was less on children than on the behaviour of wives. His consideration, too, was about the role that the state played not with respect to education, but to financial maintenance of families. Indeed, his concerns stemmed from his twin interests in social policy and a critique of feminist politics and their effects on public policy (Gilder 1981; 1982). This has most recently been reviewed by Faludi (1992).

Second, Murray, a social and political scientist, has developed similar arguments about the decline of the traditional family. He wrote two texts to popular conservative acclaim. The first, *Losing Ground: American Social Policy 1950–1980* (1984), was a reanalysis of the impact and effects of federal liberal policies to deal with social issues. He was particularly concerned to argue for a reduction in state and social intervention because of their adverse consequences on family and community. In his second text, *In Pursuit of Happiness and Good Government*, (1989), he widened his commentary to consider 'happiness' as the most important criterion of successful governmental policies. He demonstrated how liberal and neo-conservative policies had led to the persistence, rather than prevention, of social problems and, in particular, changes in family life. He used a variety of examples to make his point, including that of education:

> To return to the running example of education, the reforms in education during the 1960s and 1970s may be seen as a series of steps that 'took some of the trouble' out of educating one's child and to that degree attenuated this important source of satisfaction. Responsibility for decisions about nearly everything – curricula, textbooks, disciplinary standards, rules of attendance and suspension, selection of teachers, testing requirements, the amounts of money to be spent, guidelines for lunch menus – moved outward from the neighbourhood to the state or federal government. The argument here is not about whether these changes were substantively good or bad; rather, it is that *even if* they had been good educationally, they were still bad for parents in that they constrained and depressed the ways in which a parent with a child in public school could take satisfaction from that component of life called 'overseeing the education of one's child.' (Murray 1989: 268)

In other words, Murray was concerned that liberal social policies had, in effect, reduced individuals' personal responsibilities, including and especially those of parents for their children. These policies had generally negative effects on family life.

But Murray was more perturbed about the consequences of the loss of community for the traditional family. His argument essentially focused on the moral and social consequences of the changes. He saw the effects of such changes as the creation of an 'under-class', largely consisting of black families, which is prone to crime, indolence and having children illegitimately. Although he did not specify gender differences in the effects of the break-up of the traditional family, he was, in fact, focusing upon women, especially single mothers and particularly, on black female-headed households and their child-rearing responsibilities. He also pointed to the role of the black, unemployed 'youth' or young men who resorted to crime. However, although Murray raised the question about how children are reared in such circumstances of illegitimacy and poverty, his central remedy was not state education or social policies. Instead, it was to reduce state intervention and reinvoke individual and parental responsibilities.

Murray's thesis was a gloomy prognostication about the future of the family and community. His remedy, though, was limited to the reassertion of a particular set of *moral* values about the traditional nuclear family, which may not be effective in modern industrial societies. Nevertheless, his analysis does point to the problematic future for children of such kinds of family life, despite the dearth of evidence or positive possibilities.

His arguments, however, became so popular among conservative thinkers in Britain that he was asked by the Institute of Economic Affairs, a conservative think-tank, to give consideration to the applicability of his ideas in Britain. As a result, he wrote a sharply polemical essay entitled *The Emerging British UNDERCLASS*, published with rejoinders from British social scientists in 1990. He argued that similar social problems existed in Britain as a result of similar social policies. He wrote: 'It seems safe to conclude that as of 1989 the British underclass is still small enough not to represent nearly the problem it does in the US . . . The question facing Britain is the same haunting question facing the United States: how contagious is the disease?' (1990: 24). However, he was concerned that the long-term effects might be very similar. He continued:

> In the case of illegitimacy, it is impossible to assume the exponential curve in the trendline since 1970 will continue to steepen – if it were to do so, all British births would be illegitimate by the end of the century. But even if we assume more conservatively that the trend of the past 10 years will continue linearly, more than 40 per cent of births will be to single women by 1999 . . . In both countries, the same humane impulses and the same intellectual fashions drove the reforms in social policy. The attempts to explain away the consequences have been

similar . . . The central truth . . . is our powerlessness to deal with an underclass once it exists. No matter how much money we spend on our cleverest social interventions, we don't know how to turn around the lives of teenagers who have grown up in an underclass culture. Providing educational support opportunities or job opportunities doesn't do it. Training programmes don't reach the people who need them most. We don't know how to make up for the lack of good parents – day care doesn't do it, foster homes don't work very well. Most of all, we don't know how to make up for the lack of a community that rewards responsibility and stigmatises irresponsibility. (Murray, 1990: 33)

Despite this kind of agnosticism, Murray jumped to particular solutions and advocated a reduction in the role and responsibilities of government. He preferred a system of 'self-government', or individual and parental responsibility. He even cites this as an example:

If people in one neighbourhood think marriage is an outmoded institution, fine, let them run their neighbourhood as they see fit. But make it easy for the couple who thinks otherwise to move into a neighbourhood where two-parent families are valued. (1990: 34)

His wider analysis led him to advocate a whole range of private, rather than public, policy solutions such as education vouchers and tuition tax credits. But his solutions remain polemical and were contested for Britain by three major social scientists who pointed variously to problems in the statistical analysis of single mothers and illegitimacy, the issues about social policy, crime and indolence and the concept of the underclass itself.

Brown, in response to Murray, presents a more careful statistical picture of the characteristics of lone mothers in Britain, pinpointing differences between single, never-married, separated, widowed and divorced mothers. She writes:

The picture the figures present is of a growing population of one-parent families, mostly fatherless families dependent on benefit to quite a staggering extent. Moreover, while in 1986, 50 per cent of married mothers went out to work to help support their families, only 42 per cent of lone mothers worked, and as few as 25 per cent of single mothers, and half of them part-time only . . . [But] by 1987 . . . 27 per cent of single mothers were (more than 5 years) on benefit and 37 per cent of divorced mothers . . .

Among women aged 18–49, with and without children, the proportion cohabiting has risen from 9 per cent of single women and 39 per cent of divorced and separated women 1981 to 20 per cent of single and 52 per cent of divorced and separated women in 1988.

Given these patterns, pointing a finger at single mothers – but not at divorced or separated wives – as an especial danger to society makes little sense. If, for a child, being brought up without a father is of key importance, it is hard to see a difference of major social significance between starting life without a father and acquiring one, and starting with a father and then losing him, even though it might have been better for the child in both cases if there had been a stable union involving both natural parents. (1989: 45–6)

Brown captured a key flaw in Murray's study – that of imputing particular effects of changes in family life to child-rearing practices and responsibilities. Nevertheless, Murray's 'attractive' thesis has been used by conservative social reformers and researchers alike. It underpins recent social reforms especially towards privatisation. But little consideration was given to the links between changes in family life and education, a point to which we will return.

Other American sociologists, such as Berger and Berger in *The War Over The Family* (1984), also point up the debates between the right and the left over the future of families, particularly in the context of rapid social change. As liberals, Berger and Berger were loath to recommend intervention in the privacy of family life. They did, however, recommend a range of public policy strategies to ensure the continuation of the traditional family. They did not choose to address questions of educational reform. This brief review of the American debate on changes in family life and strategies to deal with them has once again illustrated the fact that these debates about family policy have, to a large extent, been pursued independently of those educational policy.

The same is also true in Britain. Similar arguments to those of Gilder and Murray have been developed by other right-wing writers in Britain, most particularly Mount (1982) and members of the Institute of Social Affairs (ISA) such as Anderson (1986), of the Institute of Economic Affairs (IEA) such as Green (1991), as well as members of the Centre for Policy Studies (CPS). The IEA has pursued most vigorously the arguments, as we have just noted, about changes in family life. Anderson a right-wing sociologist, has also vigorously argued (in Anderson and Dawson, eds 1986) about the demise of the traditional family and developed arguments for its resuscitation through moral censure, rather than government action. Most recently he has not seen the issue of such central significance (1991). Most of these right-wing commentaries do not link their analysis of trends in family life with educational strategies, except in general moral terms.

But all of their solutions to the social problems of changes in family life, such as divorce, separation and out-of-wedlock parenthood, have implications for education as well as social policy. Their key argument is that changes in family life have been 'caused' by state interference, rather than state intervention. In other words, the 'nanny' state has provided excessive social and economic support to families. A reduction in state intervention and an increase in private, parental responsibilities is the right's solution to a range of problems, including children's educational development. Murray's arguments chime in well with those of conservative family and educational commentators in Britain such as Sexton (1985), Anderson and Dawson (1986), Cox (1989), Flew (1989), Sexton (1990) and Green (1991, 1992).

Durham (1991) has carefully reviewed the ways in which these conservative arguments about the family and morality were constructed in Britain in the 1980s in contrast with the US. He has used five case-study examples of moral campaigns or crusades, namely sex education, abortion, Gillick and contraception for under 16-year-old girls, embryo research and 'sex and violence' campaigns. He argues, however, that the British New Right has 'relatively little interest in moral issues' (1991: 160). He goes on:

> A comprehensive account of the New Right would have to acknowledge that it does contain significant moralist strands. But this remains fundamentally different from the situation in the United States. Issues of family and morality were crucial to the rise of the American New Right in the Seventies and have remained central to major components since. The British New Right is far less focused and far more disparate on such issues. (1991: 160)

He also tries to assess the links between the various 'moral' campaigns and the Conservative governments, particularly in 'the Thatcher years'. He concludes:

> If the eighties were the decade of Margaret Thatcher, one of its many effects has been to popularise the term 'Victorian values'. A political project which was committed to privatisation . . . and the restoration of Britain's standing on the world stage was also committed to a revival of discipline and standards . . . When sex education is placed in 'a moral framework' . . . and government begins to show concern over single-parent families, then moral campaigners can believe their time has come. But on key issues the government proved to be a disappointment or even an antagonist rather than an ally, and many of the social indices which outrage campaigners – the abortion rate, the divorce rate, the illegitimacy rate – have risen and are continuing to rise . . . But what we . . . are not likely to see in the nineties, is the coming together of the political right and the moral lobby and a shift from rarely implemented government rhetoric to a sustained 'moral majority' stance. (1991: 179)

He did not fully review the Conservative government's policies, however, but focused instead on the moral crusaders on family matters. In fact, had he reviewed the strategies, he would have noted their lack of effectiveness. In other words, as Murray pointed out, even New Right politicians, in government, have not pursued effective social strategies that have reversed the changes in family life. Nevertheless, the rhetoric has been strong.

Recently, as we noted in the introduction, one conservative writer in Britain, another Dawson (1991), has raised the issue of the connection between changes in family life and children's educational performance as a basis for adding vigour to arguments about policies for families and education. He claims that the evidence of the poorer educational performance of children from single-parent families is now incontrovertible, and cites to his support work by a social-democratic sociologist, Halsey.

Indeed, it has been the case that left perspectives on the relation between parents and education have not necessarily been any less traditional than those of the 'moral' or the 'new' right. A similar rhetoric about the effects of changes in the family and family circumstances has often been pursued from left perspectives. Arguments about the family from left-wing commentators have not centred crucially on the links with education. In particular, Lasch's arguments, although couched in Marxian language, are redolent of those of the New Right. His *Haven in a Heartless World* (1967) and its sequel *The Culture of Narcissism* (1980) also mourn the passing of the traditional family, without developing notions about its effects or how to deal with it (Barrett and McIntosh 1984, 1991).

Similarly in Britain much of the evidence about changes in the family does not touch on the effects on educational performance or provision. Indeed, in one of the most recent publications from the relatively newly established left-wing policy 'think-tank' – the Institute for Public Policy Research (IPPR) – the authors consider issues about the family without reference to educational effects or strategies (Coote et al. 1990). At approximately the same time a pamphlet on education was also published by them without reference to the links with the family, despite the public policy agenda (Miliband 1991). In other words, the public policy debate on changes in family life has rarely been related to that on educational reforms, and the changes are mourned without reference to the possibility of either creating positive effects or noting their complexity.

Similarly, most of the work by social scientists concerned with family change, such as Bradshaw and Millar (1991), has only documented the changes and their financial and social consequences rather than their educational implications. But some social scientists have developed a broader perspective on changes in family life. In particular, there has been documentation of the extent and type of changes with respect to the gender and/or race or ethnicity of parents.

A critical perspective has been applied to notions originally developed in the US about 'the feminisation of poverty.' The argument developed in the US was essentially about the extent to which the growth and development of female-headed households with dependent children had thrown them into dependence on state welfare and support. 'Welfare mothers' – women rearing children alone on state support – were deemed to be a new category of the poor (Eisenstein 1984; Scott 1985). Indeed, for the most part they were also seen to be disproportionately women from racial or ethnic minorities, particularly black.

However, evidence for Britain suggests that 'family poverty' as a social category and term has been a mask for considerable poverty among women as mothers, whether or not they are dependent upon husbands or the state (Land 1986). Changing family patterns, such as marital break-up and the creation of lone-parent households consisting predominantly of mothers with dependent and often school-age children makes for different patterns of female poverty and social dependence. Millar (1989, 1990) has variously pointed to the characteristics and social needs of lone parenthood. While lone parenthood is not only the prerogative of those who are disadvantaged or in poverty, it certainly has important social repercussions for those who do become dependent upon state support (Bradshaw and Millar 1991). Lone parenthood among the middle classes has different effects and consequences, including those of education. We have already noted Brown's comments about these complexities in her rejoinder to Murray in his pamphlet.

Changes in family life from the apparently 'traditional' family composed of two natural parents with dependent children being reared in the privacy of their own homes, evoke a range of political responses. Yet they are clearly complex and diverse. It is important to consider the impact of these changes, if any, on children's education. I will consider now these issues in three respects. One is the impact upon children's educational performance, in terms not only of differential educational achievements or success but also happiness and security. Is there evidence about the effects of changes in family life on children's education in terms of happiness and/or success? Secondly, I shall also consider the question of the differential impacts on boys and girls. Thirdly, I will address the question of whether such various changes in family life had an impact upon parents' participation in their children's education, on the premise that such participation affects educational standards and outcomes. Indeed, the political argument that parents should have a voice, a choice or some involvement in educational processes, either in decision-making or the curriculum, is predicated upon the assumption that this participation leads to better educational outcomes.

The relations between changes in family life and children's education

In fact, as noted above, very little research evidence has been collected on the variety of changes in family life specifically linked to children's schooling or their educational performance. First, there is considerable evidence about women's changing patterns of paid employment, particularly when there are young or school-age dependent children present. We have referred to these substantive changes in previous chapters, drawing particularly on the work of Joshi (1989) and Melhuish and Moss (1991). The increases in maternal employment have occurred in most advanced industrial societies, regardless of whether there have been other changes in family life such as marital break-down or out-of-wedlock parenthood. However, the pattern of maternal employment varies depending upon the form and nature of public childcare and education. So maternal employment is, in fact, closely associated with responsibility for child-rearing and education. Moss noted that trends in public childcare provision have not followed on patterns of maternal employment. Mothers tend to view childcare as their prime, and often sole, responsibility, and fit in paid employment in the interstices of childcare provision.

In Britain, by contrast with other European countries and North America, paid employment for mothers of pre-school children tends to be rather limited.

Similarly, the pattern of paid employment for mothers of young, school-age children also tends to be part-time and limited to school hours and school days. As Cohen has noted, 'The hours that women work are significantly affected by parenthood. The 1980 Women and Employment Survey found that only 6% of childless women worked part-time whereas 35% women with children under 16 worked part-time' (1988: 12). These figures have barely changed since the study of women and employment by Martin and Roberts was published in 1984, despite further changes in family life. Brown has, however, noted the fact that there have been differences in the rates and types of employment for lone mothers and married mothers of dependent children. Moreover, the British patterns of maternal employment tend to differ from those in both the US and Europe. In both the latter, maternal employment, whether of 'single' or 'lone' mothers or married mothers, tends to be full-time, although of a temporary and casual rather than permanent kind. The exceptions are for more highly educated mothers, as we have seen in discussions of Holland and France in the previous chapter. This is also the case for the US and for Britain.

Apart from the clear view that mothers perforce have to take seriously the responsibilities of parenthood, there is little evidence about whether patterns of paid employment affect particular children's educational performances. But the reasons for maternal employment, ranging from the need to support a family to job or career advancement, may themselves be linked to children's educational performance. Indeed, there is some evidence to suggest links between poor home circumstances and the necessity of maternal employment, and poor educational outcomes for children. The evidence collected in the 1970s about family poverty could be generalised to the contemporary situation. Toomey (1989) has reviewed a range of evidence and shown that it is women's position, rather than social class, which affects children's scholastic achievements. The whole thrust of work on socially disadvantaged children which we have referred to earlier, as well as developments in 'parent education' for mothers of such families, was based on the assumption that maternal employment would further disadvantage such children. We shall return to this evidence later.

There is now evidence about the patterns of marital break-up, separation and divorce collected not only in Britain but also for the US and European countries. The British trends for divorce and separation mirror those of the US, followed by other European countries. Although the figures for divorce and marital separation are very dramatic, such that one in every three marriages in Britain commencing in the 1990s is likely to end in divorce, little is still known about the effects on the relations between parents and children. The focus in most of the research about the effects of divorce or marital break-up is on either the process or the emotional relationships between the partners and for their children. It is clear that complex kinds of family patterns are created, such as lone-parent families, joint custody arrangements, step-parent families, half-sibling households, etc. Indeed, given the rates of divorce, the rate of re-marriage or cohabitation are also extremely dramatic, which have the effects of creating these diverse and complicated 'family worlds'. A study conducted for the OECD by the Centre for Educational Research and Innovation (CERI) entitled *Caring for Children* attempted to document this complexity in the early 1980s.

The effects of family changes on boys' and girls' educational success

Given the complexity of families in which children now grow up and the fact that they move between a variety of families throughout their school years, it is perhaps not surprising that there are few studies of the impact of such changes upon children's educational performance. Wallerstein and Kelly did study how both parents and children in the US dealt with the immediate effects of the changes. In a book entitled *Surviving the Break-Up* (1980), they focused on the emotional and social effects. However as Lareau has pointed out, these effects have short-term, if not long-term, consequences which are not controversial. She writes:

> Parents' separation and divorce have a significant negative influence on children's socioemotional state. The impact on children differs dramatically by age, but often involves changes in behaviour, including poorer school performance. Over time, children usually revert to their predivorce status, but the turmoil introduced by divorce usually dominates the family for six months to a year. (1989a: 254)

Lareau based her evidence on three rather slender pieces of work, most of which were conducted prior to the very dramatic increases in family changes in the 1980s in the US.

In a follow-up study conducted ten years later, Wallerstein, this time with Blakeslee (1989) looked at the long-term emotional and social implications. Again, they did not look carefully at the particular educational effects. However, they did consider the general question of adjustment of both adults and children to their situation, which would have an overarching impact on performance in education. Curiously, Lawson's rather encyclopedic study of both American and British couples involved in a range of different types of marital situations and changes, entitled rather provocatively *Adultery* (1990), does not consider the effects on children, although as noted in the previous chapter, she does look at the effects of education on the men and women involved. Here she did discern some appreciable effects especially on women who became involved in education as mature students.

In Britain there has been some specific research on the effects of parental divorce on children's educational performance. The data on which this research was based were the first of three national cohort studies, developed initially by the National Children's Bureau, of one-third of all children born in one week in

1946. Subsequent studies in 1958 and 1970 attempted to replicate and reproduce the data. The main focus of the studies has been on children's general educational development and performance, related to a variety of different social factors including divorce (Elliott and Richards 1991). Wadsworth and Maclean (1986) analysed some of the data to look at the effects of parental divorce on the economic and educational achievement of adults. They demonstrated that divorce had an adverse effect on children's educational and economic achievements and attainments, through difficulties with long-term emotional adjustment. The reasons for Wadsworth and Maclean's study were very specific, since they felt that a considerable amount was known about the long-term social, emotional and financial consequences of divorce. They wrote:

> Having documented the immediate income deficit for households containing children after divorce, we now wish to examine whether there are longer term economic difficulties for divorced parents with children, with the possibility of affecting the child's educational achievements and earning capacity. In England and Wales the law has given relatively little attention to the interests of children at the time of family breakdown . . . But although divorce in England has become easier . . . Nevertheless the legal interest in the child's position has remained residual, providing no more than a safety net . . . However . . . we are accumulating evidence to demonstrate that more systematic attention needs to be given to the long-term consequences for children of parental divorce. (Wadsworth and Maclean 1986: 146–7)

They went to reanalyse some of the data collected by the original 1946 cohort study, which in effect meant taking a very long-term perspective on the analysis. However, Wadsworth and Maclean argue that, given the now extensive evidence that children involved in parental divorce either as pre-schoolers or as dependent children all experienced social and emotional trauma, the analysis of children's resultant, wider life-chances is important. Specifically, they demonstrate that:

> . . . children of divorced or separated parents were significantly more likely than other children to have no educational qualifications by the age of 26 years, and to have a significantly reduced chance of getting qualifications at any level: this association was maintained regardless of the social class of the family at the time of the family break. By comparison parental death (these are mostly deaths of fathers) seems to have had very little impact on the child's later educational achievements, and may even have increased manual social class children's chances of going to university. An important protection against the damaging effect of a family break of this kind was found in family structure, in that the educational achievements of only children from broken homes were not significantly different from those of other only children. However, first born children with siblings, and second subsequently born children made significantly lower educational achievements if they had experienced broken homes. These associations of family circumstances with achieved level of education were statistically significant for both boys and girls. (1986: 151)

They also attempted to test whether other family changes, such as remarriage, may modify these significant effects on long-term educational achievements or social class positions. They did not find that remarriage restored children from broken homes to the same levels of education achieved by children from intact homes. However, they do also argue that it is not evident that *all* children from intact homes necessarily had a suitable environment to develop their capabilities.

They also note that children below the age of five involved in marital breakups were more likely than older children to have serious long-term consequences such as delinquency and involvement in crime. They make the significant point that 'high emotional disturbance was significantly associated with lower educational achievement' (p. 155), and then draw the more general conclusion that there is:

> . . . a chain effect in which childhood experience of parental divorce and separation reduces chances of educational achievement, both because of the emotional experience and the change in socio-economic circumstances, which in turn by age 36 years reduces income earning opportunities. (p. 156)

This conclusion in indeed strong but it is also rather general in its overall implications for educational successes and is only broadly linked to social class. Moreover, the changes in divorce rates, separation and wider patterns of family life have been so dramatic, largely amongst this age group of children *as adults* given that they were all born almost 50 years ago, that the links between emotional experience and educational achievements cannot be read off nearly so neatly. The situation is far more complex and requires a more complicated form of social analysis.

Nevertheless there are important issues to consider from within this kind of study. Maclean has also tried to consider the differential effects of parental divorce on boys and girls. In a subsequent analysis, Maclean this time with Kuh (1991), demonstrated the differential effects of parental divorce on boys' and girls' educational performance and economic life. They showed, in particular, that parental divorce seemed to have a more lasting effect on females than males and to last well into adulthood. Nevertheless, this study was also based on rather limited and sketchy, old data, which were not capable of a more in-depth investigation of the particular effects of family circumstances. Their main focus was on the effects on girls and women, on the presumption that they differed considerably from men's educational and economic life-chances.

Maclean and Kuh were keen to examine these issues because of the complexities in the family situations and the dearth of previous studies. Before presenting their own analysis of new data from an old cohort study, they looked at data from both US and UK studies. One significant piece of evidence they cited was from a Michigan Panel Study of Income Dynamics looking at

2,000 women, which found substantial evidence of post-divorce poverty for mother-headed families. They noted that McLanahan (1985) had found 'poor school attendance at 17 years, and low educational attainment in mother-only families associated with economic deprivation'. This also showed that lack of educational achievement was a major factor in the subsequent likelihood of experiencing poverty (Maclean and Kuh 1991: 163). Maclean and Kuh found a similar pattern for British women. They state:

> For women from non-manual origins, those from divorced families were over twice as likely to have no educational qualifications than those from intact famil- ies. Although this pattern of educational under-achievement was also present within the manual group for women from divorced families of origin, the associ- ation with parental divorce and death was weaker than for the other groups. The level of educational qualifications achieved by women was significantly higher for those from both . . . families of origin if their mothers had gone to secondary school themselves, but women from divorced families still had a significantly higher risk of leaving school with no educational qualifications even when the effects of mothers' education and father's social class, at the time of the child's birth, were taken into account. (p. 167)

They went on to demonstrate that, for women, educational and occupational achievements were closely associated with marriage and fertility patterns. Women from divorced non-manual families were found to be significantly more like than those from intact families to experience their own marital breakdown by the age of 36 years (p. 171). The complexity of these findings led Maclean and Kuh to conclude that, despite the fact that 'these data may now be of only historical interest', parental divorce leads to substantial long-term emotional and allied or associated socio-economic disadvantages, including especially educational under-achievement. In particular they end on this note:

> The increased stress shown by the women from higher socio-economic groups may well be due to the higher aspirations which they may have had, and their mothers may have had and to the greater gap between aspirations and achieve- ment at school, at work, and in family life. (1991: 177)

In other words, despite the complexity there was a clear pattern of associa- tions between parental divorce and subsequent life-chances for women in terms of family, education and their allied economic circumstances.

These findings in both the US and Britain are clearly of immense importance, particularly given the increases in divorce and complex family patterns, for educational provisions for girls more than for boys. Nevertheless, given the fact that such changes are now more normative and less stigmatised than in the past, the direct associations between emotional trauma and education and economic achievements may become more muted. Given the fact that these data are based on a sample of people who were relatively rare and who themselves were part of not only the family changes but also liberal social and educational reforms, the future patterns, based on families reaching maturity in the Thatcher years, may be very different.

The impact of family changes on children's type of education

These studies did not look at the impact of marital changes on parental participation or choices in education. However, there is also some evidence to suggest that families in particular divorce situations attempt to stem the potentially deleterious effects on children by trying to buy forms of private education. In particular, in Britain, private boarding school education has recently become not only the preserve of extremely wealthy families but also of those in the processes of family change (Walford, 1990). Some evidence for this was adduced by both Fox (1986) and Johnson (1987). It is certainly also part of the publicity developed by the Independent Schools Information Service (ISIS). In two major educational investigations recently evidence was collated to suggest that disproportionate numbers of families in non-traditional situations were involved in these schemes. Both studies focused upon new forms of private education in England and Wales. The first was the study by Edwards, Fitz and Whitty (1989) of the assisted places scheme, mentioned in previous chapters. This scheme was developed by the government, as noted in chapter 4, to provide financial help to poor parents of academically able children so that they could benefit from private, secondary schooling. The scheme aimed to provide financial help to families, setting the income limit at one related to male earnings. However, Edwards, Fitz and Whitty found that 40 per cent of the parents in their study were lone mothers, usually divorced or separated from their spouses. They also found that these mothers were not educationally disadvantaged but had been quite well-educated, many of them the beneficiaries of higher education. These mothers were, presumably, trying to obtain what they considered high educational standards for their children. Given the kind of study conducted – of the parents of children being selected for academic, secondary schooling – no evidence was collected of the ultimate educational achievements of the children. However, one indicator of educational success is the ability to be selected, at age 11, for an academic education. Hence there is, it seems, an association between parental, or rather maternal, familial status and educational performance, albeit that this is a particular case-study sample, rather than one drawn from the wider population. On the other hand, it is of far more recent data that the longitudinal studies by Maclean and others cited above.

Another case study, also of a new form of quasi-private schooling in England – this time of the creation of the first city technology college – also found an interesting and intriguing parental group. As noted in chapter 4, the CTCs were to be schools developed in inner-city areas with industrial and entrepreneurial sponsorship rather than public or governmental support. In discussing the social characteristics of the families at the school, Walford and Miller comment:

> The college does not keep records of the identities of adults who share the household with the student and guardian. Obviously it records the names and address of legal guardians, but it does not necessarily know the marital status of the guardian, or with whom the guardian is cohabiting. It would have been inappropriate to have asked the students about this, so it is not possible to given an accurate indication of the proportion of students in single-parent families. The Principal has estimated that about half of the students are no longer living with both natural parents, and the information gained through interviews does not contradict this estimate. (1991: 113)

So there is evidence to suggest that about half of this new school are living in non-traditional households, but in this case, however, the families seem to cross class lines. As Walford and Miller note:

> Without putting too much faith in the exact numbers, it is evident that only a very small percentage of adults are from social class I or II together. The vast majority of adults have skilled manual or non-manual occupations . . . it is certain that this first intake year . . . does not include a high proportion of middle class children as many commentators had predicted. (1991: 114–15)

However, it does seem to suggest that these parents, from a variety of circumstances, but largely non-traditional families, are choosing new forms of schooling, in the hopes of obtaining a better education for their children. From this study, too, it is impossible to link parental choice or background with children's educational performance, except insofar as these children, too, were selected from a wider pool of applicants for the school.

As far as I am aware, there has been no similar study of parents in other changed family circumstances. There are a number of studies of women who choose to have children in adolescence or early adulthood. There is, for example, a plethora of such American research. Two studies have been conducted fairly recently in England. One, by Sue Sharpe, entitled *Falling for Love*, (1986), is a study directed at young women and is therefore rather didactic in approach. Rather than looking at the links between early motherhood and their children's likely educational performance, it focuses, as noted in chapter 9, on educational opportunities foregone by the mothers themselves. By implication, however, from previous studies of mothers in educationally disadvantaged circumstances such as the study by Rockhill (1987a), it is likely that these disadvantages will be passed on to the children. Rockhill argues that

> ... to frame literacy in terms of equality of opportunity, rights, or empowerment
> is absurd in the face of a fist – or, less dramatically, in a gendered society where
> the conception of rights is alien to women who have been told all their lives that
> they must obey and care for others. (1987a: 165)

Having looked at the experiences of Hispanic women in relation to their families, husbands and children, she argues that they found themselves in

> ... a double bind: to act upon their desire for change requires a choice that few
> feel they can make – a choice between love, family, home and violent upheaval.
> However, violent the love they live may be, for most, the unknown of the latter is
> more threatening. (p. 166)

Rockhill did not provide substantive evidence but rather pondered the social and cultural context and experiences of such mothers in particularly
disadvantaged circumstances and communities. The possibilities of change,
through school and/or education, were quite simply not appropriate or on the
women's agendas, as they could not be. The study by Phoenix (1991) is a more
detailed and sophisticated analysis of young mothers. Nevertheless, Phoenix
does not explore the educational consequences for the children of young
motherhood. Again her focus was on the lives and circumstances and early
effects on such mothers. But she, too, points to the educational effects for the
mothers themselves. Hudson and Ineichen have also investigated issues to do
with teenage motherhood. They write:

> Disadvantaged children are those most often from homes run by parent(s)
> who are on welfare, unemployed, disabled or sick ... It is likely that parents in
> these circumstances are ill-equipped to show interest or encouragement in their
> children's attainment at school, and at age 11 such children show typically low
> scores on basic maths, reading and comprehension. These scores reflect social
> circumstances and not ability levels. If disadvantage continues up to puberty, it
> accumulates in adolescence and seriously impedes attainment thereafter (Wedge
> and Essen, 1982). Teenage parenthood is a possible outcome at this stage ...
> (1991: 158)

They also consider the evidence about the effects of teenage motherhood on
the children, including their education. They argue that contrary to most of the
usual evidence, children of young mothers may benefit from more than one
carer. Reviewing an American study of 400 children born to teenagers in the
1960s in Baltimore in the US by Furstenberg et al. (1987), they report that the
amount of time the adolescent mother spends with her child was inversely
related to the child's cognitive abilities. They summarise the evidence by saying
that 'the effects of poverty and deprivation on a teenage mother's child seem
to be ameliorated if child-rearing is shared with another adult' (Hudson and
Ineichen 1991: 156).

Hudson and Ineichen took as given that teenage motherhood was unusual or aberrant rather than the norm. Phoenix made the point that it was not necessarily so. Indeed, Rockhill's study of migrant workers in Los Angeles was of a group of women who all married in their teens, and had several children in rapid succession, since all were Catholics (1987a: 325). There have also been several other studies of young motherhood that do not necessarily regard it as deviant. However, when linked with illegitimacy, as it has been by critics of these family patterns, it has been viewed as aberrant, despite the fact that in Britain and the US births to unwed mothers are almost one-third of all births in 1990. Nevertheless, it is the attempt to associate these trends with social and educational disadvantages, ethnicity, unemployment and crime that raises the 'moral' side of the policy debate.

There is very little evidence of the educational consequences for children in families with histories of abuse or violence, whether physical or sexual, although Hudson and Ineichen point to abuse and violence as a problem for teenage mothers. Rockhill (1987a and b) also made it a common-place in the evidence of family lives of Hispanic women in Los Angeles. However, she points to how it prevented the mothers themselves from 'going to school' rather than looking to the longer-term consequences for their children, especially their daughters.

Given that this issue in only now being discussed cautiously in the public policy arena, it is perhaps not surprising that there is little evidence of a long-term kind about the relationships between families and schools in such circumstances. By implication, however, from official British reports such as the Butler-Sloss inquiry into child sexual abuse in Cleveland, N. Yorkshire (1989) and Campbell's account (1989), such family processes have disastrous consequences for children and their lives. However, the actual interventions in family life, which tend to focus on the victims rather than the perpetrators, may themselves add to an already problematic situation. The removal of children from family settings into care may further exacerbate the situation, with emotional and social and allied educational consequences.

There is some slender evidence that children who do not live in family households of any type at all, but who are 'in care', are likely to be educationally disadvantaged. Jackson (1990) recently conducted a small-scale study of the educational needs of children in care and found them to be disadvantaged and performing under par, compared with their counterparts in conventional families. An analysis by St Claire and Osborn (1987) of the data collected in the National Children's Bureau cohort study and the Child Health and Education Study also reached similar conclusions about the educational consequences for children separated from both their parents. Of course, the lack of participation of their parents in their education is also likely to have an effect which is significantly different from that of parents from more conventional homes. In both senses, then, children in care are not able to benefit from education in the conventional ways.

Effects of family circumstances on children's education

There is considerably more evidence of the effects of particular family circumstances in terms of forms of ethnicity or race on educational performance and success. We have already noted the evidence about black female-headed households in the US. By contrast, in Britain, little of the evidence considers the twin effects of race and family patterns or circumstances.

An early study by Coard (1971) alerted educationalists to the problems of school allocation of children of West Indian background. Evidence was collected to demonstrate that children from such family backgrounds were selected for special education on the basis of conjecture and stereotype rather than careful analysis. Since this study, there has been a massive amount of data collected both for official inquiries, particularly the Rampton and Swann committees, and for social scientific investigations. Most of this evidence has been best summarised by Tomlinson (1983, 1984, 1990). In a series of careful analyses she has shown the particular effects of racial or ethnic family backgrounds on educational performance. There are, in effect, clear differences in types of educational attainment and achievement between children from different types of Asian background, and from Afro-Caribbean backgrounds.

In addition, there are differences between boys and girls within and between these various family backgrounds. Fuller's account (1983) remains one of the clearest expositions of why Afro-Caribbean girls aim to achieve well, despite their critical appraisal of the educational process. She shows how critical educational qualifications were seen by the girls to be for their adult and family life, dependent as such young women assumed they would be on being economically independent. Brah (1988) and Riley (1988) have considered similar issues both between black and Asian girls and among Asian women.

The official inquiries, particularly the Swann report *Education for All*, (1985) did not focus especially on differential educational performance, although careful reviews of the previous studies were undertaken, as we saw in the previous chapter. It did consider whether the form of education – single-sex versus co-educational, or bilingual early childhood education – would have substantial effects on children's educational success and performance. However, despite the acknowledgement of Asian parents' wishes for such forms of education, the official recommendation was against such education on liberal and ostensibly equal opportunities grounds. For example, it was argued that such single-sex girls' secondary education especially among Muslims taught a 'way of life' and restricted girls to education for motherhood. No case was made, however, to demonstrate that comprehensive secondary education does more than promote motherhood as a pre-occupation rather than as occupation for young women (David 1988). In this instance, however, parental choice was not the determinant of the recommended form of education.

Similarly, at the level of primary or early childhood education, the Swann committee argued against the 'liberal' conventional wisdom of initiation into education in mother-tongue language. Indeed, it was claimed that such bilingualism would impede educational progress. Thus only bilingual resources, consisting of secondary-school girls doing child development courses, could assist the transition to school of such young pupils. It was apparently assumed that mothers' influence on educational progress was not paramount in this case (David 1988).

Despite this conclusion, the Child Health and Education Study, in an investigation of reading and maths at infant school, reached the conclusion that 'although West Indian children live in considerably worse social conditions than white British children their educational attainments are little affected by those conditions' (Brewer and Haslum 1986, quoted in Plewis 1987: 77). Plewis' reanalysis of these data (1987) for black (West Indian but not Asian) and white children together with his own data showed that similar relations for black and white children are dependent on their mothers' educational qualifications. Mothers are, then, crucial for their children's early educational attainments. However, the precise form of the relationship between disadvantage and educational attainment requires careful study. Hartley (1989) has argued, in a review of this work, that the situation is now more complex. He has argued that the notion of 'the home and the school' is a 'paradigm lost' (1989: 253). Toomey (1989) has also argued that mothers, rather than class, are crucial to children's scholastic achievements.

The recent study of American high schools by Chubb and Moe (1990) attempted to review, as we have noted before, the various causes of educational achievement or under-achievement among students. Curiously, they were forced to argue that:

> ... we found that black students learn neither more nor less than would be predicted of them based on their initial ability, family background and the ... qualities of their schools. In short, race – at least the black, non-black distinction – has no independent consequence at either the individual or school level for student achievement ... achievement is not affected by the sex of the student either. (1990: 127)

However, they did not fully consider issues of race together with family backgrounds as having effects on children's achievements. But they did consider separately the influences of mothers' educational and economic levels. Indeed they argued first that family income and gendered parental education was directly related to school performance but it was not a strong predictor of it (1990: 107). They also found, rather equivocally, that:

> Two-parent households are also less likely to burden children with the emotional repercussions of adult problems – divorce, abandonment, unwed motherhood –

that may impair concentration on schoolwork. Yet, whatever the advantages of two-parent households, they do not really stand out in the comparisons of high and low performance schools ... There is also reason to believe that children may benefit educationally from having their mothers in the home rather than in the work place ... Nevertheless, there is only a 2 per cent difference in the employ-ment rates of mothers in successful and unsuccessful schools. And the difference is not in the commonly expected direction. Mothers in successful schools are slightly more, not less, likely to work. (1990: 108)

In other words, one of the most recent reanalyses of educational achievement in the US by two rather 'conservative' social analysts has found that mothers' employment and family circumstances do not have deleterious consequences for the contemporary achievements of their children, whether sons or daughters, black or white. This finding is indeed important given the not inconsiderable previous evidence and rhetoric about these being critical factors in the long-term if not the short-term.

Smith and Tomlinson (1989) reached a similar conclusion from a British study of multiracial and multicultural secondary schools. In a nationwide inves-tigation of 20 schools, they demonstrated that despite major differences in family and ethnic circumstances schools can achieve similar effects. In other words, they concluded that the crucial variables in educational performance are not family and/or ethnic characteristics but school ethos, management and organisation. Thus schools can alter children's educational performance and success, although they may not break down fine educational differentiation. Nevertheless they argued that school is more critical than family for children's educational performance.

It may also be asked: what effects do these various changes in family circumstances have on parents' chances to participate in decision-making or to express a choice of school? Given the complexity of the family worlds it is impossible to summarise the range of effects. However, it is perhaps important to note that the complexity of women's lives as mothers, whether in paid employment, as lone or step-parents with complex custody arrangements, or as young mothers, makes involvement in the daily work of school extremely difficult. Epstein has argued on the basis of American research that:

Most parents cannot and do not participate at the school building ... The results from several studies also point to a clear need to more broadly define the term 'volunteer' to include and to recognize the work that parents do at the school building during the school day, after school, on weekends, at home, or in the community to support school programs and student success. Research is needed on the effects on families and on schools of these different types of volunteer participation. (Epstein 1990: 108)

Lareau has also reached similar conclusions from her review of the American evidence:

Many parents did influence their children's schooling . . . Although it is difficult to quantify the contribution that parents' interventions make to children's performance, for some children the impact is not trivial . . . Parents intervened in their children's schooling in important ways, some children profited from these interventions . . . Parents' performance was linked to their educational competence, their social confidence, the information they had about their children's schooling, their conception of parents' proper role in education and their children's classroom performance. These social resources forged a closer alignment between family life and school life for upper-middle-class families than for working class families . . . It was through social practices that parents transformed social resources into profits. (1989b: 145)

However, Lareau also points to what she calls 'the dark side of parent involvement', and the difficulties that result from changes in family-life patterns and forms of employment which may cause 'stress' between families and schools.

It is also difficult to summarise the effects on parental 'voice' or 'choice'. However, parental participation in decision-making may not be confined to natural and/or cohabiting parents. On the contrary, the term 'parent' may be legally defined to include a step-parent who resides with the child as well as both natural parents. This may, though, give some children a wider network of relatives on whom to call for an educational 'say' than in the traditional two-parent family. Nevertheless, in the British educational legislation for parent governors and the parental ballot the term 'parent' has been given a wide legal connotation. On the other hand, the ability of mothers in such circumstances to become involved in educational politics – as a parent governor, for instance – is incredibly restricted. Deem (1989), for example, has demonstrated the general difficulties for 'women parent governors' – mother governors – to be involved, on the basis of time, knowledge and inclination, as we noted in chapter 6. However, Golby (1989) pointed to the more effective role of mother governors than others in the 'New Order', as we also saw in chapter 6.

As regards parental choice, there is little systematic evidence of the effects of changing family circumstances on educational provision. However, although the studies referred to in chapter 7 did not look at the differential circumstances of parents, there is some case-study evidence to suggest differences. For example, there have been at least six different *causes célèbres* about such issues in the 1980s in Britain. Two such issues, both in Yorkshire – one in Dewsbury and one in Cleveland – centred on parents wishing to choose different schools for their children than the ones allocated at the secondary-school stage. In the case of Dewsbury in Kirkless in 1987, some parents objected because the allocated school was largely Asian and they preferred a predominantly white school. Rather than compromise, they educated their children in a 'pub' for almost a year with a retired private school ex-head teacher for tutor (Naylor 1989). In the event, they were eventually allowed the school of their choice, given changes in the legislation. In this case the ethnicity of the majority of parents at the allocated school was seen as a barrier to white children's educational success.

Similarly, in Middlesborough in Cleveland, the mother a mixed-race child objected to her daughter's allocation to a predominately Asian school. In the event, she also was given the school of her choice, adding to the apparent racism in this process of decision-making. However, a High Court decision eventually decided that parental choice of education was to be preferred to issues of apparent racial discrimination.

Some Sikh parents have received public support for their educational intervention:

> The leading case of the interpretation of 'ethnic origins' is that of *Mandla v Dowell Lee*. The issues was whether a Sikh father who wished his son to be able to wear a turban as a pupil in a private school was entitled to the law's protection against indirect discrimination. The House of Lords decided in his favour. The court held that for a group to constitute an 'ethnic group' for the purpose of the 1976 Act it had to regard itself, and be regarded by others, as a distinct community by virtue of certain characteristics . . . Gypsies and Rastafarians have since been held to be groups which made what are now called 'the Mandla Conditions'. (Banton 1991: 119)

In other words, parental choice is both complex and complicated by the variety and range of situations of families in different circumstances. What can be said is that despite the complexity there is a patterning to parental effects on children through the educational process, which remains linked to class, whether through gender or ethnicity.

Conclusions

We have discussed the various circumstances and changes in family life that have occurred over the last two or three decades in parallel with developments in educational policies. The strategic developments in education have been predicated, whether from a left or right political perspective, on notions of the importance of a close link between parents and their children's schooling. The main argument has been that this would lead to more effective education and educational performance of children. However, these arguments were not linked to the evidence about the impacts of family changes and patterns and circumstances. Indeed, different arguments were developed about how to cope with family changes independently of the educational strategies. The main thrust of these arguments, especially from the right, was about how to stem the tide of family changes on the assumption that they were necessarily 'bad', especially for children and community. We have reviewed the range of political debates both in the US and Britain about how to deal with these issues, especially those of the New Right.

However, the evidence that has been collected on the impacts and effects of a ranges of family circumstances and changes indicates that the situation is now so complex that 'historical' effects cannot necessarily be read off from old data to new circumstances. Nevertheless, there remains a patterning to some of the effects, such as that parental divorce or separation may have particular impacts for women's family and educational circumstances in their adulthood. Moreover, women in socially disadvantaged communities and from ethnic minority backgrounds may continue to pass their disadvantages on to their daughters. However, these effects are not necessarily entirely universal, and larger studies such as those of Chubb and Moe (1990) in the US and Smith and Tomlinson (1989) in Britain have found that school is far more important than family, race and/or ethnicity, or gender for school-based educational achievements.

What is clear is that family circumstances and family life are now so complex that the old 'verities' about families and education for children's life-chances cannot easily be adduced. Policies that take no account of such complexities may, as Lareau (1987, 1989a and b) has so well argued, reproduce old social class effects rather than develop a system that does not disadvantage 'new' social groups based on new patterns of family life, incorporating racial and/or mother-run households. It is, however, important that future research agendas attempt to consider the range and variety of these issues and their implications for policy.

11

Conclusions: Family Changes, Social Research and Education Reforms

Introduction

Given the contemporary public debates about families and schools, the aim of this book has been to consider the relations between parents and education, as they have been understood from the perspective of the social sciences. This has meant taking a rather circuitous journey through the history of the social sciences to understand the origins of this perspective. I have shown how the developments in social and educational reforms and the research on which they were based occurred together. I have presented this as a two-way process of interactions between policy-makers and the social sciences. My particular 'example' has been the relationships between families and education to illustrate the ways in which policy-makers or social reformers and social scientists, especially social researchers, have together developed strategies, reforms and the conceptual apparatus for understanding and evaluating them. I have wanted to show how a particular body of social scientific knowledge has been developed to understand and interpret these reforms.

This study of parents and education has been conducted in a particular set of contexts. First, I have used British social and educational reforms as the main focus, where possible drawing comparisons and contrasts with the United States, Canada, Australia and other advanced industrial societies in Europe such as Germany and France. Secondly, I have specifically chosen to focus on the period of social change and reforms from the Second World War to the present day. I believe this period is crucial for understanding the complex interplay between social and educational reforms and the developments in the social sciences. It is also a period in which there have been massive social and economic changes which have themselves influenced and been influenced by policy developments and social reforms.

My argument has been that a particular framework has been used by policy-makers and social scientists alike to inform and interpret social and educational reforms. This framework has tended to ignore, or not to make explicit, questions of gender or race. However, despite both the gender-neutral and race-neutral language, reforms and research have been constructed around gender and racial divisions. I have pinpointed how gender and race have been incorporated into strategic policy developments and yet have remained largely implicit in social scientific research.

More important, perhaps, is the fact that our understandings and our strategic policy developments and reforms, given this framework, have been and will remain narrow. They do not, and perhaps will not, take into account the full complexity of social and economic changes and their effects on men's and women's lives, inside and outside the family, and whether black or white. In other words, we can only fully understand both the past complex developments and their implications for the future if we adopt a critical perspective which includes gender and race. Looking to the future is, in any event, a hazardous process, given that we cannot predict either future knowledge or social and economic developments. However, without a wide remit, which takes into account gender and race questions, and sexual as well as social divisions, the picture will necessarily be incomplete. It will provide a scenario of social diversity, without patterns of gender and race. Some of the crucial social and economic changes have been around men's and women's roles and relationships in both private family life and public economic life.

Social-democratic reformers and researchers' perspectives on parents and education

In the immediate aftermath of the Second World War, 'liberal' or 'social-democratic' policy-makers and social scientists were together involved in creating a new social policy context and educational reforms. Their joint aim was to create an appropriate socio-economic system to ensure economic growth. This perspective entailed the greater involvement of the state in the provision of social and economic services, and supports to families and industry to enhance economic growth. To this end, social scientists were incorporated into the policy process to advise on and aid it. As a corollary, these social scientists began to reflect upon their involvements and develop an understanding of the social and educational policy process. A body of social scientific knowledge develop which was intimately associated with these policy reforms and yet remained analytically distinct. Banks (1955, 1975), for example, has shown most forcefully how the sociology of education was born in this context. Similarly, she has contributed to our understanding through her later work on family and gender.

Banks' own academic career illustrates the general argument. She began as a sociologist, at the LSE in the early 1950s, interested in the development of educational reforms from the turn of the century to the Second World War. She then turned her attention to a broader study of the sociology of education. Later in life, she adopted a more explicitly feminist perspective, considering the role that feminists had played in public arenas. Most recently, she tried to account for the role that feminists have played in the sociology of education, concluding that, although their perspectives have been vital for broadening our understanding of social and sexual divisions, they have remained, at best, marginal to the mainstream developments.

The perspective taken by social-democratic reformers and researchers alike was that the state should develop a particular partnership with families for the provision of social and economic services. This notion underpinned the array of public and social services known particularly in Britain as the welfare state. However, the partnership between state and families for the provision of social welfare was not confined to Britain, as we have already seen. It was also crucial to the development of public policies especially for education and social welfare in most advanced industrial societies, as Mishra (1984), amongst others, has argued. *Pace* the apparently unique development of the British welfare state on the Fabian model, this partnership between state intervention, families and socio-economic policies is relatively universal in advanced industrial societies.

It drew from a set of political ideologies social scientists both studied and developed. These ideas centred upon notions of the privacy of the family and, at the same time, the need for state services to ensure equality of opportunities in the public arena. In other words, there were two interlocking notions in social-democratic political ideologies: family privacy and equality of opportunity. Given their complexity, social scientists were called upon to aid strategies and reforms across the array of social, educational and economic services.

As we have seen, the partnership between social reformers and social researchers was particularly significant in respect of educational policies. However, the perspective was specific, to ensure economic growth by reducing social and economic barriers to social and occupational mobility. Educational policies were oriented to that goal. This has meant a particular perspective developed on our understanding of the relationships between parents and education.

The vast majority of the social scientific research, since these early origins, has been about the impact and effects of families, family roles and relationships, and family characteristics on education, educational progress, performance, attainment or achievements, rather than the other way round. We have learnt relatively little about the impact and effect of education and educational policies on families, their circumstances and characteristics, and family life. We know much less about what education does to different members of families than about what effects family socio-economic circumstances have on educational progress. However, as we have seen, in recent years, given a broader perspective, this latter kind of study has developed, especially by feminists such as Rockhill (1987), D. Smith (1987), and Walkerdine and Lucey (1989). Even so, it has not been particularly significant for strategic policy developments, but rather has been part of a more critical perspective in our social scientific knowledge.

The partnership between social-democratic reformers and researchers led to the development of a partnership between families and the state over education. Essentially this hinged on special roles for parents in relation to their children's education. In that respect, the term parent was and remained gender-neutral, despite the fact that in public policy rhetoric and in social scientific research the traditional family, with a clear sexual division of labour between parents, was paramount. In other words, gender-differentiated roles for parents as mothers or fathers were clearly expected and specified. Nevertheless, in the developing framework, they became gender-neutral. In the pre-war period in policy rhetoric and analysis such notions of parent and family had been more explicitly defined in gender terms (David 1985).

In the early post-war social-democratic period, the partnership between parents and education was clearly developed. As we have seen, social-democratic reformers and researchers implemented the goal of equality of educational opportunity by a variety of strategies to reduce parental privilege in access to educational provisions. First, that meant limiting the advantages of social class, defined in terms of parental socio-economic circumstances or home backgrounds. As a corollary, it also entailed expanding educational opportunities at various ages and stages, namely secondary and higher education, for children from working-class family backgrounds. However, early social scientific investigations of a broadly statistical kind tended to demonstrate the persistence of the effects of parental income or material circumstances on educational progress, performance or achievements. Indeed, despite the gradual sophistication of the social scientific tools of analysis *and* the deployment of more complex indicators of family and socio-economic circumstances, these effects have not yet been transformed. Moreover, strategic developments such as the expansion of years of schooling and opportunities for higher education do not appear to have modified very much the patterning of these processes.

Social and economic changes, such as the increasing complexity and diversification of the labour market and kinds of skilled manual and non-manual occupations, have also *not* had a major impact on the broad social class patterns in relation to education and families. These patterns, to some extent, have become more difficult to interpret, given policy changes and other parallel, and interrelated, familial changes. In other words, although there has been a continuation of broad, social class patterns in relation to educational and economic opportunities, these have been intersected by familial and other related socio-economic changes, such as women's roles, so that the patterns of class, gender and race are far more complex.

A second 'stage' in the developments by social-democratic reformers and researchers was to 'compensate' socially and economically disadvantaged children through educational provision, to enable them to compete on a par with children from more financially secure home backgrounds. This led social researchers to pursue a whole panoply of strategies to 'educate' such disadvantaged families. This eventually developed into schemes to develop 'home–school' relations or parental participation in education. Different strategies were proposed by social psychologists, sociologists and educational researchers, but all within the broad framework of trying to reduce the disadvantages of 'parental poverty' and the dissonance between home and school, on the premise that this would enhance educational performance. The vast majority of social and educational research, as we have seen, became oriented to developing or evaluating these notions about home–school relations and parental participation, both in concert with, and independently of, social-democratic reformers.

Some of the most theoretically and statistically sophisticated sociological research in and on education drew from these policy-oriented concepts. In particular, Bernstein's seminal work was born from an initial dialogue with social reformers. Similarly, the other social critiques grew out of an engagement with the more policy-related work of social-democratic reformers and researchers. The social sciences drew their strength from these kinds of critical engagements. Nevertheless, despite the increasingly complex and sophisticated social analysis that developed in this context, it did not include perspectives on race or gender. Curiously, although social research was framed within the social-democratic notions of equality of opportunity, this led only to more detail of social class, through indicators of parental socio-economic circumstances. It did not mean consideration of the gendered or racialised character of parenthood. It led into an engagement with the broader notions of equal opportunities for children, especially at school, on the basis not only of class, but also race and gender. But the complexity of inter-generational notions of equal opportunities was rarely, and is still barely, considered.

However, 'home–school' relations or parental participation in education as issues both for strategic development and for social research blossomed into a veritable industry. From individual parental involvement at home either in the pre-school or school years, or at school, engaged in general forms of child development or particular subjects – reading, writing and language, mathematics – a whole panoply of issues was reviewed and advocated. As we have already seen, various typologies of parental involvement were developed to take account of the range of strategies.

In the 1970s, such strategies became harnessed not only to issues about equal opportunities but also to broader notion of political participation to enhance local democratic or community control. It was in this respect that political scientists became engaged with the previous, more individualistic notions of social psychologists and sociologists. The diversification of social scientific research led to the differentiation of strategies. The idea of *participation* became more complex and took on the meaning of *political* involvement in decision-making processes through the interplay both within the social sciences and between social research and social reform. Beattie (1985) neatly analysed the notion of parental participation in education as a form of political concern either by government or political pressure groups and social movements. He compared and contrasted these strategic developments in four European countries.

By the late 1970s, the political consensus around social-democratic or liberal approaches to social welfare and reforms was beginning to break down in the public arena. Nevertheless, a strand of social research remained committed to the strategic development of ideas about parental participation, integrating both individualistic and political aspects. However, the balance in the relations between home and school began to shift in research from an emphasis on home and parents to that of schools and education. At the primary or elementary-school level, educators began to develop ideas about how to involve parents more closely in educational processes at home from the school. In other words, teachers' expectations about parental pedagogies have grown, influenced by the growing evidence of social and educational researchers (Lareau, 1989; Epstein 1990; Merttens and Vass 1991). At the secondary-school level, the key research theme has shifted to 'school effectiveness' from that of 'home improvement' to enhance educational performance. Nevertheless, in all these areas it is now taken as a given that 'good' home–school relations are a necessity for effective education.

There have been more subtle sleights of hand. The focus has moved from equality of opportunity, regardless of class, race or gender of the children, to effective schooling. In other words, it appears to have been accepted that schools cannot, in themselves and alone, change society or the social structure. The aims have therefore become more modest in the changed policy context – to ensure that schools, within the social and economic resource constraints, reach given standards. This kind of shift is most evident in the recent large-scale statistical analyses of schooling, namely those of Smith and Tomlinson for England and Wales (1989) and Chubb and Moe of the Brookings Institution in the US (1990). These more recent social research developments are rather different from those of the past. The close partnership with social reformers is not as evident and the social researchers have not been as influential on policy as hitherto.

Social researchers themselves have rather more diverse ambitions and no longer represent a homogeneous community of scholars. Smith and Tomlinson remain within the social-democratic research tradition, but given the changed policy context, they have put their emphasis on school-based, rather than national governmental, strategies. Chubb and Moe, although they conducted their study for the traditionally 'liberal' Brookings Institution, have moved away from that social-democratic tradition in their conclusions. They have opted for a radically 'liberal' set of proposals which diverge from any governmental strategy at all, towards a thoroughgoing market solution. However, their position remains relatively rare even among more 'conservative' or 'New Right' thinkers. For example, the Institute of Economic Affairs, bastion of the New Right in Britain, recently argued a similar theme to that of Chubb and Moe – how best to 'empower the parents' and 'break the schools monopoly' (Green 1991). Yet their analysis led them to advocate the relatively classic scheme of education vouchers, provided through state mechanisms. The editor, Green, carefully compared and contrasted the applicability of Chubb and Moe's analysis to the British situation, and concluded that it needed modification or an alternative to be appropriate to the British context (Green 1991: 12).

Despite the proliferation of social-democratic research, little of it has, in fact, demonstrated the significant impact or effectiveness of strategies for parental participation or involvement. Rather, the emphasis in the social-democratic researcher and reformer partnership has shifted from equality of opportunity in education or in economic life, to the more modest one of school effectiveness. Nevertheless, parental roles have been transformed in the process, albeit that this has not been shown to have a major impact upon social or sexual differentiation. Indeed, the persistence of class-based, or home-background, inequalities, has been the more remarkable given the plethora of strategies for parental participation from pre-school, through to higher, education. Connell et al.'s Australian research, using the most complex form of qualitative and quantitative analysis, is vital in this respect. If confirms the importance of parental 'cultural capital', including its impact on race and gender, for the continuation of patterns of social difference.

However, the burgeoning feminist social research has offered a critique of how social-democratic research into parental participation has reinforced particular forms of gendered parenthood. The effects of the social-democratic researcher and reformer partnership may not have been achieved in terms of educational outcomes for children but they have resulted in changes, especially for mothers. Mothers of dependent children, especially those in early childhood, have, as we have seen, been expected to play increasing 'educational' roles with respect to their children, both at home and at school. They have had to prepare their children for the rigours of school; to aid their early educational development such as learning to read. They have been expected to contribute widely, and in diverse circumstances, to their children's schooling – financially, as volunteers, as 'teachers', and so on.

This has not necessarily altered the class-based effects of schooling, as both feminists and more traditional social researchers have noted (Walkerdine and Lucey 1989; Lareau 1989). It has, however, altered mothers' roles in a class context. It may even have made the relationships between mothers, and mothers and teachers, more difficult, given that some mothers have come to be expected to regulate other mothers (Manicom 1984; David 1985; Walkerdine and Lucey 1989). In other words, mothers' roles have become more heavily circumscribed through the strategies recommended by social researchers in partnership with social-democratic reformers. Although mainly modelled on the notion of middle-class mothers' 'invisible pedagogies', as Bernstein (1974) named them, the strategies – especially those of parent education – have required tremendous work and the foregoing of other opportunities for mothers' successful accomplishment of them. We have little proof of the differential effects of 'maternal pedagogies' on children's educational outcomes in either the short or longer term. Rather the evidence, such as it is, points to the effects on mothers' lives.

There is evidence from Germany (Ulich 1989) that they have made family life in general, and for mothers in particular, more stressful. Edwards (1991) has shown how the effects have influenced mothers' strategies to enter higher education to provide better for their children both economically and financially. On the other hand, others (Rockhill 1987a and b; Lawson 1990) have argued that mothers' involvement in education, even for the sake of the children, may have disastrous consequences on their own marital and/or family lives. The consequences of these strategic developments, despite the close relationships between social researchers and reformers have not, then, been in the expected direction of achieving equal opportunities for children or parents.

Right-wing reformers and social researchers' perspectives on parents and education

The transformation of the policy context to a more right-wing one led to parallel and revised forms of social research. In particular, the New Right's political ideologies of *freedom* and *choice*, especially with respect to parents and education, influenced a different research agenda. Indeed, the right-wing educational reformers developed close associations, on the whole, with different social scientists from those in the social-democratic tradition. For the most part, social scientific researchers such as psychologists, social administrators and sociologists developed critical evaluations of strategic developments, including those from within a given system of bureaucracy (Kelly 1987). In some curious way, this social-democratic research became more clearly tied to policy analysis than hitherto when more broad-ranging statistical or theoretical analyses had developed.

Another set of social scientists, more usually economists, philosophers or political scientists, began to contribute to strategic developments for right-wing reformers. They were concerned to aid the policy process through their involvement as social researchers. In the US, however, the shifting policy context was partly attributable to the changed role that some social scientists themselves chose to play. For example, many prominent 'liberal' or left-wing sociologists of 1960s and 1970s changed their allegiances and became neo-conservatives, advocating new social and economic strategies (Glazer 1975; Coleman et al. 1977). They were closely involved in the process of political transformation, insofar as it was based upon social scientific appraisal. Moynihan, Glazer and Coleman were prominent social scientists who had contributed to the liberal-democratic policy developments of the 1960s, and who, in the 1970s, moved to the right, providing cogent strategies for a Republican administration, especially in terms of education. Coleman, for instance, was famous amongst those advocating family choice in education, particularly in terms of the system of vouchers (Coleman et al. 1977). He had previously been the advocate of schemes to provide equality of educational opportunity, through 'compensatory education', educational equity programmes and racial integration.

The keynote strategy of right-wing reformers was 'choice' in education, making parents the consumers of education in a marketplace, and/or the guardians of educational standards, rather than these being the professional educators. As we have seen, these strategies were devised in conjunction with social researchers. However, the rationale for such policy developments was no longer equality of educational opportunity or educational equity but rather the maintenance of educational standards, through parental demands in the educational marketplace and the 'empowerment of parents'. These implied a changed balance between social researchers and reformers, as well as in the very evidence on which the arguments were based. Indeed, the evidence about the effectiveness of the strategies did not weigh heavily in the development of the policies. Rather, philosophical principles, centring on parental rights rather than social equity, began to dominate the debates and influence educational research (Macleod, ed. 1989).

The right-wing perspective influenced the kinds of role expected of gendered parents in education. However, the rhetoric relied again on gender-neutral language, but beneath that lay the traditional notion of the family of two natural parents, with dependent children, in which the man is breadwinner and the woman home-maker and housewife. In that respect, freedom of choice has less meaning for the housewife/mother than for the breadwinner father. However, there is a dearth of literature in this area compared to that on previous issues, despite the enormous fanfare of publicity about the importance of choice for the family. Social critics have not been particularly to the forefront in demonstrating the implications of these particular strategies for social and sexual differentiation. To the extent that they add to the pre-existing social and sexual inequalities, they do not alter the pattern of effects of the classic influence of home or family background on educational success. However, the shift in political ideology is such that social and sexual diversity and difference are now celebrated rather than being a cause for concern. Any supportive public policy research would seek to demonstrate effectiveness in terms of social and sexual differentiation among families, rather than its reduction. In other words, social and sexual inequality is regarded as a spur to economic advancement rather than the reason for careful evaluation of ways to reduce it.

The changing social and economic context

During the social-democratic period of educational and social reform there were also economic policy changes and developments. As we have argued, the social-democratic strategy was of economic growth through state intervention in economic and social life, with a particular partnership with private families. In fact, the evidence indicates that economic and social changes did result from these early strategies. In particular, the labour market expanded and became increasingly diversified, especially with respect to types of service and non-manual occupations. The study by Halsey, Heath and Ridge (1980) carefully documented these kinds of changes in Britain, with regard to the role played by the expansion of educational opportunities for boys in access to a transformed labor market. Similar accounts have been presented for the US (Jencks et al. 1972; Bowles and Gintis 1976), and Australia (Connell et al. 1982). These studies tended to be relatively traditional and did not focus on the trans-formations with respect to race or gender, especially not with regard to women's opportunities for paid employment.

Other authors have indicated the impact of social democracy on labour-market opportunities and broader issues of economic life, especially form the point of view of blacks and/or women. By the late 1960s and early 1970s, it had become commonplace to note the transformations in economic life and women's involvement in the labour market. In Britain, moreover, there was also a conventional wisdom about economic opportunities for black immigrants (Miles and Phizacklea 1978).

The partnership between social reformers and social-democratic researchers was not confined to educational strategies alone. It influenced much broader social and economic strategic developments, encompassing a whole area of public and social policies, from education to social services, especially for children, to income maintenance strategies, especially for families, to economic policies, including support for industry. It also influenced the ways in which social scientists construed these developments and their significance. Analysis of the effectiveness of strategies also remained within these parameters, namely issues about the expansion of social and economic opportunities. As we have already argued, the evidence from within this respective tended to indicate a continuation rather than reversal of traditional patterns, albeit complicated by social and economic restructuring. Concern about family poverty, for instance, as the mainstay of social-democratic research, remained within these given parameters, rather than opening up to debate broader questions about the characteristics of the family, in terms of gender and race.

However, critical perspectives did develop, as Williams (1989) has cogently pointed out. On the one hand, they pointed to the limited effectiveness of social-democratic strategies. On the other, they provided a broader framework for the analysis of such strategic developments, incorporating race and gender perspectives. They tended not to pinpoint the crucial issue of the partnership between families and education and the impact of strategic developments on economic and social life from the point of view of blacks and women.

A third strand, however, was that of the development of a critical feminist perspective, which pointed to the lack of attention to gender and race. It began also to highlight the ineffectiveness of social-democratic strategies with respect especially to women's opportunities outside the home, in public and/or economic life. This perspective touched on girls' opportunities in school and in education, but did not, at the same time, address the inter-relationships with their mothers' lives.

Despite the growth of social scientific research, little attention was paid to family changes, in particular mothers' roles within a changed family as well as employment context. These issues remained marginal. A clear and coherent study of women's position in public and private life developed, which paid attention more significantly to issues within the privacy of the family and the broader questions of the relationships between the sexes in public life – politics, employment, social and economic services. These approaches documented changes in family life, especially with respect to women's family and employment opportunities. Such social researchers also developed prescriptions for changes such as childcare, equal employment and educational opportunities, and family rights with respect to marriage, divorce and birth control. A complex interplay between feminist social researchers and social reformers resulted. Again, policies on equal pay and employment, changes in divorce and family maintenance were strategies that developed. Effectiveness remained a much more complicated issue to measure and account for. Inevitably, differing social and political ideologies focused on different kinds of effectiveness.

A fourth critical perspective that developed was that of the New Right. This perspective argued not only that social-democratic strategies had not been effective in their own terms, not achieving economic growth as had been expected, but also that they had led to increased bureaucracy at the expense of individual freedom and choice, and that therefore they inhibited economic development. The whole panoply of social-democratic strategies, based upon the principles of equality of opportunity and the practice of a particular partnership between state and families, as well as social reformers and social researchers, was called into question. Most important were the ways in which social-democratic strategies inhibited the free play of market forces, the development of individual

freedom of choice, the pursuit of educational excellence. In other words, families were denied opportunities to pursue their own ends by the bureaucratic
stifling and inhibiting of individual initiative. These kinds of arguments and the
allied evidence of economists and social researchers contributed to the shifting
policy context.

The contemporary socio-economic context and family life changes

By the late 1970s and the demise of social democracy as the dominant political
ideology, the nature of social, economic and family life had been transformed
dramatically from its origins in the aftermath of the Second World War. Our
understandings had also been transformed. Nevertheless, there are some key
features of these that are worth mentioning. First, the state had become
increasingly involved in providing social and economic services, which in some
respects took the form of the regulation of family life. Second, family life,
particularly from the perspective of women, had become, on the whole, more
diverse. For example, there were greater chances for women as mothers to be
involved in forms of paid employment as well as, and at the same time as, being
home-makers, mothers and carers of husbands and children. Equally important,
there was greater likelihood of women as mothers being involved in a range of
family and marital situations, from being lone (and/or separated or single)
parents, to being divorced, remarried or cohabiting parents, to being teenage
parents or widowed mothers.

Third, the range of social and economic supports provided by the state bore
with them particular expectations of standards of parental behaviour and role
with respect to children. Parents were given more clearly defined responsibilities with linked social and economic sanctions, through policy, law, the
courts. This was especially the case with respect to childcare responsibilities. It
was also true that these parental responsibilities were increased through the
system of education, particularly the developments in home–school relations.

As a corollary, as Donzelot (1987), among others, has argued, there had
developed a range of professional and state services and employees to regulate
these parental responsibilities. At the same time as the growth in such activities,
there was the concomitant blossoming of service and professional positions
– teachers, social workers, lawyers, professional educators – to manage and
regulate these services. As part of the expansion of women's employment
opportunities, these service occupations became available to women, even
themselves as mothers. Women, for instance, form the majority of teachers,
especially in early childhood and primary education; of social workers; of
nursery and childcare workers. Most of them are mothers, often of dependent
children. In that respect, relations between 'professional' mothers and 'amateur'
mothers have become increasingly complex.

The state has also encouraged women, especially those with dependent children, into the labor force or the further-and higher-education system as a prelude to paid employment to ensure a sufficiently large labour force to cater for the needs of the dependent population. Given changing demographic trends, especially in terms of family formation and increases in average life expectancy, governments in the 1980s have become concerned about the balance between the labor force and dependent children, handicapped and elderly people. It has been recognised that, as a result of previous socio-economic and familial changes, the balance may have tipped too far away from a strong and regular labor force. These 'problems' may also have been exacerbated by governmental policies to privatise and remove an economic infra-structure of social supports. Whatever the reasons, mothers' economic and social lives have been altering dramatically. Women now also form the majority in certain forms of higher education, especially as mature women students, and with dependent children. They also form the majority of the students on courses of access to higher education.

At the same time, a majority of women as mothers are not conventional 'home-makers' in the traditional sense. They are involved in education as students, as mothers of school-children in terms of unpaid volunteer activities or as helpers as paid and professional teachers or educators, as political activists, such as mother-governors, school board trustees or managers of schools. They may be involved in one or more of these kinds of activity at the same time.

Given right-wing policies towards more family and parental choice, and yet more involvement through required home–school relations and information, as well as volunteer and 'political' activities especially in decision-making, what are the effects in this context likely to be?

It is clear that there is already far more social and sexual diversity in terms of family and economic life than in the past. The lives of women as mothers of dependent children are far more diverse than appeared to be the case at the end of the Second World War. As a corollary, children by the age of 16 may have been involved in a diversity of social and familial situations, having experienced parental divorce, separation, or lone parenthood, cohabiting or remarried parents, and maternal employment. They may also have acquired new and varied siblings and relatives or wider kin. Many may also have experienced a variety of forms of care, including neglect, abuse or violence, as well as the more usually discussed adequate parental care.

Given that there is already tremendous social and sexual diversity and difference, rather than socio-economic equality, and that right-wing governments aim to encourage further familial and socio-economic diversity as a spur to economic advancement, it can be extrapolated that social and economic differences between families will continue. Even right-wing commentators such as Murray (1990) or Green (ed. 1991) have already noticed how difficult it has been for governments to stem the trends towards family change in terms of lone and/or single and young parenthood. They have advocated less, rather than more, governmental intervention, seeing it as interference rather that support. In that context, socio-economic diversity will surely increase rather than lead to a halt in these trends. Non-action by government, punitive though it may be intended to be, could not in fact stop the trends. Interestingly, of course, these right-wing social commentators also separately advocate family choice to increase educational diversity while appearing not to condone particular family choices of lone parenthood (Quest 1992).

Given these trends, which have continued unabated for two decades, despite competing political strategies to stem family-life changes (especially in forms of lone parenthood), mothers' responsibilities for children, their care and education, must increase. They are already poised to increase, at least as parental duties, given the moves towards a stronger home–school partnership, with greater parental political roles in educational decision-making, e.g. as parent governors or through choice of school. In Britain, the Education (Schools) Act of 1992, giving legal effect to the Citizen's Charter as a Parent's Charter, adds flesh to this. This must inevitably lead not only to a bifurcation between families on the basis of the traditional patterns of social class, but also between and within social classes on the basis of types of parenthood – lone or 'natural', two-parent, divorced, separated, widowed, cohabiting, etc. Although the scant evidence indicates that social class patterns continue to be most marked, within those patterns differences between types of mother-run families must be accentuated. If current trends, and current right-wing policies, continue up to the year 2,000, social and sexual differences will clearly be exacerbated rather than eroded.

The import of these trends in family and educational life may, however, be somewhat less significant than that hailed by right-wing commentators fearing for the future, especially in terms of traditional family morality. The evidence, also scanty, that has so far been collected on the effects of parental divorce and lone parenthood on children's educational performances and achievements has not been unequivocal. Most of it has been about the long-term effects on men and women in relation to economic rather than educational achievements. Of course, there is a clear correlation between educational attainment and economic success, but it has never been shown to be as unequivocal as suggested. Indeed, Jencks and his co-authors (1972) were castigated for pouring cynicism on these close effects, arguing that the associations were based more on serendipity than policy. Jencks' argument pertained to the overarching effects of family and social class, rather than within family situations on educational success. Given his careful analysis, it is unlikely that he would have found more sustained effects for children of parental divorce. Bowles and Gintis' reanalysis of the Jencks data showed mainly a class-based pattern to the effects.

What has been seen as more important is whether such trends in family life contribute to the erosion of social and sexual equality in subsequent generations. Murray (1990) and others have argued that they lead to particular forms of criminal activity, especially among juveniles, given that mothers of illegitimate children do not adequately care for or socialise them. Murray's prognosis may be more of a moralistic than analytical position. As we have already argued, there are logical and statistical flaws to the argument that do not bear detailed scrutiny. Inadvertently he, among others, draws attention to the gendered nature of these issues, although he does not render them problematic. Young women's behaviour in producing illegitimate children is, in his eyes, one source of the problem. The other unconnected 'problem' from his point of view is indolence, unemployment and juvenile crime, almost invariably committed by young men. His solution is to isolate these groups both physically and through lack of government support, in the hope of stemming the tide.

A more optimistic solution comes from a more sophisticated feminist analysis, which has been developed and applied to some extent in countries of Europe, such as Sweden, Denmark, Holland and France. It is to develop forms of state social and economic supports for parents and children, from maternity or paternity leave and entitlements to public childcare and parental leave for the care of sick children (Melhuish and Moss, eds 1991). These have been provided regardless of parental circumstance or gender and aim to provide social support for a variety of forms of family life. Even more imaginative schemes of community development in terms of time for paid employment and family care are developing in Italy (Saraceno 1991; Sassoon 1991). In these respects changes in family life and circumstances are accepted as irreversible givens, which may not destroy the fabric of social life, but rather may contribute to an interesting new tapestry of social and economic life, valued for its challenges, rather than penalised for its paucity.

Families, social change and social science

In the preceding sections, I have tried to illustrate the complex interplay in our understandings of parents and education of social reforms, social changes and the social sciences. I have argued that what we know of the relations between parents and education can only be understood through particular perspectives. I have also shown that our knowledge developed in a particular way, through the application of the social sciences in a changing policy context. It was with the development of a partnership between social-democratic reformers and researchers that a partnership between parents and education was elaborated. There was an intimate interrelationship between the two partnerships. The social-democratic reformer–researcher partnership also influenced the growth and extent of social and family-life changes and our understandings of them.

These perspectives initially excluded any questioning of the nature of the private family or family life. The social and educational reforms introduced by professional educators, social scientists and reformers, were all predicated on the importance of professional expertise. Moreover, the need to educate families to conform became part and parcel of these developments.

These perspectives also ignored issues of race or gender and the understanding of the significance or import of these matters. However, some of the social and educational changes bore crucially on women's lives and those of minority ethnic groups. Although never part of what Eichler (1986) called the 'business-as-usual' paradigm in the social sciences, new non-sexist or feminist perspectives grew out of social movements to understand these changes. Such critical perspectives were fundamental to a broader understanding of the extent of social, economic and familial transformations in the era of social democracy.

They have also been important to our understanding of the right-wing policy changes often dubbed the 'new era'. Despite their importance, feminist and critical perspectives remain marginal to our understanding of right-wing approaches to social and educational reform. This means that, in the policy arena, we only have a partial understanding of the dynamics of family and social change, and social and educational reform. Without the incorporation of such critical perspectives into the mainstream of policy analysis, our understanding of the dynamics of the partnership of parents and education will remain partial. We will not have a full possibility of interpreting the effects on family and economic life, or the reverse. In that framework, it will be possible to add to the responsibilities of motherhood, with its attendant social and economic implications, without understanding the range of social and sexual consequences. Nor will mothers' experiences of their roles as parents, in the family and in the public world, be incorporated into a broader perspective.

Parents and education are indeed central issues on the public agenda, both in concert and in tandem. Given the ways in which the social sciences have developed and been incorporated into the public policy arena, these two will remain partial questions until such time as gender is also included explicitly on the agenda.

Bibliography

Abel-Smith, B. and Townsend, P. (1965): *The Poor and the Poorest*. London: Bell.

Acland, H. (1972): Streaming in British junior schools. Cambridge, Mass.: Harvard Center for Educational Research.

Adler, M., Petch, A. and Tweedie, J. (1989): *Parental Choice and Educational Policy*. Edinburgh: Edinburgh University Press.

Altbach, P. (1985): The great education 'crisis': In P. Altbach, G. Kelly and L. Weis (eds) (1985).

Altbach, P., Kelly, G. and Weis, L. (eds) (1985): *Excellence in Education: Perspectives on Political Practice*. Buffalo, NY: Prometheus Books.

Altschuler, A. (1967): *Community Control: The Black Demand for Participation in Large Cities*. New York: Pegasus.

Anderson, B. (1989): The gender dimension of home – school relations. In F. Macleod (ed.) (1989).

Anderson, D. (1991): Plenary address to the *Social Policy Association Annual Conference*. Nottingham University, 7–9 July.

Anderson, D. and Dawson, G. (eds) (1986): *Family Portraits*. London: Social Affairs Unit.

Apple, M. (1979): *Ideology and the Curriculum*. London: Routledge and Kegan Paul (2nd edition, 1990).

—— (1982): *Education and Power*. Boston: Routledge and Kegan Paul.

—— (ed.) (1982) *Cultural and Economic Reproduction in Education: Essays on Class, Ideology and the State*. London: Routledge and Kegan Paul.

Arnot, M. and Weiner, G. (eds) (1987): *Gender and the Politics of Schooling*. London: Hutchinson.

Arnove, R. F., Altbach, P. G. and Kelly, G. (eds) (1992): *Emergent Issues in Education: Comparative Perspectives*. Albany, NY: State University of New York Press.

Arnstein, S. (1969): A ladder of citizen participation. *Journal of American Institute of Town Planners*, July.

Aronowitz, S. and Giroux, H. (1986): *Education Under Siege: The Conservative, Liberal and Radical Debate over Schooling*. London: Routledge and Kegan Paul.

Ashworth, J., Papps, I. and Thomas, B. (1988): *Increased Parental Choice: An Economic Analysis of Some Alternative Methods of Management and Finance of Education* London: Institute of Economic Affairs.

Atkin, J., Bastiani, J. with Goode, J. (1988): *Listening to Parents: An Approach to the Improvement of Home–School Relations*. London: Croom Helm.

Atkin, J. and Goode, J. (1982): Learning at home and at school: *Education*, 3–13, 10, 17–70.

Backett, K. (1982): *Mothers and Fathers: A Study of the Development and Negotiation of Parental Behaviour*. London: Macmillan.

Bacon, W. (1978): *Public Accountability and the Schooling System*. London: Harper and Row.

Balbo, L. (1987): Crazy quilts. In A. S. Sassoon (ed.) (1987).

Ball, S. (1990a): *Politics and Policy Making in Education*. London: Routledge and Kegan Paul.

—— (1990b): *Education, Inequality and School Reform: Values in Crisis*. Inaugural Lecture. London: King's College, 15 October.

—— (1991): *Markets, Morality and Equality*. Hilcole Group Papers No. 5, London: Tufnell Press.

Banks, O. (1955): *Parity and Prestige in Secondary Education*. London: Routledge and Kegan Paul.

—— (1976): *The Sociology of Education*. London: Batsford.

—— (1982): Sociology of education. In Cohen L., et al. (eds), *Educational Research and Development in Britain 1970–80*, Windsor: NFER.

Banton, M. (1991): The race relations problematic. *British Journal of Sociology*, 42/1: 115–30.

Barrett, M. and MacIntosh, M. (1982): *The Anti-Social Family*. London: New Left Books. (Second Edition 1991).

Barton, L. and Tomlinson, S. (eds) (1981): *Special Education: Policy, Practices and Social Issues*. London: Harper and Row.

—— (1983): *Special Education and Social Interests*. London: Croom Helm.

Bash, L. and Coulby, D. (1989): *The Education Reform Act: Competition and Control*. London: Cassell.

Bastiani, J. (1986): *Your Home-School Links*. London: New Education Press.

—— (ed) (1987): *Parents and Teachers, Vol. 1: Perspectives on Home–School Relations*. Windsor: NFER-Nelson.

—— (ed) (1988): *Parents and Teachers, Vol. 2: From Policy to Practice*. Windsor: NFER-Nelson.

—— (1989): *Working with Parents: A Whole School Approach*. Windsor: NFER-Nelson.

—— (1991): Home–school contract: a moving target? In *Home–School Contract of Partnership*, Newsletter 2, Spring.

Beattie, N. (1985): *Professional Parents: Parent Participation in Four West European Countries*. London: The Falmer Press.

Benn, C. and Simon, B. (1971): *Half Way There: Report on the British Comprehensive School Reform*. Harmondsworth: Penguin.

Berger, B. and Berger, P. (1984): *The War over the Family: Capturing the Middle Ground*. Harmondsworth: Penguin.

Bernardes, J. (1985a): Family ideology. *Sociological Review* 33/2: 275–97.

—— (1985b): Do we really know what 'the family' is? In P. Close and R. Collins (eds), *Family and Economy*, London: Macmillan.

—— (1987): Doing things with words: sociology and 'family policy' debates. *Sociological Review*, 35/4: 679–702.

—— (1988): Founding the *new* family studies. *Sociological Review* 36/1: 57–86.

Bernstein, B. (1968): Education cannot compensate for society. *New Society*.

—— (1971): *Class, Codes and Control, Vol. 1: Theoretical Studies Towards a Sociology of Language*. London: Routledge and Kegan Paul.

—— (1973): *Class, Codes, and Control, Vol. 2: Applied Studies Towards a Sociology of Language*. London: Routledge and Kegan Paul.

—— (1975): *Class, Codes and Control: Vol. 3: Towards a Theory of Educational Transmissions*. London: Routledge and Kegan Paul.

—— (1977): *Class, Codes and Control, Vol. 4*. London: Routledge and Kegan Paul.

—— (1990): *The Structuring of Pedagogic Discourse*. London: Routledge and Kegan Paul.

Berube, M. R. and Gittell, M. (eds) (1969): *Confrontation at Ocean Hill-Brownsville*. New York: Praeger.

Best, R. (1983): *We've All got Scars Now*. Bloomington: Indiana University Press.

Beveridge, Sir W. (1942): *Social Insurance and Allied Services, Cmd 6404*. London: HMSO.

Blackstone, Baroness T. (1990): Interview on Radio 4, Today Programme, 15 November.

Bloom, W. (1987): *Partnership with Parents in Reading*. London: Hodder and Stoughton.

Boudon, R. (1974): *Education, Opportunity and Social Inequality: Changing Prospects in Western Society*. New York: Wiley.

Bourdieu, P. (1974): The school as a conservative force: Scholastic and cultural inequalities. In J. Eggleston (ed.), *Contemporary Research in the Sociology of Education*, London: Methuen.

—— (1977): *Outline of a Theory of Practice*. Cambridge: Cambridge University Press.

Bourdieu, P. and Passerow, J. C., trans. R. Nice (1977): *Reproduction in Education, Society and Culture*. London: Sage.

Bowe, R. and Ball, S. (1992): *Reforming Education and Changing Schools.* London: Routledge and Kegan Paul.

Bowles, S. and Gintis, H. (1976): *Schooling in Capitalist America.* London: Routledge and Kegan Paul.

Boyd, W. (1991): Some parallels between British and US education reforms. SIPS Seminar, Centre for Educational Studies, King's College, London University, 1 February.

Boyson, R. (ed.) (1972): *Education: Threatened Standards.* Enfield: Churchill.

Bradshaw, J. (1989): *Lone Parents: Policy in the Doldrums.* London: Family Policy Studies Centre.

Bradshaw, J. and Millar, J. (1991): *Lone Parent Families in the UK.* London: HMSO.

Brah, A. (1988): Black struggles, equality and education. *Critical Social Policy*, 24: 83–90.

Brannen, J. and Moss. P. (1988): *New Mothers at Work: Employment and Child Care.* London: Unwin Hyman.

—— (1990): *Managing Mothers: Dual Earner Households After Maternity Leave.* London: Unwin Hyman.

Brehony, K. J. and Deem, R. (1990a): Charging for free education: an exploration of a debate in school governing bodies. *Journal of Education Policy*, 5: 333–47.

—— (1990b) The legitimation of education reform – the role of school governors. Paper given to the International Sociological Association Conference, Madrid, July.

—— (1992): The participating citizenry: a comparative view from education. Paper presented to the British Sociological Association Conference, University of Kent, April.

Brown, A. (1991): Participation, dialogue and the reproduction of social inequalities. In R. Merttens and G. Vass (eds), *Ruling the Margins: Issues in Parental Involvement*, London: The Falmer Press.

Brown, P. (1990): The 'third wave': education and the ideology of parentocracy. *British Jornal of the Sociology of Education*, 11/1; 65–85.

Brown, P. and Lauder, H. (eds) (1991): *Education for Survival.* London: Routledge and Kegan Paul.

Bruner, J. (1980): *Under Five in Britain.* London: Grant McIntyre.

Bull, D. (1980a): School admissions: a new appeals procedure. *Journal of Social Welfare Law*, 10/4 pp. 209–33.

—— (1980b): *What Price 'Free' Education? London: CPAG.*

—— (1985): Monitoring education appeals: local ombudsmen lead the way. *Journal of Social Welfare Law*, 15/4 pp. 184–226.

Bull, D. and Glendenning, C. (1983): Access to 'free' education: erosion by statute and stealth. In D. Bull and P. Wilding (eds), *Thatcherism and the Poor*, London: CPAG.

Bunzel, J. (ed.) (1985): *Challenges to America's Schools*. Oxford: Oxford University Press.

Burke, V. and Burke, V. (1974): *Nixon's Good Deed*. New York: Columbia University Press.

Butler-Sloss, Lord Justice C. (1988): *Report of the Inquiry into Child Abuse in Cleveland 1987*. London: HMSO, Cm. 412.

Campbell, B. (1989): *Unofficial Secrets*. London: Virago.

Castelain-Meunier, C. and Fagnini, J. (1991): Beyond contradictions: family and professional strategies of highly educated women in France. Paper presented to the European Feminist Research Conference, University of Aalborg, Denmark, 18–22 August.

Centre for Contemporary Cultural Studies (CCCS), (1981): *Unpopular Education*. London Hutchinson.

Centre for Educational Research and Innovation (CERI) (1983): *Caring for Children*. Paris: OECD.

Chubb, J. and Moe, T. (1990): *Politics, Markets and America's Schools*. Washington, DC: Brookings Institution.

—— (1992): Special issue: The classroom revolution: how to get the best from Britain's schools. In *Sunday Times* magazine, 9 February, pp. 18–36.

Clark, P. and Astuto, T. A. (1989): The disjunction of federal education policy and educational needs in the 1990s. In D. Mitchell and M. Goertz (eds) (1989).

Coard, B. (1971): *How the West Indian Child is made Educationally Subnormal in the British School System*. London: New Beacon.

Cohen, B. (1988): *Caring for Children: Services and Policies for Child Care and Equal Opportunities in the United Kingdom*. London: Commission of European Communities.

Coldron, J. and Boulton, P. (1991): Happiness as a criterion of parents' choice of school. *Journal of Education Policy*, 6/2: 169–78.

Coleman, J. S. (1961): *The Adolescent Society*. New York: The Free Press.

Coleman Report (1966): *On Equality of Educational Opportunity*. Washington, DC; US Office of Education.

Coleman, J. S. (1990) *Equality and Achievement in Education*. Boulder, Colo: Westwood.

Coleman, J. S., Hoffer, T. and Kilgore, S. (1982): *High School Achievement: Public, Catholic and Private Schools Compared*. New York: Basic Books.

Coleman, J. S. et al. (1977): *Parents, Teachers and Children: Prospects for Choice in American Education*. San Francisco: Institute for Contemporary Studies.

Community Development Foundation (CDF) (1990): *Minority Ethnic Communities and School Governing Bodies*. National Consumer Council with AGIT (Action for Governors Information and Training), October.

Connell, R. W., Ashenden, D. J., Kessler, S. and Dowsett, G. W. (1982): *Making the Difference; Schools, Families and Social Division*. London: Allen and Unwin.

Coons, J. E. and Sugarman, S. D. (1978): *Education by Choice: The Case for Family Control*, London: California University Press.

Coote, A. and Campbell, B. (1982): *Sweet Freedom*. London: Fontana.

Coote, A., Harman, H. and Hewitt, P. (1990): *The Family Way*. London: Institute of Public Policy Research.

Coward, R. (1991): *Our Treacherous Hearts: Why Women Let Men Get Their Way*. London: Faber and Faber.

Cox, C. (1991) Review of J. E. Chubb and T. M. Moe's *Politics, Markets and America's Schools*. *British Journal of Sociology of the Education*, 12/3; 385–8.

Cox, C. B. and Boyson, R. (eds) (1975): *Black Paper 1975: The Fight for Education*. London: J. M. Dent.

—— (eds) (1977): *Black Paper 1977*. London: Temple Smith.

Cox, C. B. and Dyson, A. E. (eds) (1969a): *The Fight for Education: A Black Paper*. London: The Critical Quarterly Society.

—— (eds) (1969b): *Black Paper 2: The Crisis in Education*. London: The Critical Quarterly Society.

—— (eds) (1970): *Black Paper 3: Goodbye Mr Short*. London: The Critical Quarterly Society.

Cremin, L. (1961): *The Transformation of the School: Progressivism in American Education* 1876–1957. New York: Vantage Books.

—— (1970): *American Education: The Colonial Experience 1607–1788*. New York: Harper Torchbooks.

Crittenden, B. (1988): *Parents, the State and the Right to Education*. Ashford, Middlesex: Melbourne University Press.

Cronin, J. (1973): *The Control of American Schools*. Boston: Little Brown.

Cullingford, C. (ed.) (1985): *Parents, Teachers and Schools*. London: Royce.

Cyster, R., Clift, P. and Battle, S. (1979): *Parental Involvement in Primary Schools*. Windsor: NFER-Nelson.

Dale, J. and Foster, P. (1986): *Feminists and State Welfare*. London: Routledge and Kegan Paul.

Dale, R. (1989): *The State and Educational Policy*. Milton Keynes: Open University Press.

David, M. E. (1971): (with M. H. Peston) Planning in LEAs. *Local Government Studies*, 2; 39–46.

—— (1975): *School Rule in the USA*. Cambridge, Mass.: Ballinger.

—— (1976): Professionalism and participation in school budgetting in the USA. *Journal of Social Policy*, 5/2: 151–66.

—— (1977): *Reform, Reaction and Resources: The 3Rs of Educational Planning*, Slough: NFER.

—— (1980): *The State, The Family and Education*, London: Routledge and Kegan Paul.

—— (1985): Motherhood and social policy – a matter of education? *Critical Social Policy*, 12: 28–44.

—— (1986): Moral and maternal: the family in the right. In R. Levitas (ed.), *The Ideology of the New Right*, Cambridge: Polity Press.

—— (1988): Home–school relations. In S. Ball and D. Green (eds), *Inequality and Progress in Comprehensive Education: A Reconstruction for the 1980s.* London: Croom Helm.

—— (1989): Education. In M. McCarthy (ed.), *The New Politics of Welfare: An Agenda for the 1990s*, London: Macmillan.

—— (1990): *What is Education For?* Inaugural Lecture, London: South Bank Polytechnic.

—— (1991a): Putting on an Act for Children? In M. Maclean and D. Groves (eds) (1991).

—— (1991b): Comparisons of 'education reform' in Britain and the USA: a new era? *International Studies in the Sociology of Education*, 1: 87–111.

—— (1991c): A gender agenda: women and family in the new ERA. *British Journal of the Sociology of Education*, 12/4: 433–46.

—— (1992): Parents and the state: how has social research informed education reform? In M. Arnot and L. Barton (eds), *Voicing Concerns: Sociological Perspectives on Contemporary Education Reforms*, Wallingford, Oxon: Triangle Books.

—— (1993 forthcoming): Theories of family change, motherhood and education reform. In M. Arnot and K. Weiler (eds), *Education, Gender and Social Justice*, London: The Falmer Press.

David, M. E., Edwards, R., Hughes, M. and Ribbens, J. (1993, forthcoming): *Mothers and Education: Inside Out? Exploring Family-Education Policy and Experience.* London: Macmillan.

David, M. E. and West, A. (1992, forthcoming) *Parental Choice of Secondary School.* Final Report to the Leverhulme Trust.

Dawson, P. (1991): in the *Daliy Telegraph*, 8 August, p. 12.

De'Ath, E. (ed.) (1984): *Working Together: Parents and Professionals as Partners.* London: NCB.

Deem, R. (1989): The new school governing bodies: are gender and race on the agenda? *Gender and Education*, 1/3: 247–61.

—— (1990): The reform of school of governing bodies: the power of the consumer over the producer? In M. Flude and M. Hammer (eds) (1990).

Delphy, C. and Leonard, D. (1992): *Familiar Exploitation.* Cambridge: Polity Press.

Domanico, R. J. and Genn, C. (1992): *Creating the Context for Improvement in New York City's Public Schools.* Paper presented to JSSRU Conference on the *Quality of Life in London and New York*, London, March.

Donzelot, (1987) *The Policing of Families.* New York: Pantheon.

Douglas, J. W. (1967): *The Home and the School.* London: Fontana.

Douse, M. (1985): The background of assisted place scheme students. *Educational Studies*, 11/3: 211–17.

Durham, M. (1991): *Sex and Politics: The Family and Morality in the Thatcher Years*. Basingstoke: Macmillan.

Echols, F., McPherson, A. and Willms, J. D. (1990): Parental choice in Scotland. *Journal of Education Policy*, 5/31: 207–22.

Edwards, J. and Batley, R. (1978): *The Politics of Positive Discrimination: An Evaluation of the Urban Programme: 1967–77*. London: Tavistock.

Edwards, R. (1989): Pre-school home visiting projects: a case study of mothers' expectations and experiences. *Gender and Education*, 1/2: 165–181.

—— (1990a): Access and assets: the experiences of mature mother-students in higher education. *Journal of Access Studies*, 5/2, pp. 188–202.

—— (1990b): Connecting method and epistemology: a white women interviewing Black women. *Women's Studies International Forum*, 13/4: 477–90.

—— (1991): *Degrees of Difference: Mature Women Students in Higher Education*. Unpublished Ph.D., South Bank Polytechnic.

Edwards, T., Fitz, J. and Whitty, G. (1989): *The State and Private Education: An Evaluation of the Assisted Places Scheme*. Basingstoke: The Falmer Press.

Edwards, V. and Redfern, A. (1988): *At Home in School: Parent Participation in Primary Education*. London: Routledge and Kegan Paul.

Eichler, M. (1986): The relationship between sexist, non-sexist, women-centred and feminist research. In T. McCormack (ed.), *Studies in Communication*, Vol. 3, Toronto; JAI Press.

—— (1988): *Nonsexist Research Methods: A Practical Guide*. London: Allen and Unwin.

Eisenstadt, N. (1986): Parental involvement: some feminist issues. In N. Browne and P. France (eds), *Untying the Apron Strings*, Milton Keynes: Open University Press.

Eisenstein, H. (1984): *Contemporary Feminist Thought*. London: Allen and Unwin.

Eisenstein, Z. (1982): The sexual politics of the New Right: on understanding the existing crisis of liberalism. *SIGNS: Journal of Woman and Culture*, 7/3: 567–88.

Elliott, B. J. and Richards, M. P. M. (1991) Children and Divorce: Educational Performance and behaviour before and after parental separation *International Journal of Law and the Family*, 5: 258–78.

Elliott, J. (1982): How do parents choose and judge secondary schools? In R. McCormack (ed.) (1982).

Elliott, J., Bridges, D., Gibson, R. and Nias, J. (1981a): *School Accountability* London: Grant McIntyre.

Elliott, J., Bridges, D., Gibson, R. and Nias, J. (1981b): *Case Studies in School Accountability*, Vol. 1. Cambridge: Cambridge Institute of Education.

Epstein, J. (1990): School and family connections: theory, research and implications for integrating sociologies of education and family. *Marriage and Family Review*, 15/1–2: 99–126.

Evans, T. (1988): *A Gender Agenda*. Sydney: Allen and Unwin.

Faludi, S. (1992): *Backlash: The Undeclared War Against Women*. London: Chatto and Windus.

Fantini, M., Gittell, M. and Magat, R. (1970): *Community Control and the Urban School*. New York: Praeger.

Fein, L. (1971): *The Ecology of Public Schools*. New York: Basic Books.

Ferri, E. (1976): *Growing Up in a One-Parent Family: A Long-Term Study of Child Development*. Windsor: NFER.

Ferri, E. and Saunders, A. (1991): *Parents, Professionals and Preschool Children*. London: National Children's Bureau.

Finch, J. (1984): The deceit of self-help: preschool playgroups and working class mothers. *Journal of Social Policy*, 13/1, pp. 1–21.

—— (1989): *Family Obligations and Social Change*. Cambridge: Polity Press.

Fitz, J. and Halpin, D. (1990): Researching grant-maintained schools. *Journal of Education Policy*, 5/2: 167–80.

—— (1991): From policy to workable scheme: grant-maintained schools and the DES. *International Studies in the Sociology of Education*, 1: 129–53.

Flett, M. (1991): Community education and parental involvement. Unpublished Ph.D., Aberdeen University.

Flew, A. (1983): *Education Tax Credits*. Surrey: IEA Education Unit.

Flew, A. (1987): *Power to the Parents: Reversing Educational Decline*. London: Sherwood Press.

Flew, A. et al. (1981): *The Pied Piper of Education*. London: Social Affairs Unit.

Floud, J., Halsey, A. H. and Martin, F. M. (1956): *Social Class and Educational Opportunity*. London: Heinemann.

Flude, M. and Hammer, M. (eds) (1990): *The Education Reform Act 1988: Its Origins and Implications*. London: The Falmer Press.

Fox, I. (1986): *Private Schools and Public Issues: The Parents' Views*. London: Macmillan.

Freire, P. (1972): *Pedagogy of the Oppressed*. London: Steel and Ward.

Fuller, M. (1983): Critical qualifications, qualified criticism. In J. Purvis and M. Hales (eds), *Achievement and Inequality in Education*, London: Routledge and Kegan Paul.

Furstenberg, F. (1987): *Recyling the Family: Remarriage after Divorce*. Newbury Park, Ca.: Sage.

Gerwitz, S., Miller, H. and Walford, G. (1991): Parents' individualistic and collectivist strategies at the City Technology College, Kingshurst. *International Studies in the Sociology of Education*, 1: 173–93.

Gilder, G. (1974): *Sexual Suicide*. London: Millington.

—— (1981): *Wealth and Poverty*. New York: Basic Books.

—— (1982): *Wealth and Poverty*, London: Buchan and Enright.

Gilligan, C. (1984): *In a Different Voice*. Cambridge, Mass.: Harvard University Press.

Gittell, M. and Berube, M. (1967): *School Boards and School Policy*. New York: Praeger.

Glass, D. (1961): Education and social change in modern England. In A. H. Halsey et al. (eds) (1961).

Glatter, R. (ed.) (1989): *Educational Institutions and their Environments: Managing Boundaries*. Milton Keynes: Open University Press.

Glazer, N. (1975): *Affirmative Discrimination*. New York: Basic Books.

Gleeson, D. (1989): *The Paradox of Training*. Milton Keynes: Open University Press.

—— (1990): *Training and its Alternatives*. Milton Keynes: Open University Press.

Glenn, C. L. (1989): *Choice of Schools in Six Nations*. Washington, D.C.: US Department of Education.

Goertz, M. (1989): Education politics for a new century: introduction and overview. In D. Mitchell and M. Goertz (eds) (1989).

Golby, M. (1989): Parent governorship in the new order. In F. Macleod, (ed.) (1989).

Golby, M. and Brigley, S. (1989): *Parents as School Governors*. Tiverton, Devon: Fair Way Publications.

Golby, M. and Lane, B. (1989): *The New School Governors*. Exeter Papers in School Governorship, Tiverton, Devon: Fair Way Publications.

Golby, M. et al. (eds) (1990): *The New Governors Speak*. Exeter Papers in Schools Governorship, Tiverton, Devon: Fair Way Publications.

Gordon, T. (1990): *Feminist Mothers*. Basingstoke: Macmillan Education.

Gray, J., McPherson, A. and Raffe, D. (1982): *Reconstructions of Secondary Education: Theory, Myth and Practice since the War*. London: Routledge and Kegan Paul.

Green, D. (1987): *The New Right: The Counter Revolution in Political, Economic and Social Thought*. Brighton: Wheatsheaf.

—— (ed) (1991) *Empowering Parents: How to Break the Schools' Monopoly*. London: IEA Health and Welfare Unit.

Gregory, J. (1987): *Sex, Race and the Law: Legislating for Equality*. London: Sage.

Guthrie, J. W. and Pierce, L. C. (1990): The international economy and national education reform: a comparison of education reforms in the US and GB. *Oxford Review of Education*, 16: 179–204.

Hall, S. (1979): 'The great moving right show'. *Marxism Today*.

—— (1983): 'Education in crisis'. In J. Donald and A. M. Wolpe (eds), *Is There Anyone Here From Education?*, London: Pluto Press.

Halsey, A. H. (1961): *Ability and Educational Opportunity*. Paris: OECD.

—— (ed.) (1972): *Educational Priority*, Vols 1–6. London: HMSO.

Halsey, A. H., Floud, J. and Anderson, C. A. (eds) (1961): *Education, Economy and Society*. Glencoe: The Free Press.

Halsey, A. H., Heath, A. and Ridge, M. J. (1980): *Origins and Destinations*. Oxford: Oxford University Press.

Halsey, A. H. and Sylva, K. (eds) (1987) Plowden twenty years on. *Oxford Review of Education*, 13/1.

Halsey, A. H. and Sylva, K. (1987): Plowden: history and prospect. *Oxford Review of Education*, 13/1: 3–13.

Hamilton, D. and Griffiths, A. (1984): *Parent, Teacher, Child*. London: Methuen.

Hannon, P. and Cuckle, P. (1984): Involving parents in the teaching of reading. *Educational Research*, 26/1, pp. 2–11.

Hannon, P. and Jackson, A. (1987): *The Belfield Reading Project Final Report*. Rochdale: Belfield Community Council.

Hansard (1987) 1 December.

Hargreaves Report (1984): *Improving London's Secondary Schools*. London: ILEA.

Hargreaves, D. (1985) *The Challenge of the Comprehensive School*. London: Routledge and Kegan Paul.

Hartley, D. (1989): The home and the school: paradigm lost. *British Journal of the Sociology of Education*, 10/2: 253–63.

Haskey, J. (1989): Families and households of ethnic minority and white populations of Great Britain. *Population Trends*, 57; 8–19.

Hawkins, R. B. (1985): Strategy for revitalizing public education. In J. Bunzel (ed.) (1985).

Her Majesty's Inspectorate (HMI) (1991): *Parents and Schools: Aspects of Parental Involvement in Primary and Secondary Schools 1989–90*. London: Department of Education and Science.

Heron, L. (ed) (1985): *Truth, Dare or Promise: Girls Growing up in the Fifties*. London: Virago.

Hewison, J. (1985a): Home environment and reading attainment: a study of children in a working class community.

—— (1985b): The evidence of case studies of parents' involvement. In C. Cullingford (ed.) (1985).

Hickox, M. (1991): Review of J. C. Chubb and T. M. Moe's *Politics, Markets and America's Schools. British Journal of the Sociology of Education*, 12/3: 393–6.

Hicks, C. (1988): *Who Cares: Looking After People at Home*. London: Virago.

Higgins, J. (1978): *The Poverty Business*. Oxford: Blackwell/Robertson.

Higgins, J., Peakin, N., Edwards, J. and Wicks, M. (1983): *Government and Urban Poverty*. Oxford: Blackwell.

Hillgate Group (1986): *Whose Schools? A Radical Manifesto*. London: Claridge Press.

—— (1987): *Reform of British Education: From Principles to Practice*. London: Claridge Press.

Hirshman, A. O. (1970): *Exit, Voice and Loyalty: Responses to Decline in Firms, Organisations and States*. Cambridge, Mass.: Harvard University Press.

—— (1981): *Essays in Trespassing*. Cambridge: Cambridge University Press.

Hudson, F. and Ineichen, B. (1991): *Taking it Lying Down: Sexuality and Teenage Motherhood*. Basingstoke: Macmillan.

Hughes, M., Wikeley, F. and Nash, T. (1990a): *Parents and the National Curriculum: An Interim Report*. School of Education, University of Exeter.

—— (1990b): Business partners: relationship between parents and schools. *TES*, No. 3836, 5, Jan. 1990, p. 20–1.

Hunter, J. (1989): *Parental choice of secondary school* (RS 1230/89). London: ILEA.

—— (1991): Which school: a study of parents' choice of secondary school. *Educational Research*, 33/1: 31–5.

Hurt, J. S. (1985a): *Education and the Working Classes from the Eighteenth to the Twentieth Centuries*. London: Michael Argyles.

—— (1985b): Parental involvement in schools. In C. Cullingford, (ed.) (1985).

Ingham, M. (1981): *Now We are Thirty: Women of the Breakthrough Generation*. London: Eyre Methuen.

James, P. (1980): *The Reorganisation of Secondary Education*. London: Allen and Unwin.

Jefferies, G. and Streatfield, D. (1989a): *Recruitment of School Governors under The Education Act (2) 1986*. Slough: NFER.

—— (1989b): *Reconstitution of School Governing Bodies*. Slough: NFER.

Jencks, C. et al. (1972): *Inequality: A Reassessment of the Effects of Family and Schooling in America*. Harmondsworth: Penguin.

Johnson, D. (1987): *Private Schools and State Schools: Two Systems or One?* Milton Keynes: Open University Press.

—— (1990): *Parental Choice in Education*. London: Unwin Hyman.

Johnson, D. and Ransom, E. (1983): *Family and School*. London: Croom Helm.

Joshi, H. (1987): Pay differentials and parenthood: analysis of men and women born in 1946: a research report.

—— (ed.) (1989): *The Changing Population of Britain*. Oxford: Blackwell.

—— (1991): 'Sex and motherhood as handicaps in the labour market. In M. Maclean and D. Groves (eds) (1991).

Jowett, S. (1990): Working with parents – A study of policy and practice. *Early Child Development and Care*, 58: 45–50.

Jowett, S. and Baginsky, M.(1988): Parents and education: a survery of their involvement and a discussion of some issues. *Educational Research*, 30/1: 36–45.

Judd, D. and Parkinson, M. (eds) (1990): *Leadership and Urban Regeneration: Cities in North America and Europe*. Newbury Park, Ca.: Sage.

Katz, M. (1971): *Class, Bureaucracy and the Schools: The Illusion of Educational Change in America*. New York: Praeger.

—— (ed) (1971): *School Reform: Past and Present*. Boston: Little Brown.

Kelly, G. (1985): Setting the boundaries of debate about education. In P. Altbach et al. (eds) (1985).

Kelly, G. (1987) 'Comparative Education and the Problem of Change: An agenda for the 1980s' Presidential Address *Comparative Education Review*, 13/4: 477–89.

Keuzenkamp, S. (1991): Demographic implications of Dutch emancipation policy. Paper presented to the European Feminist Research Conference, University of Aalborg, Denmark, 18–22 August.

Keys, W. and Fernandes, C. (1990): *A Survey of School Governing Bodies*, Vol. 1. Slough: NFER.

Kiernan, K. and Wicks, M. (1990): *Family Change and Future Policy.* York: J. Rowntree Memorial Trust and Family Policy Centre.

Knight, C. (1989): *The Making of Tory Education Policy in Post-War Britain 1950– 1986.* London: The Falmer Press.

Kogan, M. (1975): *Educational Policy Making.* London: Allen and Unwin.

—— (ed.) (1984): *School Governing Bodies.* London: Heinemann Educational.

—— (1986): *Educational Accountability: An Analytical Overview.* London: Hutchison.

Kogan, M. and Eyken, W. Van der (1973): *County Hall.* Harmondsworth: Penguin.

Land, H. (1976): Women: supporters or supported? In D. L. Barker and S. Allen, (eds), *Sexual Divisions and Society: Process and Change*, London: Tavistock.

—— (1989): Time to care. In M. Maclean and D. Groves (eds) (1989).

Land, H. and Parker, R. (1978): Family policy in Britain. In S. Kamerman and A. Kahn (eds), *Family Policy: Government and Families in Fourteen Countries*, New York: Columbia University Press.

Land, H. and Ward, S. (1986): *Women Won't Benefit.* London: NCCL.

Lareau, A. (1987): Social class differences in family–school relationships: the importance of cultural capital. *Sociology of Education*, 60: 73–85.

—— (1989a): Family-School Relationships: A View from the Classroom *Educational Policy*, 3/2: 245–59.

—— (1989b): *Home Advantage, Social Class and Parental Intervention in Elementary Education.* London: The Falmer Press.

Lasch, C. (1967): *Haven in a Heartless World: The Family Besieged.* New York: Basic Books.

—— (1980): *The Culture of Narcissism.* London: Abacus Books.

Lawson, A. (1990): *Adultery: An Analysis of Love and Betrayal.* Oxford: Oxford University Press.

Leonard, D. and Hood-Williams, J. (1988): *Families.* Basingstoke: Macmillan Education.

Levin, H. M. (ed.) (1970): *Community Control of Schools.* New York: Simon and Schuster.

Levin, M. (1987): Parent-teacher collaboration. In D. W. Livingstone (ed.), *Critical Pedagogy and Cultural Power*, Basingstoke: Macmillan Education.

Levine, D. M. and Bane, M. J. (eds) (1975): *The Inequality Controversy: Schooling and Distributive Justice.* New York: Basic Books.

Lightfoot, S. L. (1978): *Worlds Apart: Relationships between Families and Schools.* New York: Basic Books.

Litt, M. and Parkinson, M. (eds) (1979): *US and UK Educational Policy: A Decade of Reform*. New York: Praeger.

MacBeath, J., Mearns, D. and Smith, M. (1986): *Home From School*. Glasgow: Jordanhill College of Education.

MacBeath, J. and Turner, M. (1990): *Learning Out of School: Homework, Policy and Practice*. Glasgow: Jordanhill College of Education.

Macbeth, A. (1989): *Involving Parents: Effective Parent–Teacher Relations*. Oxford: Heinemann Educational.

—— (1990): *Parents and Education: Priorities for Research*. Edinburgh: Scottish Council for Research in Education.

Macbeth, A. et al. (1984): *The Child Between: A Report on School–Family Relations in the Countries of the European Community*. Luxembourg: Office of Official Publications of the EEC.

Macbeth, A., Strachan, D. and Macaulay, C. (1986): *Parental Choice of School*. Glasgow Department of Education, University of Glasgow.

Macbeth, A., Strachan, D. and Macaulay, C. (1986): *Summary of Parental Choice of School in Scotland*. The public report of the Parental Choice Project, Glasgow, Department of Education, University of Glasgow.

McCormack, R. (ed.) (1982): *Calling Education to Account*. London: Heinemann Educational.

Maclean, M. and Groves, D. (eds) (1991): *Women's Issues in Social Policy*. London: Routledge and Kegan Paul.

Maclean, M. and Kuh, D. (1991): The long term effects for girls of parental divorce. In M. Maclean and D. Groves (eds) (1991).

Maclean, M. and Wadsworth, M. (1988): Children's life chances and parental divorce. *International Journal of Law and Family*, 2: 155–66.

Macleod, F. (ed.) (1989): *Parents and Schools: The Contemporary Challenge*. London: The Falmer Press.

Maclure, S. (1989): *Education Reformed*. London: Hodder and Stoughton.

McPherson, A. and Raab, C. (1988): *Governing Education: A Sociology of Policy since 1945*. Edinburgh: Edinburgh University Press.

Manicom, A. (1984): Feminist frameworks and teacher education. *Journal of Education*, 166/1: 77–88.

Marris, P. and Rein, M. (1966): *Dilemmas of Social Reform*. Harmondsworth: Penguin.

Martin, J. and Roberts, C. (1984): *Women and Employment: A Lifetime Prespective*. London: HMSO.

Mayall, B. (1990): *Parents in Secondary Education: The Parent Organiser Project at Westminster City School*. London: Calouste Gulbenkian Foundation.

Melhuish, E. and Moss, P. (eds) (1991): *Day Care for Young Children: International Prespectives*. London: Routledge and Kegan Paul.

Merttens, R. and Vass, J. (1987a): IMPACT – a learning experience. *Primary Teaching Studies*, 21 pp. 263–71.

—— (1987b): Parents in schools: raising money or raising standards? *Education*, 3–13, June, pp. 23–7.

—— (1990): *Sharing Maths Cultures IMPACT: Inventing Maths for Parents and Children and Teachers*. London: The Falmer Press.

—— (1991): *Bringing School Home: Children and Parents, Learning Together*. London: Hodder and Stoughton.

Midwinter, E. (1980): *Education Choice Thoughts*. London: Advisory Centre for Education.

Miles, R. and Phizacklea, A. (1980): *Labour and Racism*. London: Routledge and Kegan Paul.

—— (1984): *White Man's Country: Racism in British Politics*. London: Pluto Press.

Miliband, D. (1991): *Learning by Right: The Entitlement to Paid Education and Training*. London: Institute for Public Policy Research.

Millar, J. (1990): *Poverty and the Lone Parent: The Challenge to Social Policy*. London: Avebury.

Millar, J. and Glendenning, C. (1989): Gender and poverty. *Journal of Social Policy*, 18/3: 363–83.

Mishra, R. (1984): *The Welfare State in Crisis*. Brighton: Wheatsheaf.

Mitchell, D. (1989): Education politics for the new century: past issues and future directions. *Journal of Education Policy*, 4/5: 133–67.

Mitchell, D. and Goertz, M. (eds) (1989): *Education Politics for a New Century: The Twentieth Anniversary Politics of Education Yearbook*, Special Issue of *Journal of Education Policy*, 4/5.

Morgan, V., Dunn, S., Cairns, E. and Fraser, G. (1991): *Breaking the Mould*. Final Report of the ESRC Funded Project, 'The Roles of Parents and Teachers in the Integrated Schools in Northern Ireland', Coleraine: University of Ulster, Centre for the Study of Conflict.

Moroney, R. (1976): *The Family and the State*. London: Tavistock.

Mortimore, J. and Blackstone, T. (1980): *Disadvantage and Education*. London: Heinemann Educational.

Mortimore, J. and Mortimore, P. (1984): Parents and school. *Education*, Special Report, 5 October.

Mortimore, P. and Mortimore, J. (1991): *The Primary Head: Roles, Responsibilities, Reflections*. London: Chapman.

Mortimore, P., Sammons, P., Stoll, L., Lewis, D. and Ecob, R. (1988): *School Matters: The Junior Years*. Wells: Open Books.

Moss, P. (1988): *Childcare and Equality of Opportunity*. London: The European Community.

—— (1989): The costs of parenthood. *Critical Social Policy*, 24, pp. 20–38.

—— (1990): Childcare in the European Communities, 1985–1990. *Women of Europe Supplements*, 31, Brussels: Commission of the European Communities.

—— (1991): Day care for young children in the United Kingdom. In E. Melhuish and P. Moss (eds) (1991).

Moss, P. and Melhuish, E. (1991): *Current Issues in Day Care for Young Children: Research and Policy Implications*. London: HMSO.

Mosteller, F. and Moynihan, D. (eds) (1972): *On Equality of Opportunity*. New York: Vintage Books.

Mount, F. (1982): *The Subversive Family*. Harmondsworth: Penguin.

Mountfield, A. (1991): *State Schools – A Suitable Case for Charity?* London: Directory of Social Change.

Moynihan, D. P. (1966): *The Negro Family*. New York: Basic Books.

—— (1970): *Maximum Feasible Misunderstanding*. New York: The Free Press.

Murray, C. (1984): *Losing Ground: American Social Policy 1950–1980*. New York: Basic Books.

—— (1989): *In Pursuit of Happiness and Good Government*. New York: Basic Books.

—— (1990): *The Emerging British UNDERCLASS*. London: IEA Health and Welfare Unit.

Naylor, F. (1989): *The School in a Pub*. London: Allen and Unwin.

New, C. and David, M. (1985): *For the Children's Sake: Making Child Care More Than Women's Business*. Harmondsworth: Penguin.

Noddings, N. (1985): *Caring: A Feminine Approach to Ethics and Moral Education*. Berkeley: University of California Press.

Oakley, A. (1973): *The Sociology of Housework*. London: Tavistock.

—— (1974): *Housewife*. Harmondsworth: Penguin.

—— (1983): *Taking it Like a Woman*. London: Cape.

O'Donnell, L. (1985): *The Unheralded Majority: Contemporary Women as Mothers*. Boston, Mass.: Lexington Books.

Orfield, G. (1978): *Must We Bus?* Washington, DC: Brookings Institution.

Owen, U. (ed.) (1983): *Fathers: Reflections by Daughters*. London: Virago.

Parkinson, M. (1970): *The Labour Party and the Reorganisation of Secondary Education 1918–1965*. London: Routledge and Kegan Paul.

Pascal, C. (1988): Democratised Primary School Government: policy in practice *British Educational Research Journal*, 14/1.

Pascall, G. (1986): *Social Policy: A Feminist Analysis*. London: Tavistock.

Pateman, C. (1970): *Participation and Democratic Theory*. London: Tavistock.

Peele, G. (1986): *Revival or Reaction: The Right in America*. Oxford: Oxford University Press.

Pennock, J. R. (1979): *Democratic Political Theory*. Princeton, NJ: Princeton University Press.

Peterson, P. (1972): The politics of educational reform in England and the USA *Comparative Education Review*, 17/1.

—— (1985): Did the Education Commissions say anything? In P. Altbach et al. (eds) (1985).

Peterson, P. E. (1985): *The Politics of School Reform 1810–1940*.

Phillips, A. (1987): *Divided Loyalties: Dilemmas of Sex and Class*. London: Virago.

—— (1991): *Engendering Democracy*. Cambridge: Polity Press.

Phoenix, A. (1991): *Young Mothers?* Cambridge: Polity Press.

Phoenix, A., Woollett, A. and Lloyd, E. (eds) (1991): *Motherhood: Meanings, Practices and Ideologies*. London: Sage.

Piven, F. F. and Cloward, R. (1971): *Regulating the Poor*. New York: Vintage.

—— (1976): *Poor People's Movements*. New York: Vintage.

Plewis, I. (1987): Social disadvantage, educational attainment and ethnicity: a comment. *British Journal of the Sociology of Education*, 8: 77–83.

Plowden Report (1967): *Children and Their Primary Schools*. Central Advisory Council for Education, London: HMSO.

Plowden, B. (1987): 'Plowden' twenty years on. *Oxford Review of Education*, 13/1: 119–25.

Poulton, G. (1983): Origins and development of pre-school home visiting. In G. Aplin and G. Pugh (eds), *Perspectives on Pre-School Home Visiting*, London: National Children's Bureau.

Pugh, G. and De'Ath, E. (1984): *The Needs of Parents: Practice and Policy in Parent Education*. Basingstoke: Macmillan.

Quest, C. (ed.) (1992) *Equal Opportunities: A Feminist Fallacy*. London: Institute of Economic Affairs.

Rampton, Sir W. (1981): *The Education of West Indian Children*. London: HMSO.

Ranson, S. (1990): *The Politics of Reorganising Schools*. London: Unwin Hyman.

Ravitch, D. (1976): *The Great School Wars*. New York: Basic Books.

Ray, F. and Mickelson, R. (1989): Business leaders and the politics of school reform. In D. Mitchell and M. Goertz (eds) (1989).

Raywid, M. A. (1985): Family choice arrangements in public schools: a review of the literature. *Review of Educational Research*, 55: 435–67.

Reynolds, D. (ed.) (1985): *Studying School Effectiveness*. London: The Falmer Press.

Ribbens, J. (1990): *Accounting for Our Children: Different Perspectives on 'Family Life' in Middle Income Households*. Unpublished Ph.D., South Bank Polytechnic.

Riddell, S. and Brown, S. (eds) (1991): *School Effectiveness Research: Its Messages for School Improvement*. Edinburgh: HMSO.

Riley, D. (1985): *War in the Nursery*. London: Virago.

Rockhill, K. (1987a): Gender, language and the politics of literacy. *British Journal of the Sociology of Education*, 8/2, 153–69.

—— (1987b): Literacy as a threat/desire: longing to be SOMEBODY. In J. S. Gaskell, and A. T. McLaren, (eds), *Women and Education: A Canadian Perspective*, Calgary: Detselig.

Rutter, M. and Madge, N. (1976): *Cycles of Disadvantage: A Review of Research*. London: Heinemann.

Rutter, M., Maughan, B., Mortimore, P. and Ouston, J. (1979): *Fifteen Thousand Hours: Secondary Schools and their Effects on Children*. Wells: Open Books.

St. Claire, L. and Osborn, A. (1987) The ability and behaviour of children who have been 'in care' or separated from their parents. *Early Child Development and Care*, 28/3: 187–364. Special Issue.

Sallis, J. (1979): *School Governors: Partnership in Practice*. London: Advisory Centre for Education.

—— 1988: *Schools, Parents and Governors*. London: Routledge and Kegan Paul.

Salter, B. and Tapper, E. (1981): *Education, Politics and the State*. London: Grant McIntyre.

Saraceno, C. (1991): Women and care. Paper presented to the European Feminist Research Conference, University of Aalborg, Denmark, 18–22 August.

Saran, R. (1973): *Policy-Making in Secondary Education*. Oxford: Clarendon Press.

Sassoon, A. S. (ed.) (1987): *Women and the State*. London: Hutchinson.

—— (1992): Equality and difference: the emergence of a new concept of citizenship. In D. McLellan and S. Sayers (eds), *Democracy and Socialism*, London: Macmillan.

Scott, G. (1990): Parents and preschool services: issues of parental involvement. *International Journal of Sociology and Social Policy*, 10/1: 1–13.

Scott, H. (1984): *Working Your Way to the Bottom: The Feminisation of Poverty*. London: Pandora Press.

Scruton, R. (1980): *The Meaning of Conservatism*. Harmondsworth: Penguin.

—— (1986): *Sexual Desire*. London: Weidenfeld and Nicholson.

—— (1988): *Conservative Thoughts: Essays from the Salisbury Review*. London: Claridge.

Scruton, R., Ellis Jones, A. and O'Keefe, D. (eds) (1987): *Education and Indoctrination*. Harrow: Education Research Centre.

Segal, L. (ed.) (1983): *What is to be Done About the Family?* Harmondsworth: Penguin.

—— (1987): *Is The Future Female?* London: Virago.

Sexton, S. (1990): Reward, responsibility and results, the new 3Rs. *Sunday Times*, 21 October, p. 9.

Shakeshaft, C. (1988): *Women in Educational Administration*. London: Sage.

Sharpe, S. (1976): *Just Like a Girl: How Girls Learn to be Women*. Harmondsworth: Penguin.

—— (1984): *Double Identity*. Harmondsworth: Penguin.

—— (1986): *Falling for Love: Teenage Mothers Talking*. London: Virago.

Silver, H. (1990): *Education, Change and the Policy Process*. London: The Falmer Press.

Simon, B. (1988): *Bending the Rules: the Baker 'Reform' of Education*. London: Lawrence and Wishart.

Smith, D. E. (1987) *The Everyday World as Problematic: A Feminist Sociology*. Boston, Mass: Northeastern University Press.

Smith, D. E. (1988): *The Everyday World as Problematic: A Feminist Sociology.* Milton Keynes: Open University Press.

—— (1987): 'Women's work as mothers'. In R. Miliband (ed.), *Socialist Register,* London: Lawrence and Wishart.

Smith, D. and Tomlinson, S. (1989): *The School Effect: A Study of Multi-Racial Comprehensives.* London: Policy Studies Institute.

Smith, G. (1987): Whatever happened to educational priority areas? In A. H. Halsey and K. Sylva (eds) (1987).

Smith, G. and Smith T. (1973): Educational home visitors. In A. H. Halsey .(ed.) (1973).

Smith, T. (1980): *Parents and Preschool: Oxford Research Project.* London: Grant McIntyre.

Social Trends 19, (1989): London: HMSO.

Social Trends 20, (1990): London: HMSO.

Social Trends 21, (1991): London: HMSO.

Social Trends 22, (1992): London: HMSO.

Spender, D. (1980): *Manmade Language.* London: Routledge and Kegan Paul.

—— (ed.) (1981): *Men's Studies Modified.* Oxford: Pergamon Press.

—— (1989): *Invisible Women: The Schooling Scandal.* London: Women's Press.

Spender, D. and Sarah, E. (1980) (eds): *Learning to Lose: Sexism and Education.* London: Women's Press.

Sperling, G. (1991): Can the barriers be breached? Mature women's access to higher education. *Gender and Education,* 3/2: 199–215.

Steedman, C. (1982): *The Tidy House.* London: Virago.

—— (1986): *Landscape for a Good Woman.* London: Virago.

—— (1990): *Childhood, Culture and Class in Britain: Margaret Macmillan, 1860 1931.* London: Virago.

Steedman, C., Unwin, C. and Walkerdine, V. (eds) (1985): *Language, Gender and Childhood.* London: Routledge and Kegan Paul.

Stillman, A. (ed.) (1986): *The Balancing Act of 1980: Parents, Politics and Education.* Windsor: NFER-Nelson.

Stillman, A. and Maychell, K. (1986): *Choosing Schools: Parents, LEAs and the 1980 Education Act.* Windsor: NFER-Nelson.

Streatfield, D. (1988): *School Governor Training and Information.* Slough: NFER.

Streatfield, D. and Jefferies, G. (1989): *Reconstitution of School Governing Bodies– Survey 2: Schools.* Slough: NFER.

Swann, Lord (1985): *Education for All: The Report of the Committee of Inquiry into the Education of Children from Ethnic Minority Groups.* London: HMSO Cmnd 9453.

Sylva, K. (1987): Research: the child in the school. *Oxford Review of Education,* 13/1: 8–11.

Tapper, T. and Salter, B. (1978): *Education and the Political Order.* London: Macmillan.

Tawney, R. H. (1924): *Education: The Socialist Policy*. London: Independent Labour Party.

—— (1931): *Equality* (Rpt.1983), London: Routledge and Kegan Paul.

Taylor, G. (1977): *A New Partnership for Our Schools*. London: HMSO.

Taylor-Gooby, P. (1991): *Social Science, Social Change and Social Policy*. Brighton: Harvester-Wheatsheaf.

Thernstrom, S. (1967): *Poverty and Progress*. New York: Atheneum.

Thomas Report (1985): *Improving Primary Schools*. London: ILEA.

Tizard, B. and Hughes, M. (1984): *Young Children Learning: Talking and Thinking at Home and at School*. London: Fontana.

Tizard, B., Blatchford, P., Burke, J., Farquhar C. and Plewis, I. (1988): *Young Children at School in the Inner City*. London: Lawrence Erbaum Associates.

Tizard, B., Mortimore, J. and Burchell, B. (1981): *Involving Parents in Nursery and Infant Schools*. London: Grant McIntyre.

Tomlinson, S. (1983): *Ethnic Minorities in British Schools: A Review of the Literature 1960–82*. London: Heinemann Educational.

—— (1984): *Home and School in Multicultural Britain*. London: B. T. Batsford.

—— (1990): *Multicultural Education in White Schools*. London: B. T. Batsford.

—— (1991): *Teachers and Parents: Home–School Partnership*. London: Institute for Public Policy Research.

Toomey, D. (1989): Linking class and gender inequality: the family and schooling. *British Journal of the Sociology of Education*, 10/4: 389–403.

Topping, K., Thomas, A. and Dennison, B. (1991): Parental or pupil choice – who really decides in urban schools? *Educational Management and Administration*, 19: 243–51.

Topping, K. and Wolfendale, S. (1985): *Parental Involvement in Children's Reading*. Reading: Hodder and Stoughton.

Townsend, P. (1979): *Poverty in the UK*. Harmondsworth: Penguin.

Tyack, D. (1974): *The One Best System: A History of American Urban Education*. Cambridge, Mass.: Harvard University Press.

Ulich, K. (1989): Parents and students: the impact of the school on education in the family. In *Zeitschrift für Socialisations Forschung und Erzietungssociologie*, 9/3: 179–84.

Ungerson, C. (1988): *Policy is Personal: Sex, Gender and Informal Care*. London: Tavistock.

United States National Commission on Excellence in Education (1983): *A Nation at Risk: The Imperative for Educational Reform*. Washington, DC: The Commission on Education.

University of Glasgow (1986): *Parental Choice of School in Scotland*. Glasgow Department of Education, University of Glasgow.

Useem, M. (1988): *Liberal Education and the Corporation*. New York: de Gruyter.

Valentine, C. (1968): *Culture and Poverty: Critique and Counter Proposals*. Chicago: University of Chicago Press.

Wadsworth, M. and Maclean, M. (1986): Parental divorce and children's life chances. *Children and Youth Services Review*, 8: 145–61.

Walford, G. (1986): *Life in Public Schools*. London: Methuen.

—— (1990): *Privatisation and Privilege in Education*. London: Routledge.

—— (1991): Choice of school at the first City Technology College. *Educational Studies*, 17/1: 65–75.

Walford, G. and Miller, H. (1991): *City Technology College*. Milton Keynes: Open University Press.

Walkerdine, V. and Lucey, H. (1989): *Democracy in the Kitchen: Regulating Mothers and Socialising Daughters*. London: Virago.

Wallerstein, J. and Blakeslee, S. (1989): *Second Chances*. London: Bantam.

Wallerstein, J. and Kelly, J. (1980): *Surviving the Break Up*. New York: Basic Books.

Watt, J. and Flett, M. (1985): *Continuity in Early Education: The Role of Parents*. Aberdeen: Department of Education, Aberdeen University.

Watt, J. S. (1989): Community education and parent involvement: a partnership in need of a theory. In F. Macleod, (ed.) (1989).

Weiner, G. (1986): Feminist education and equal opportunities: unity or discord? *British Journal of the Sociology of Education*, 7/3: 265–74.

Weiner, G. and Arnot, M. (eds) (1987): *Gender Under Scrutiny: New Inquiries in Education*. London: Hutchinson.

West, A. (1992): *Choosing Schools: Why Do Parents Opt for Private Schools or Schools in Other LEAs?* Commissioned by Islington Education Department, London: Clare Market Papers No. 1, Centre for Educational Research.

West, A. and Varlaam, A. (1991): Choosing a secondary school: parents of junior school children. *Educational Research*, 33/1: 22–30.

West, A., Varlaam, A. and Scott, G. (1991): Choice of high school: pupils' perceptions. *Educational Research*, 33/3: 205–15.

Westoby, A. (1988): *Culture and Power in Educational Organisations*. Milton Keynes: Open University Press.

—— (1989): Parental choice and voice under the 1988 Education Reform Act. In R. Glatter (ed.), (1989).

Wicks, M. (1991): Social Politics 1979–1992: Families, Work and Welfare, Plenary Address to the Social Policy Association Annual Conference, University of Nottingham, 7–9 July.

Williams, F. (1989): *Social Policy: A Critical Introduction. Issues of Gender, Race and Class*. Cambridge: Polity Press.

Wilson, E. (1978): *Only Half Way to Paradise: Women in Postwar Britain: 1945–68*, London: Tavistock.

—— (1982): *Mirror Writing*, London: Virago.

—— (1983): *What is to be Done About Violence in the Family?* Harmondsworth: Penguin.

Wolfendale, S. (1983): *Parental Participation in Children's Development and Education*. New York: Gordon and Breach.

—— (ed.) (1989): *Parental Involvement: Developing Networks between School, Home and Community*. London: Cassell Educational.

Woodhead, M. and McGrath, A. (eds) (1988): *Family, School and Society*. London: Hodder and Stoughton.

Woods, P. (1988): A strategic view of parent participation. *Journal of Education Policy*, 3: 323–34.

—— (1992): Changing schools? responses to parental choice and competition. *Management in Education*, 6/1.

Wragg, E. (1988): *Education in the Marketplace: The Ideology behind the 1988 Education Bill*. London: NUT.

—— (1989): *Schools and Parents*. London: Cassell.

Wright, N. (1977): *Progress in Education*. London: Routledge and Kegan Paul.

Young, H. (1991): *One of Us: A Biography of Margaret Thatcher*. London: Macmillan.

Young, M. (1961): *The Rise of the Meritocracy*. Harmondsworth: Penguin.

Zaretsky, E. (1976): *Capitalism, the Family and Personal Life*. London: Pluto Press.

Index

Index of Authors